FIRST MANHATTANS

Also by Robert S. Grumet

Native Americans of the Northwest Coast (1979)
Native American Place Names in New York City (1981)
The Lenapes (1989)
Historic Contact (1995)
(ed.) *Northeastern Indian Lives* (1996)
(ed.) *Journey on the Forbidden Path* (1999)
Bay, Plain, and Piedmont (2000)
(ed.) *Voices from the Delaware Big House Ceremony* (2001)
(ed.) *Revitalizations and Mazeways* (2003)
(ed.) *Modernity and Mind* (2004)
The Munsee Indians: A History (2009)

FIRST MANHATTANS

A Brief History of the Munsee Indians

Robert S. Grumet

University of Oklahoma Press : Norman

Publication of this book is made possible through the generosity of
Edith Kinney Gaylord.

Library of Congress Cataloging-in-Publication Data
Grumet, Robert Steven.
First Manhattans : a brief history of the Munsee Indians / Robert S.
Grumet.
    p. cm.
Rev. ed. of: The Munsee Indians, 2009.
Includes bibliographical references and index.
ISBN 978-0-8061-4163-3 (pbk. : alk. paper)
1. Munsee Indians—History. 2. Community life—Northeastern States—
History. 3. Northeastern States—History. 4. Northeastern States—Ethnic
relations. I. Grumet, Robert Steven. Munsee Indians. II. Title.
E99.M93G77 2011
305.897'345074—dc22

2010030566

The paper in this book meets the guidelines for permanence and durability
of the Committee on Production Guidelines for Book Longevity of the
Council on Library Resources, Inc. ∞

1 2 3 4 5 6 7 8 9 10

For Mark and Mr. Lockett

CONTENTS

ILLUSTRATIONS

FIGURES

MAPS

PREFACE AND ACKNOWLEDGMENTS

Like most books, this one is the end result of a project started many years ago. I first became interested in the Indians of Greater New York as a child growing up in the Bronx. This initial interest crystallized into my first research project, a study of Indian place-names in New York City submitted as a senior honors thesis in anthropology at the City College of New York in 1972, and published in a much revised form in 1981 by the Museum of the City of New York. Reciprocity and many of the other explanatory concepts used to make sense of patterns in historical records about life in the Munsee homeland during the colonial era were initially developed in my 1979 doctoral dissertation, entitled "We Are Not So Great Fools," for the Department of Anthropology at Rutgers University. Fellowships at the Newberry Library Center for the Study of the American Indian and experiences as a visiting scholar at several colleges and museums helped me bring many of these ideas to maturity. Although I was occasionally able to squeeze out enough time to publish some of the results of this research during my subsequent career as a National Park Service Archeologist, a heavy workload put production of a book summarizing my findings on hold for many years.

I finally began work on this book as a cultural affiliation study for the National Park Service Northeast Region Ethnography Program, under Cooperative Agreement CA4560B0028, shortly after my retirement in 2002. Regional Anthropologist Chuck Smythe administered this study with Daniel K. Richter, professor of history at the University of Pennsylvania and director of the university's McNeil Center for Early American Studies. Adrienne Gruver drafted the study's maps and kinship graphs. The final report, entitled "From Manhattan to Minisink," was submitted to the National Park Service in 2007. At the University of Oklahoma Press, Senior Associate Director and Publisher John Drayton, Acquisitions Editor Alessandra Jacobi Tamulevich, Managing Editor Steven B. Baker, and Marketing Assistant Lauren Ballard helped see the scholarly hardbound version of the book (*The Munsee Indians: A History*) into print in 2009. Copyeditor Melanie Mallon significantly improved the hardbound edition and provided good guidance for making the book more accessible to general readers. The same team at the University of Oklahoma Press, this time working with copyeditor Kirsteen E. Anderson, developed this much-shortened, revised paperback version. Julie Thompson Margulies passed a sharp reader's eye over several paperback-version chapters, making the ideas presented in the book's pivotal fourth chapter significantly clearer and more understandable. Acknowledgments of help provided by institutions and colleagues, as well as endnotes and bibliographies documenting sources for information in this volume, may be found under the appropriate headings in *The Munsee Indians*.

This volume is dedicated to Mark D. Dornstreich, who looked out for me like a patient elder brother, and to the late Lambert P. Lockett, Sr., who was a father to me.

FIRST MANHATTANS

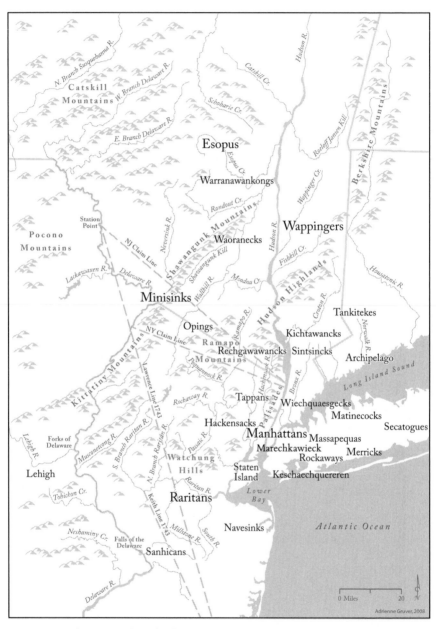

Map 1. The Munsee homeland.

INTRODUCTION

Once, and not all that long ago, Manhattan was Indian country, as it had been for thousands of years. Today, most people tracing descent to the first Manhattans live scattered along the many trails leading into their exile on small reservations in Ontario, Wisconsin, and Oklahoma. Four centuries ago, when Europeans like Henry Hudson began sailing to their shores, Manhattans and their kin held sole, sovereign sway over a homeland that took in a broad swath of the Mid-Atlantic seaboard. It stretched from Manhattan to the nearby mainland and adjacent parts of Long Island and the Jersey shore, across meadows and pine barrens along the coastal plain, and inland through forest-covered valleys. Above them rose ascending tiers of ridges extending from the Palisades, Ramapos, Hudson Highlands, Kittatinys, Shawangunks, and Taconics to the high peaks and plateaus of the Berkshire, Catskill, and Pocono uplands. Then as now, winds constantly blew moisture-laden storm clouds over these front ranges of the Appalachians, a mountain chain that runs like a spine across eastern North America from Acadia to Alabama (see map 1).

The winds that blew from the four cardinal directions across these mountain ramparts were regarded by the region's first people as grandparents. The south wind was affectionately called "Our Grandmother Where It Is Warm"; the others were addressed as grandfathers. Changes in the seasons were thought to reflect the changing fortunes of the winds as they played against one another on their celestial gambling mat. Spring came when South Grandmother defeated North Grandfather; autumn signaled a change in his luck.

Wooded places still scented with pine tar, fallen leaves, and wood smoke hint at how beautiful the entire region was before loggers cut down the ancient forests two centuries ago. Dirtied and dammed as they are, the rivers and streams that flow into freshwater wetlands, saltwater sounds, and sheltered bays preserve much of their old allure. The land itself retains its naturally scoured look, the sharp contours of its rocky uplands worn smooth by the mile-thick ice sheets that have ground their way back and forth over the region for the past million years. Sands and gravels left when glaciers last receded north some twenty thousand years ago still collect in low places, mixing with the forest litter of ten thousand summers to molder into deep, rich soils.

The forests that rise from these valleys to cover the Greater New York region's highest hilltops were much taller, deeper, and denser when Manhattan was Indian land. During warm months when the ancient oaks and maples were in leaf, forest floors were shade-dappled, the sunshine falling directly only on open places such as beaches, lakes (far fewer when only beavers built dams), and the main courses of rivers, winding like brightly lit highways through the forest gloom.

The two greatest of these river-highways, the Hudson and the Delaware, still flow from the Appalachian uplands to the sea through spectacular gorges: the Delaware at the Water Gap where it forces its way through the Kittatiny Ridge, and the Hudson where it cuts across the Highlands at Storm King. Two islands just beyond the line of sight from the highest points overlooking these gorges mark the borders of this Indian homeland: Manhattan, some thirty miles south of Storm King on the east, and Minisink, about the same distance above the Delaware Water Gap to the west.

The destinies of these two islands at the margins of this beautiful land could not have diverged more. Minisink, still tucked comfortably along the stretch of flats that lines both banks of the Delaware, is just another piece of sleepy rural real estate barely noticed by the rafters and canoeists who paddle past it every summer. Like the rest of the land protected from development within the Delaware Water Gap National Recreation Area, Minisink seems little changed from what it was when Indians called the place home. The same cannot be said for Manhattan. There are still some wilder spots where you can imagine what the island once looked like if you squint your eyes just so when the light is just right. The rest of the place is utterly urban, an artificial landscape of skyscrapers and high-rises lined up like so many banks of gaming slots where a lucky gambler can still strike it rich like the Dutchman who first bought the island from the Indians in 1626 for the fabled bargain sum of twenty-four dollars (actually sixty guilders, more like several hundred present-day dollars).

As for the Indians who sold Manhattan, they're mostly overlooked, like that other island at the far end of their homeland. When thought of at all, they're mostly remembered as naifs, poster children for the kind of guileless innocence that doomed their people to dispossession and dispersal at the hands of more cunning colonists. The rest—their culture, their place in history, even their identity—is forgotten.

But not totally forgotten. Today, Manhattan and Minisink are only two of many Indian names still on regional maps. Hackensack, Passaic, Musconetcong, and Neversink still grace local rivers. Watchung, Taconic, and Shawangunk are only some of the region's hills and mountains that also retain their Indian names. People commute to and from communities called Massapequa, Maspeth, and Rockaway. Oratam Parkway, Lake Oscawanna, the villages of Katonah and Mamaroneck, and Mounts Teedyuscung and Nimham bear names of formerly prominent local Indian leaders.

Linguists think these words and many more like them come from a language they call Munsee. Munsee, most agree, is the northernmost dialect of Delaware, one of the Eastern Algonquian family of languages that were spoken by all coastal Indians between Canada and the Carolinas four hundred years ago. The word itself means "People from Minisink." Still used by many of their descendants today, the term "Munsee" only first came into use just as colonists forced the region's first people from their last refuges in their homeland around Minisink during the early 1700s.

"Manhattan," "Minisink," and "Munsee" all evidently bear some relationship to the word "island" in English. The Munsee homeland between Manhattan and Minisink was truly an island world, a succession of clearings that spread like a chain of archipelagos across the region's oceanlike woodland expanses. Like all forests (and oceans, for that matter), the woodlands of Munsee country were mosaics. Access to resources scattered like the individual tiles of a mosaic across the floors of these forests required periodic changes of residence within, and sometimes beyond, home territories.

Four hundred years ago, Munsees hacked and burned clearings at favorable locales throughout their homeland. Some of the largest were on well-drained terraces overlooking fertile floodplains ideal for farming. Others bordered pools above and below falls and rapids where migrating shoals of shad, herrings, and eels gathered seasonally on their way to and from spawning grounds. Wherever they lived, Munsees tended to avoid locations along major rivers where unexpected visitors could suddenly drop by unannounced. Instead, Munsee people preferred to cut clearings for their towns and camps out of the forests alongside smallish streams. Fast-running creek currents brought fresh water and fish while washing away eggs and larvae of mosquitoes and other pests. Streambeds also provided the fine-grained, waterworn cobbles that Indians fashioned into pecked-stone axes for clearing more trees. Wood from felled trees was used to make everything from axe handles to dugout canoes. Smaller cobbles that did not burst when heated were just right for hot-rock cooking and saunalike sweat lodges.

Men and women used stone tools to girdle and fell trees on land intended for garden plots. They then burned the tangled masses of branches and brush to clear the land for planting. Women and children swung wooden-handled hoes of horn, bone, or shell to till and weed low mounds where they grew corn, beans, and squash. Although their help was not required by custom, loving husbands and accommodating grandfathers nevertheless often took turns guarding fields, driving away pests, and pitching in during harvesttime. Some men also tended private tobacco plots.

When harvesttime came, visionary dreamers called people together for prayer and thanksgiving. Persuasive visionaries often convinced people to move to more promising locales. Some might relocate to newly cleared lands nearby. Others might move farther away, sometimes beyond ancestral borders.

Although gardens could briefly produce bumper crops, cultivation quickly exhausted forest soils. New plots constantly had to be cleared while old fields lay mostly fallow for several years to recover their fertility. Uncultivated fields were not unproductive places, however. Edible berries, greens, and roots flourished there, along with milkweed pods bursting with soft down perfect for twisting into sewing thread and yarn. Young trees growing in sunlit fallow fields provided firewood and willow, yew, and maple saplings for bows, skin-drying frames, tool handles, and weapon shafts. Glues made from tree sap, boiled fish bones, and animal fat were used to secure pecked-stone axes, adzes, and gouges, and chipped-stone knife blades, scrapers, drills, and arrow points, tied by thin rawhide and sinew strips to sapling shafts and handles. Skillful stone-knappers produced carefully crafted arrows and spears used in war, on hunts, and in ambushes of deer, bear, and other animals drawn to greens, grasses, and berries growing in fallow fields close to home.

Women used chipped-stone knives and scrapers to prepare meat and fish for cooking and storage. Similar tools removed fat and hair from animal skins so that they could be tanned and tailored to make skirts, shirts, loincloths, shoes, and other apparel. Hats and other headgear were not needed for sun protection in this shady forest world and were rarely worn. Shoes and blanket-like mantles, on the other hand, were important. Capes of animal skin or woven turkey feathers were worn over the shoulders to protect against branches and brambles, ward off rain and snow, provide warmth in winter, and absorb sweat in hot weather. Moccasins protected the feet of people whose only ways of getting around were on foot or by canoe.

The constant press of moccasin-clad feet beat otherwise soft forest soils into hardened pavements in the clearings where people lived and worked. Woodworkers, stone-knappers, and lounging townsfolk sheltered from wind, rain, and sunlight beneath small skin- or bark-covered tents and lean-tos roofed with grass mats. Smoky fires drove away insects and broiled cuts of meat and fish cooked on skewers or wooden racks. Leaf-wrapped corn cakes baked in hot ashes. Women used flexible sapling tongs to place fire-heated rocks into clay pots filled with fixings for stews and soups.

Townsfolk spent most of their time outdoors in the open air. Couples often made love in planting fields, in the hope that their exertions might somehow increase both their own and the soil's fertility. Almost everyone enjoyed sleeping beneath light shelters cooled by gentle evening breezes when weather permitted. Their settlements had no plumbing. Water was drawn from the neighboring creek or nearby springs. People bathed in the creek or took sweat baths in hot-rock-heated lodges. They relieved themselves in the woods. Refuse was thrown into the fire, buried in pits, and scavenged by dogs living with every family. There also was no cemetery. Those who died when the ground was frozen were often buried beneath fireplaces until spring thaws permitted decent interments in the forest. Bodies of infants and young children were frequently buried beneath trails in the belief that their spirits could reenter wombs of passing women and so get another chance at life. Tiny pots or bows and arrows hung in nearby trees and bushes often marked their graves.

Children ran and played around the one or two longhouses that stood at the center of most town clearings. The average longhouse was sixty to eighty feet long, about ten feet wide, and eight to ten feet in height. Each was covered with bark sheets and grass mats fixed onto frames of bent poles whose sharpened ends were inserted into post holes dug in the ground. Sapling-framed doorways along the sides of each house, often covered with hanging skins, opened into dark windowless interiors lit only by hearth flames and overhead smoke holes. Fireplaces located at intervals along a central corridor marked the centers of small apartments divided from one another by bark and mat walls. Food storage containers—fired clay pots, woven baskets and bags, and sewn pitch-sealed bark buckets—along with tools and other possessions, were placed in pits dug into house floors or were stashed beneath sleeping platforms. Plaited corncobs and strips of dried squash, meat, and fish hung from apartment ceilings, preserved for later consumption. Dried herbs also hung there, for brewing appetite-suppressing teas during lean times when everyone tightened their belts.

Each longhouse sheltered several families belonging to a lineage centering around successive generations of women and children related by blood to a common ancestor. Each lineage was named after the spirit, person, phenomenon, or event crucial in its founding. Blood-related lineages belonged to larger kinship groups that anthropologists call phratries, which bore the names of animals. Families, lineages, and phratries held the land in trust for ancestral spirits. They retained rights to use the land so long as they maintained a degree of cohesion sufficient to keep their population up and their affairs (both sacred and secular) in order. Two phratries, Turkey and Wolf, played dominant roles in ordering kin-group membership and lineage land rights in Munsee country during colonial times A third, Turtle, later grew in importance among Munsees after they intermarried with people belonging to that phratry who lived with them in exile.

Marriages between people belonging to the same phratry were considered incestuous no matter how distant their blood relationship. Instead, the women found partners from lineages belonging to other phratries in different clearings. The new husband moved in with his wife's family after marriage. Even though lineage members always considered the men in-laws, the most capable men were chosen as leaders of the kin group and expected to make life-and-death decisions affecting the future of their wife's extended family.

Men and boys moved to different clearings at various points in their lives. Raised in their mother's hometown until puberty, most boys then moved in with maternal uncles regarded and addressed as fathers. Their uncles taught them the kinds of skills that brought them to the attention of women in other lineages. Men tended to marry early and often, and moved to different settlements accordingly. Marriage ties were strong but brittle and easily broken, the wife divorcing her husband simply by piling his possessions in front of

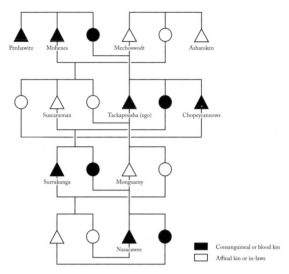

Figure 1. Cross-cousin marriage among Tackapousha's kin on western Long Island.

the longhouse. Although some men cohabited with one woman until separated by death, most men quietly moved on to new families in other settlements after finding themselves evicted. The most influential leaders might support several families at once, shuttling to and from their various households.

When making decisions people sought the guidance of particularly influential members of society: men called *sachems,* women addressed as *squaw sachems,* and spiritually blessed *metewak* of either sex. Colonial settlers referred to these individuals as doctors, magicians, and, much later, as medicine men or women. Depending on the situation, the roles of sachems, squaw sachems, and metewak could be, and often were, combined in one person. Sachems tended to be drawn from families and lineages showing evidence of being on good terms with the spirit world and having proven track records for leadership. Ability usually trumped heredity in matters of succession. Influential families, however, used their society's preferential marriage patterns and orchestrated kinship terms and connections to transfer authority and maintain politically advantageous linkages among themselves.

A chart of Massapequa sachem Tackapousha's genealogical connections (see figure 1) shows how members of prominent lineages on Long Island used kinship and marriage rules to keep power and authority within their families. Tackapousha was one of the most widely known Indian culture brokers of his time. His evident ability to mediate between colonists and Indians helped him rise to the rank of paramount sachem of western Long Island, a position he held for more than fifty years.

Mechoswodt and his cousin Penhawitz, Tackapousha's immediate predecessors, were two of the most influential sachems in the region when the Dutch began colonizing western Long Island in earnest during the 1630s. Penhawitz was a leader of the Keschaechquereren community in the present-day Canarsie section of Brooklyn. Mechoswodt was leader of the Massapequa community farther west in present-day Queens and Nassau counties. Both men referred to Tackapousha as a son. This relationship makes sense because western Long Island Indians employed what anthropologists call a Crow kinship system. In the Crow system, children born into a matrilineal kin group use their word for father to address both their mother's husband (who is a member of a different phratry and therefore considered unrelated by blood to his own children) and their mother's brothers (who are related by blood). People using such a system often contract cross-cousin marriages between children of a mother and those of her brothers that in American society would be considered incestuous unions of first cousins. This, however, was not the view among Munsees. Children belonged to their mother's lineage and inherited the rights and privileges of their mother's brothers, not necessarily the rights and obligations of their mother's husband, who passed his own rights and obligations on to his sister's children.

Multiple unions of cross-cousins, either through polygyny (marriage to more than one wife at one time) or by marrying brothers to wives from different phratries, helped particular lineages in each phratry retain power and influence over several generations. Tackapousha

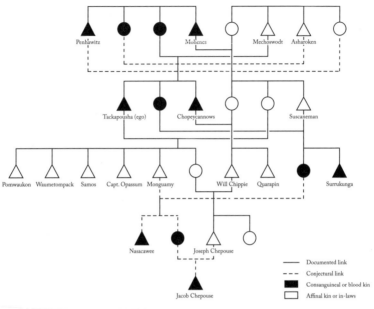

Figure 2. Tackapousha and his kin.

was adept at extending and maintaining his lineage's influence by contracting strategic marriages and arranging for sons born from these unions to be sachems of their communities. The marriage of his younger brother Chopeycannows to the sister of the influential sachem Suscaneman of the nearby Matinecock community, for example, assured close relations between the Massapequa and Matinecock communities. Most of the men identified in colonial records as Tackapousha's sons (see figure 2), served as sachems of various western Long Island Indian communities at one time or another. Thus Tackapousha, maternal nephew ("son") of Penhawitz of Keschaechquereren, could inherit the sachemship of Massapequa from another maternal uncle, the Massapequa sachem Mechoswodt. Tackapousha, in turn, could refer to both men as his fathers. As the son of the area's two most important sachems, Tackapousha would have been ideally situated to inherit the most influential leadership position on western Long Island if he could show that he was up to the job, which he did.

Sachems like Tackapousha could maintain authority, however, only by demonstrating skill and ability. They were authoritative, not authoritarian. As William Penn, the founder of Pennsylvania, put it in 1683, Indian leaders were moved "by the breath of their people." Those capable of demonstrating leadership won their people's support. Those that did not could swiftly lose followers, who were free to vote with their feet and move elsewhere. Relying more on the power of persuasion than on the persuasion of power, sachems worked together with councilors to hammer out community consensus. Consensus in Indian societies in the region did not mean unanimity. Rather, it meant consent, sometimes grudgingly given, from those who elected to stay and relocation elsewhere for those who dissented.

Sachems used consensual agreements to organize production, redistribute goods, and mediate disputes. They could also exact fines, order exile or execution, select experienced warriors to serve as captains during wartime, and order them to step down when it came time to make peace. Often represented by orators blessed with superior rhetorical skills, civil sachems conducted public business in councils. These were occasions for stately rituals to organize relations between people who were sometimes enemies, who often spoke different languages, and who frequently lived far from one another. The soothing rhetoric of the condolence ceremony and formal exchanges of pleasingly powerful gifts like wampum (small shiny cylindrical shell beads) smoothed relationships between strangers and friends everywhere in Munsee country and throughout the Indian Northeast.

A mixture of blood ties to maternal kin and marriage links with paternal relatives helped Munsees preserve community knowledge and secure and share the tools needed to support a hunting, gathering, fishing, and farming society living in a region of widely scattered, seasonally available resources. Networks formed through these ties helped people move in and around their homeland as resources played out in one place and new opportunities presented themselves in another. Munsees did what they could to sustain social ties when it made sense to do so and altered them when changed circumstances warranted. They came together, moved apart, and gathered again into different social, political, and ritual groups in different places at different times, organizing themselves at different levels of what anthropologists often call sociopolitical integration.

Munsees did not maintain strictly static or hermetically sealed social boundaries beyond the blood ties of their matrilineages. Constantly reconciling personal autonomy with community needs, they had to make decisions about which task groups to join, what work to do, and how long to remain with particular companions. Unlike citizens of more rigidly structured societies where bureaucrats give orders and where walls, visas, and border-crossing guards limit movement, Munsees could and did pursue wider ranges of individual freedoms. Yet the range of available choices was still limited by a combination of individual idiosyncrasies, social conventions, political realities, and environmental constraints that did not always neatly coincide.

Traditions that mandated hospitality, reinforced out-marriage, and eased movement helped Munsees sustain what anthropologist Edward H. Spicer called a persistent identity system. As Spicer put it, such systems help people "maintain continuity in the experience and conception of themselves in a wide variety of socio-cultural environments." This way of looking at how Munsee people saw themselves as a distinct nation at different times in their history is important. It helps explain how a people going by various names and living in different places with different people at different times could still maintain a coherent sense of their own identity. Munsees' experience and conception of themselves as a unique people and culture developed, persisted, waned, and recovered as the specific circumstances of their lives changed. It survived even as their tools, clothing, languages (both Indian and European), locations, religious beliefs, national allegiances, memories, and even their names for themselves evolved.

The idea that cultures are, as anthropologist Anthony F. C. Wallace points out, organizations of diversity, is important here. People identified by a certain name in one context and a different one in another did not suddenly become members of different cultures. Neither did the fact that people were known under different names necessarily suggest social confusion or disorganization. The existence of multiple names for individuals and groups can reflect what may be called situational identity. In Munsee society, lineage and phratry names were the only ones that remained unchanged throughout a person's life. Other names changed as the person's locations, status, and affiliations required. Names flexibly used as markers in fluid social situations helped people function as members of different communities at different times. Flexibility has its limits, of course. As Wallace also points out, too much or too little can destabilize social organization to the point where revitalization, a re-sorting of identities and their underlying customs and beliefs, is necessary if cultural values essential for solidarity are to endure.

Few indicators convey cultural continuity in the midst of changing contexts more graphically than the many and various names Munsees used to identify themselves as a distinct people at various times in their history. Although sources are far from clear on the subject, the Munsees probably used a form of the Mahican word *nenapa* (related to *lenape,* from the Unami and Northern Unami dialects of Delaware spoken from central and southern New Jersey to southeastern Pennsylvania) probably most closely reflected their shared sense of ethnicity in their home country. Nenapa means "man." When talking about a woman, Munsees and other Delaware speakers used varieties of their word *xkwe,* similar to the widely adopted and originally inoffensive Massachusett word *squaw.* Words like *nenapa* were used when referring to family, friends, or fellows much as people today use words like "mensch" (German and Yiddish for "man") and expressions like "she is a real human being" when talking about someone they really like.

Today, many writers regard "Lenape" as the most appropriate term to use when talking about Munsees, Unamis, and other Delaware-speaking people. That word, however, only rarely appears in colonial-era documents. Both Indians and colonists evidently found it too blunt an instrument for everyday use. Indians in particular tended to identify themselves as people from a particular place or a certain river.

This practice is reflected in the way they used "Delaware," itself a loan word from English. Delaware comes from the name of Thomas

West, Baron de la Warr, second governor of the Virginia colony. Early Virginian explorers gave his name to the river that Unami-speaking Delawares called Lenapewihittuck and that Munsees called Kithanne, "Large River." Colonists and Indians both began calling the river Delaware by the early 1700s. At about the same time, most Unami- and some Munsee-speaking people living along the river began using the word when referring to themselves. Most of their descendants continue to identify themselves as Delawares, as do numerous municipalities, towns, counties, corporations, and the small state at the river's mouth.

As might be imagined, the absence of a single universally accepted term for Munsees, Unamis, Lenapes, and Delawares is a source of confusion. This is particularly true for those who believe that names are unequivocal reflections of stable social systems. Most early writers struggled to impose order on seemingly contradictory documentation marked by the use of different and sometimes confused names. To that end they tended to choose what they considered the earliest or most suitable appellation for a town, region, or nation as the appropriate name for all inhabitants subsequently associated with the locale, feature, or polity in question. Thus, new arrivals from different places were often identified as members of since defunct or relocated nations. This practice also led to the invention of communities and confederacies where none existed. The persistent belief that all Indians living between the Hudson and Connecticut rivers belonged to a Mahican-speaking Wappinger Confederacy represents the best-known and most enduring example of the impact of this practice.

Just as no clearly unambiguous name collectively identifies the original inhabitants of the Munsee homeland, no reliable figures tally their aboriginal population. This, however, is not unusual either. Few societies of any sort kept track of population numbers before modern times. Some numbers do exist. Most colonists, evidently preoccupied with matters of safety and security, took note only of what they called "fighting men." Writing in 1628, a Dutch colonial official named Isaack de Rasiere penned the only known enumeration of Indian communities in the Munsee homeland that counted both sexes.

He estimated that eighty to ninety people lived on Staten Island, while another two hundred to three hundred people he called Manhattans, "women and men, under different chiefs," lived farther north.

The dynamic nature of Indian settlement patterns in the Munsee homeland placed further obstacles in the way of would-be census takers. Settlements of particular extended families, which usually sheltered only a few households, occasionally became sites of substantial gatherings of hundreds or even thousands. The same places could be totally abandoned at other times. Demographic impacts of wars, epidemics, and other disasters are even harder to determine in the absence of hard numbers. Although nearly every colonial commentator recognized declines in Indian populations, almost all observations were little more than guesswork. Writing in his journal in 1680, the visiting missionary Jasper Danckaerts noted that he had "heard tell by the oldest New Netherlanders that there is now not one-tenth part of the Indians there once were, indeed, not one twentieth or one-thirtieth."

By their own accounts, settlers claimed to have killed between one and two thousand Indian men, women, and children in attacks on communities in Munsee country during the costliest conflict in the region, known as Kieft's War, fought between 1640 and 1645. Hundreds more Munsees died in other wars with colonists. Uncounted others were killed in battles with other Indians. Drink also exacted its toll. An Indian story recalling first contact at Manhattan as the "place where we all got drunk" indicates that the particularly dramatic effects of alcohol on Indians were clear from the start. Fights broke out over it, accidents and exposure killed those befuddled by it, leaders complained about it in public (and quietly asked for it in private), and colonial authorities tried to stop settlers from selling it.

Whatever the effects of booze and bullets, microbes were the biggest killers in Munsee country. Elders with weakened immune systems and children who had yet to develop resistance were particularly susceptible to new epidemic diseases brought by colonists, like influenza, measles, and smallpox. These struck communities throughout the region with increasing frequency and dreadful regularity as the pace of European intrusion into Indian lands quickened. Epidemiological research shows that diseases like smallpox and influenza can kill as much as 90 percent of a population never previously exposed to them. The people of Munsee country and their neighbors were clearly afflicted by successive waves of these epidemic contagions throughout the first centuries of contact, although repeated infections by the same disease did not necessarily cause the same rates of mortality.

Attempts to assess the effects of war and disease usually start from baseline population figures. Most estimates of the aboriginal Munsee population range between ten thousand and thirty thousand. All estimates yield a total population that was tiny compared to the multimillion home populations of the colonizers who entered Munsee country.

Notions of population size directly influence how we think about other aspects of society Nowhere is this fact more evident than in arguments over whether Indians in Munsee country lived in comparatively populous, densely settled farming communities or organized themselves into more thinly populated nomadic bands. Many writers refer to Indian communities as bands only because they find alternative terms like "tribe" and "chiefdom" even more of a problem. This issue is more than a mere academic quibble; words like "band," "nomad," and "tribe" pack powerful conceptual punches. Even their casual use evokes vivid images of the way of life followed by the people whose social organization is categorized in those terms.

If one must categorize Munsee society at all, anthropologist Morton C. Fried's term "egalitarian" provides the closest fit. According to Fried, egalitarianism is not equality. The term instead describes the kind of society in which hereditary inequalities are not institutionalized. Ability tends to trump heredity in such societies. Egalitarian attitudes helped people select leaders demonstrating sufficient flexibility to take advantage of opportunities and rise to challenges. Leaders possessing such abilities helped their people deal with ambiguities of contact that often overwhelmed others belonging to more rigidly regimented societies.

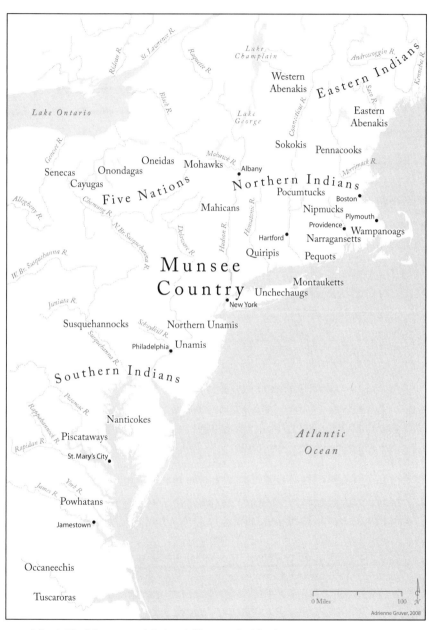

Map 2. The Munsees and their neighbors in the Northeast.

Archaeologists think Munsees and other Northeastern Indians followed an egalitarian way of life they call the Late Woodland cultural tradition for at least five hundred years before Europeans arrived. Evidence for this is preserved in sites indicating movements from old locales to new homesites cut into clearings ten, twenty, or more miles away, presumably after soils lost fertility and surrounding forests were stripped of readily accessible firewood and workable timber. The general contours of Late Woodland lifeways—a neither randomly nomadic nor completely sedentary way of life supported by forest hunting, fishing, foraging, and subsistence farming—persisted throughout the colonial era.

Contacts with colonists almost immediately brought change, however. Europeans visiting Munsee clearings in the decades following erection of the first Dutch trading fort on Manhattan in 1626 were struck by the number of Munsee mothers tending to blue-eyed and curly-haired children. They also noted the many fresh graves dug in and around Munsee clearings, evidence of the devastating epidemics brought by colonists. Pockmarks scarring the faces of survivors testified as much to the protection of spirit guardians as to immunological good fortune. The towns remained populous despite the epidemics as outsiders moved in to take the place of the deceased.

Some of these incoming Indians spoke closely related Eastern Algonquian languages like Mahican and Quiripi-Unchechaug, spoken just beyond the northern and eastern reaches of Munsee country. Others spoke the various Unami dialects of Delaware originating in clearings farther south and southwest. On occasion other, more distant languages could be heard. Some, like Narragansett, Pequot, and Mohegan from New England, and Powhatan and Nanticoke from Chesapeake Bay, were also Eastern Algonquian tongues. Others, like Mohawk and Susquehannock—Iroquoian dialects from beyond the Appalachian front ranges—differed from Eastern Algonquian as much as English differs from Japanese (see map 2).

A new patois mixed Dutch with words from Eastern Algonquian nations into a trade jargon used throughout the region. Trade brought other changes as well, as Indians produced increased amounts of goods for barter. Deer carcasses in excess of domestic needs hung from hooks, and more pelts than formerly dried on frames. Larger and more substantial gardens were planted around Munsee towns, producing corn and other crops needed by colonists. Indians exchanged furs, deer meat, and garden produce for Dutch goods. At first, they could get only a few glass beads, some iron nails, and a few scraps of copper and brass from visiting sailors. Later, settlers offered finished goods like wool blankets; iron knives, axes, and awls; and copper pots. Initially treated as raw materials cut up into triangular arrowheads or tube-shaped beads, such pots only became primarily cooking implements when Indians stopped producing their own clay pots later in the seventeenth century.

Some items were more difficult to obtain than others. Dutch laws, for example, prohibited trade of guns, lead, and powder to Munsees. Colonists did, however, give them beer, brandy, and wine, also banned by law. Drink made Indians part with goods as readily as it separated them from their senses. Bad feelings escalated as colonial lust for Indian furs and Indian desire for drink fueled arguments and encouraged abuses. Fights broke out, and people were soon hurt and killed. Although condolence presents and soothing words restored harmony for a time, fear and resentment began to build everywhere Munsees and colonists came into contact with one another.

The Indians of the lower Hudson and upper Delaware river valleys found themselves increasingly compressed between Iroquois nations in the interior and colonists from the British Isles and the Netherlands claiming the coast as colonial possessions. The coming of Europeans presented unique challenges to Indian people in this region. Wars with the newcomers, along with the highly lethal diseases they brought with them, would devastate Indian communities. The vast numbers of settlers flooding into their homeland overwhelmed and ultimately drove these coastal Indians from their ancestral lands.

Relations between Natives and newcomers in Munsee country during the centuries that passed between first European entry into the region in the early 1500s and final dispossession of the Munsee people by the late 1700s were not simple, and their outcome not inevitable.

The story of contact in the region is neither a triumphant march of civilization nor an edifying morality play pitting oppressed victims or heroic resisters against rapacious colonial intruders. Albeit outnumbered and technologically outclassed, the people of Munsee country were not hopelessly outmatched by all-powerful Dutch and English invaders who could take their lands any time they wanted. Drawing on their own resources with an effectiveness often unrecognized by their would-be conquerors, Munsees managed to hold on to their ancestral lands against fearful odds for a very long time. The story of how they did so unfolds in the pages that follow.

1

CONTACT, 1524–1640

Munsees knew nothing of the people beyond the ocean or of the challenges their coming would present when Giovanni da Verrazano first sailed into New York Harbor. Verrazano hove into the bay one blustery day in early March 1524, piloting his ship through the Narrows separating Brooklyn from Staten Island. Beyond, in the upper harbor, he saw people "clothed with feathers of birds of various colors." He described the harbor as "a beautiful lake with a circuit of about three leagues; over which [Indians] went to and fro in thirty of their little boats, with innumerable people who passed from one shore to the other in order to meet us." A rising breeze blew his ship back out to sea before he had a chance to speak with anyone.

Bits of news describing other visits by seaborne strangers probably made their way to the lands around New York Harbor in the decades that followed. Reports of French voyages up the St. Lawrence River in 1535 and 1542 almost certainly made their way south along the Lake Champlain–Hudson River corridor linking Canada to the Mid-Atlantic coast. Messengers probably also brought word of the founding of the Spanish mission of Ajacán on the James River in present-day Virginia in 1570 and destroyed a year later by local Indians. Indians living around the harbor may also have seen or met Englishmen who began sailing along Mid-Atlantic shores following the disappearance of their Roanoke Colony in North Carolina in 1585. And they almost

certainly knew that some Englishmen had built a small fort they christened Jamestown even closer to home on the Virginia coast in 1607.
Sustained direct contact, however, did not begin along the bay until
a few years after Hudson sailed his ship, *de Halve Maen* (*Half Moon*),
from the harbor into what he called the River of the Mountains, what
we now call the Hudson, in 1609.

Starting in 1614, the Dutch government commissioned a series of
private merchant companies to raid Spanish shipping and to trade
for furs with Indians. The new companies, in turn, began granting licenses to independent free traders, allowing them to make voyages to
what shortly became known as New Netherland. Few records document these initial voyages. What was written was terse and almost
wholly devoted to matters of trade and navigation, using only the
broadest terms to describe the local inhabitants.

This incurious attitude did not matter much so long as contacts
were infrequent, brief, and conducted over ships' rails or on sandy
shores. Most of the writers of these logs and diaries were neither ready
penmen nor much interested in guiding potential rivals to favored
trading spots. Because of this, little can be gleaned from their writings.
This silence does not mean that nothing happened, nor that what did
happen was entirely peaceful. Log entries record that, on occasion,
Indians attacked voyagers, while sailors stole from, kidnapped, and
killed Indians. Even Hudson's voyage was marred by violence that
claimed the lives of several Indians and one member of his crew.

Despite this, both Hudson and one of his ship's officers, Robert Juet, recorded the first Munsee word documented in European
chronicles: "Manhattan," penned in the forms "Manahata" and
"Manahatin." Other Munsee words soon appeared on maps drawn
by the free traders who were next to arrive. These men initially limited
themselves to a shipborne commerce carried on in open bay and river
waters, at safe anchorages. Only later, in 1614, did traders build their
first permanent settlement in the region, a tiny outpost christened
Fort Nassau in present-day Albany. Indians doing business with visiting Dutchmen wanted implements of iron and copper, including
pots, pans, knives, awls, and axes. Those intending to fashion or repair

their own tools and implements also accepted sheets of scrap metal. Woven wool, flax, and cotton textiles traded in bolt rolls; cut into sections called blankets; or tailored into shirts, coats, and other apparel were also desirable, as were glass beads, mirrors, and vermilion. In return, the Indians offered beaver and other pelts and gave the visitors food, fresh water, information, and supplies.

The era of free-trading ventures commanded by captains whose word was law did not last long. In their place came men employed by a group of influential merchant-investors who formed themselves into the Dutch West India Company in 1621. The company started up just as the Twelve Year Truce with Spain ended. Like its counterparts, the already-established Dutch East India Company and the English Virginia Company (chartered by King James I in 1606), the Dutch West India Company was expected to challenge Spanish dominance on the Atlantic and funnel booty and trade goods back to the mother country. The Dutch West India Company's outposts in West Africa, Brazil, the Caribbean, and New Netherland were intended to be self-governing profit centers. They were also depots used to supply and shelter Dutch privateers and warships sailing against Spain and other hostile powers.

Manhattan was the first place formally purchased by the company in Munsee country. From the start, Manhattan was more than just a place-name. In his *Nieuwe Wereldt* (New World), a promotional pamphlet first published in 1624, a company director named Johannes de Laet presented the first account referring to Manhattans as a people. De Laet himself never visited New Netherland. Staying at home in Holland, he based his account of goings-on at Manhattan on voyagers' accounts. Writing about the Hudson River, "called by some the Manhattes River," he observed that "on the east side, upon the main land, dwell the Manatthans, a bad race of Indians, who have always been very obstinate and unfriendly toward our countrymen." De Laet reflected the general Dutch attitude toward the people of the bay, who had been tagged with a bad reputation after warriors there retaliated for the killing of several of their people by attacking the *Halve Maen*'s crew.

Few documents—and, significantly, no deed or bill of sale—chronicle the purchase of Manhattan. In the 1633 edition of his pamphlet, De Laet noted that "our people have bought from [the Manatthans] the island separated from the rest of the land by the Hellgate." The best known evidence of this Indian sale is a letter from a company agent notifying the Dutch government of the safe arrival of the ship *Arms of Amsterdam* from New Netherland on November 5, 1626. In it, the agent dryly observes that company officials "purchased the island Manhattes from the Indians for the value of sixty guilders; it is eleven thousand morgens [twenty-two thousand acres] in size." Only afterward did another early pamphleteer who never set foot on New Netherland, a man named Nicolaes Janszoon van Wassenaer, write that the company established its newly purchased settlement among "a nation called Manates."

The identity of the Indians who sold the island is not known. The few extant references subsequently mentioning Manhattan Indians by name indicate that they evidently did not immediately leave their island or its surrounding hinterland after the sale. In 1628, then-resident company secretary de Rasiere may have been writing about those Indians in a passage describing development opportunities on Manhattan Island. He noted that "up the river the east side is high, full of trees, and in some places there is a little good land, where formerly many people have dwelt, but who for the most part have died or been driven away."

De Rasiere went on to note that the Manhattan nation consisted of several communities: "the old Manhatesen are about 200 to 300 strong, women and men, under different chiefs, whom they call Sackimas." In 1655, a settler named Adriaen van der Donck listed Manhattan among the four Indian languages spoken in New Netherland. Van der Donck described what he thought was the extent and composition of this language community, writing, "with the Manhattans, we include those who live in the neighboring places along the North River, on Long Island, and at the Neversink."

No document specifically identifies a particular individual as a Manhattan Indian. This does not mean that a person identified by

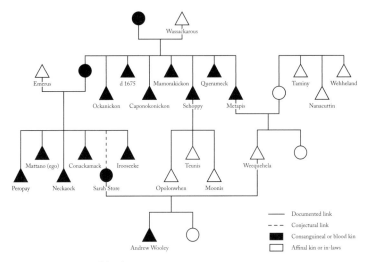

Figure 3. Mattano and his kin.

name in colonial records cannot be linked with Manhattans. An affidavit written on February 14, 1652, talks about "Manhattan Indians of New Netherland, living at Nayack, a place on Long Island directly opposite Staten Island." Other documents penned around the same time identify a man named Mattano as the sachem of both Nayack and Staten Island.

Mattano belonged to a particularly influential lineage (figure 3), several of whose more prominent members were sachems along the borderlands between Northern Unami– and Munsee-speaking communities stretching from the Falls of the Delaware (at present-day Trenton, New Jersey) to Raritan Bay. Mattano, his relatives, and their descendants figure prominently in accounts of later land sales and conflicts. A genealogical reconstruction of prominent members of this lineage reveals that Mattano could claim rights to lands extending from the western end of Long Island across the Narrows through Staten Island to the Raritan and Navesink country and beyond. This reconstruction linking the Manhattans of Nayack with Mattano and his kin also represents the first documentary link in a genealogical chain that joins members of present-day Munsee-descended communities with ancestral Manhattan Indians.

It seems clear that Manhattan country embraced more than the island at its center. People speaking languages belonging to Van der Donck's Manhattan speech community also lived along both banks of the lower Hudson River estuary as well as on the western end of Long Island. Although early records preserve Indian names like Suanhacky, which applied to all of Long Island, there is no surviving general term that collectively identifies Munsee-speaking people living on the island's western end. Records instead document names of individual communities like Rockaway, Massapequa, and Matinecock. All were situated on good pieces of well-watered upland close to fertile planting fields and seasonally available resources.

Other polities belonging to Van der Donck's Manhattan language community had territories centered on places like Wiechquaesgeck in the present-day Westchester County community of Dobbs Ferry, New York, and Hackensack, on the river of the same name in nearby New Jersey. It is not known if people living in these and nearby towns considered themselves Manhattans. The Dutch did not begin carefully linking particular communities or locations with Native people identified by personal names until after they began systematically buying land from Indians in 1630. Increasing amounts of information soon began to flow into New Amsterdam as land sales and other business contacts with local Indians became more frequent.

News tended to travel faster and farther whenever violence flared. Dutch writers ground out an unprecedented volume of paperwork in 1628 after Mohawks killed the commander and several members of the garrison at Fort Orange (built in 1624 to replace Fort Nassau), who had joined a Mahican expedition on its way to attack Mohawk towns. Another Dutch commander, at Fort Hope in today's Hartford, Connecticut, brought on another considerable round of wordsmithing when he murdered a visiting Pequot sachem a few years later. Surviving documents show that company officials were strategic in their responses. Refusing to pile one mistake on top of another by retaliating, they swallowed their pride and quickly restored peace in both places. In so doing, they managed to avoid the interminable fighting that devastated Indian and colonial communities in Virginia between 1610 and 1646 and to sidestep the brief but vicious war that ended in the defeat, dispersal, and near destruction of the Pequot nation in nearby New England in 1637.

In 1630, Dutch settlers began offering Indians in and around Munsee country goods in exchange for handwritten marks made on sheets of paper—deeds that to the Dutch signaled absolute transfers of title and ownership. What they meant to the Indians we will never know. Earlier agreements, like the 1626 Manhattan purchase, were probably informal accommodations sealed with gift exchanges and handshakes or their equivalent. Indians probably regarded these deals as temporary arrangements that could be renewed or cancelled by either party at any time.

The situation changed in 1629 after the Dutch West India Company passed an act allowing directors to set up largely self-governing estates of their own. The new law gave investors willing to use their own capital to buy Indian land and settle fifty colonists on it the right to establish what the Dutch called a patroonship. Similar in concept to English manors, patroonships conferred rights of limited self-government to private landowners known as *patroons* ("patrons" or "masters"). Around this time the company also began issuing permits to private persons wishing to purchase lands directly from the Indians. This established three interest groups competing for Indian territory in New Netherland: the Dutch West India Company, the patroons, and private purchasers acting alone or banding together in syndicates.

On July 12, 1630, agents for a prospective patroon named Michiel Pauw made the first land purchase from Indians in Munsee country to be formalized with a deed. It was followed by several others. These documents, signed by the first sachems in the region identified by name in Dutch records, gave Pauw title to Staten Island, the Bayonne Peninsula, and present-day Jersey City. Pauw, who never visited his estate in New Netherland, named the new patroonship Pavonia after himself. The venture did not prosper. Unable to attract a sufficient number of settlers to the place, he sold his land rights to the Dutch West India Company in 1635.

Patroons went through the trouble of obtaining deeds from Indians in order to secure their estates against the possibility that the company might later make competing claims. Sachems soon accommodated other colonists, placing their marks next to their names on six deeds conveying lands in and around present-day Brooklyn to private purchasers between 1636 and 1637. New Netherland director Wouter Van Twiller obtained three of these deeds (including one for Governor's Island) as a private citizen before being recalled to Holland in 1637 to answer charges that he was improperly profiting from his position.

Van Twiller's replacement, Willem Kieft, obtained the first Dutch West India Company deed to land near Manhattan, this one in the Bushwick section of Brooklyn, on August 1, 1638. During the following year, he would obtain for the company one tract of land in the southwest corner of the Bronx and another taking in the whole of western Long Island. The latter deed's wording guaranteed Indians the right to continue occupying their land. This suggests that it was more like a promissory note protecting the company's right to land being eyed by New Englanders than an outright purchase. Ambiguities surrounding the wording of this deed would make it a major bone of contention between Indians and colonists for generations to come.

2

CONFLICT, 1640–1645

Although hindsight shows that the first seeds of discord had been sown early, relations between Indians and colonists were generally amicable, at least superficially, during the first decade and a half of intensive colonial settlement on and around Manhattan. Signs of serious tension appeared only after English settlers moving west from New England began approaching Indians to purchase lands on the still-unsurveyed eastern border of New Netherland. New Englanders began looking to acquire land beyond the borders of Massachusetts Bay, Plymouth, and Connecticut during the late 1630s. In late March 1638, for example, Connecticut government emissaries met near Norwalk with a gathering of "old [Indian] men and captains from about Milford to Hudson River" to talk about extending their colony's authority over their lands. They told the assembled sachems that they had been sent to establish a protectorate over "the Indians along the coast from Quilipioke [Quinnipiac; today's New Haven] to the Manhatoes." After consulting among themselves, the sachems reached consensus and agreed to place themselves, their people, and their lands under Connecticut protection.

Within two years, English colonists from Connecticut were purchasing their first tracts of land from Indians around Norwalk. News of these purchases alarmed Kieft and his council in New Amsterdam. On April 19, 1640, Kieft dispatched his second-in-command,

Cornelis van Tienhoven, to the Norwalk Archipelago with an order "to purchase the adjacent lands there; to set up the arms of the Lords States-General; to take the Indians under our protection, and to prevent any other nation from committing any usurpation on our limits and encroaching further on our territory."

Van Tienhoven failed to purchase any Indian land at Norwalk. Instead, he appears to have spent much of his time trying to confirm rumors that other men from Connecticut and New Haven (separate colonies at the time) were founding settlements on Long Island, on land placed under Dutch authority the previous year. Sailing across Long Island Sound from Norwalk to Hempstead Harbor to meet with Penhawitz, Van Tienhoven found that the rumors were true. Kieft immediately dispatched troops, who succeeded in evicting the English homesteaders. Needing settlers to buffer his colony's exposed eastern frontier, Kieft soon invited the English back. Those accepting the invitation were neither numerous nor entirely strangers to the Dutch. Many families in New Netherland knew and liked their Protestant English coreligionists. English soldiers had fought alongside the Dutch in their long war against Catholic Spain, and dissident families took refuge in Dutch cities when facing persecution in England. Although England and Holland would go to war against each other at least three times during the following decades, a Dutch stadtholder named Willem Hendrijck would marry Mary Stuart, the future English Queen Mary II, and become King William III of Scotland and England in 1689. Kieft allowed colonists forced from Puritan New England to settle in the Dutch colony so long as they lived quietly and obeyed West India Company laws.

Among these émigrés was the prominent Puritan nonconformist Anne Hutchinson. Banished from New England along with Hutchinson was John Underhill, one of the commanders of the force that had indiscriminately massacred men, women, and children taking shelter in the fort at Mystic, Connecticut, during the recent Pequot War. Like Hutchinson, he had fallen afoul of Puritan authorities in Massachusetts. Kieft permitted both to settle in his colony, Hutchinson in Westchester and Underhill in Hempstead.

Like other new immigrants, Hutchinson and Underhill obtained company permits allowing them to begin land-purchase negotiations with the Indians. Kieft permitted those successfully getting deeds to establish their own communities, issuing patents for the lands and assuming jurisdiction over the towns. The arrangement benefited both parties: New England exiles found a haven in New Netherland while the Dutch gained fighting men, goods, and business in a colony ill-supported by its mother country.

Kieft's determination to get Indians to give up their goods without compensation brought on the colony's first crisis. It started on September 15, 1639, when Kieft and his council ordered collection of "peltries, maize or wampum from the Indians residing hereabout, whom we have hitherto protected." No one asked if Indians who had not submitted to Dutch authority wanted their protection. Wording in the act ominously authorized levy collectors to use "the most suitable means" to get Indians along the lower Hudson to pay up. It was an open invitation to violence.

In 1642, Wiechquaesgecks joined Tappans and other Indians from the Manhattan area meeting with Kieft to protest the tax. It soon became apparent that Dutch authorities were not the only ones extorting protection money from them. Other Indian nations from far upriver were doing so as well. Armed with Dutch muskets, these nations regarded Indian towns around the bay, mostly defended by warriors denied similar weapons by the West India Company, as easy pickings. Imagining that the Manhattans had heaps of wampum, pelts, and trade goods piled up in their longhouse rafters and storage pits, Mohawks and Mahicans demanded a cut of the in fact nonexistent bounty.

The maize levy was just the most visible problem threatening the peace between Indians and Dutch colonists at this time. The theft of a hog on Staten Island sparked open war. It later turned out that the pig had been stolen by a servant of David Pieterszen de Vries, a noted ship captain and prominent patroon sympathetic to the Indians. The report reaching Fort Amsterdam, however, mistakenly identified the culprits as Raritans. On July 16, 1640, Kieft dispatched

Van Tienhoven with some troops to sort things out. To hear Van Tienhoven tell the tale, the troops refused to obey his orders to deal peaceably with the Indians. They instead broke into Indian houses and storage pits, burned the Indians' fields, tortured a sachem's son, and killed several townspeople before returning to Manhattan. Outraged Raritans left the island, returning a year later to kill or carry off De Vries's tenants and burn his farms to the ground. The war started by Van Tienhoven's men now bears the name Kieft's War, for the governor who dispatched them to the island.

Kieft responded by calling for help from the same Indians he was taxing for protection. Realizing that people forced to pay for protection might not be anxious to die for the privilege, Kieft offered a bounty of ten fathoms (sixty feet) of wampum to anyone bringing him the head of any Raritan, and twice that for the head of an Indian who had killed a settler. One report noted that Indians from western Long Island taking up Kieft's offer "voluntarily killed some of the Raritans, our enemies." Another, dated November 2, 1641, recorded that a Tankiteke sachem named Pacham, from up the Norwalk River, brought the hand of a dead Raritan to Fort Amsterdam. Long Islanders were not the only Indians accepting Kieft's bounty.

Tankiteke and Long Island Indian attacks on behalf of the colonists evidently compelled Raritan people to make peace sometime in late 1641. This did not, however, put an end to the troubles. Settlers moving onto lands sold by Indians put Natives and Europeans in closer contact than ever before. Settlers' horses and cattle trampled nearby Indian gardens, while pigs broke into homes and fields of Indian neighbors. Colonists demanded compensation for livestock shot by Indians or killed by their dogs. Authorities ordered Indians to fence their fields, close their doors, and kill their dogs.

Relations worsened as rumors of Indian conspiracies, fueled by the realities of Indian wars in Canada, Virginia, Connecticut, and elsewhere, spread insidiously throughout New Netherland. Arguments, petty thefts, and drunken brawls further poisoned the atmosphere. Finally, a string of killings brought matters to a boiling point. Claiming that he was avenging the earlier murder of a relative by a Dutch colonist, a Wiechquaesgeck man randomly killed a settler he came across along a road in northern Manhattan. Other Indians reportedly "made crazy" by drink killed two Dutchmen in Pavonia.

De Vries wrote that a Hackensack sachem, probably the leader colonists would soon know as Oratam, quickly moved to defuse the situation. Meeting with Kieft at Fort Amsterdam, the sachem publicly promised that his people would turn over the suspect, who had fled inland to the Tankitekes, as soon as possible. Privately, he told De Vries that the killer was a chief's son and would not be given up.

The conciliatory note sounded by the Hackensack leader was not repeated by the Wiechquaesgeck sachem who subsequently met with Kieft at the fort. Complaining about traders' abuses and justifying the homicide as a vengeance killing, he angrily refused to turn the killer over, adding "that he was sorry that 20 Christians had not been murdered." The response infuriated Kieft, who dispatched two expeditions in the spring of 1642 to punish the Wiechquaesgecks for their defiance. Both forces got lost and returned after capturing and killing some Indians they stumbled across in the woods. Frustrated by these failures, Kieft waited for an opportunity to, as he put it, "put a bit into the mouth of the heathen."

The opportunity came during the winter of 1642–43, two weeks after a party of eighty or ninety musket-bearing Indians from the upper Hudson River attacked Tappan and Wiechquaesgeck towns. Sources differ on who the attackers were. Some claim they were Mahicans. Others think they were Mohawks. Whoever the raiders were, they claimed that the Indians had not paid their accustomed tribute, reportedly killed between seventeen and seventy people, and took an unspecified number of captives back to their towns.

Terrorized Indians from every community around Manhattan fled through deep snow to the Dutch settlements. Settlers at Pavonia let them put up shelters; brought them food, fuel, and blankets; and helped tend children, elders, and the wounded. On Manhattan, western Long Island Indians whose warriors had helped hunt down Raritans two years earlier took shelter in a small cluster of huts usually used to accommodate Indians visiting New Amsterdam. The little settlement, called Nechtanck, was located at Corlaers Hook, a neck of land jutting into the East River just beyond the northeast end of the Dutch town.

Past services provided by the Indian refugees did not prevent Kieft from ordering surprise attacks on both camps. Company soldiers and armed settlers carried out the order on the night of February 24, 1643. By the time the shooting stopped, eighty Indian people lay dead at Pavonia. Another forty were killed at Nechtanck. A graphic description of the Pavonia attack, best known in the version later published in De Vries's memoirs of his time in New Netherland, still shocks and appalls readers.

Outraged by the brutality of the attack and anxious to know why their people had been massacred in their sleep, Indians living around New Amsterdam quickly pressed for talks. Two coalitions appear in records documenting the meetings that followed. A delegation from a group of Long Island communities arrived at the fort a few days after the massacre. They asked De Vries to come with them to Rockaway to start negotiations. Arriving there together on March 5, 1643, they were greeted by a man identified as the one-eyed sachem (probably Penhawitz).

De Vries wrote that two hundred to three hundred people from Long Island were taking refuge at Rockaway. After hearing grievances presented by a speaker representing the sixteen Long Island chiefs attending the meeting, Penhawitz agreed to accompany them to Fort Amsterdam to reestablish peace with Kieft. At the fort on March 25, 1643, Penhawitz signed a peace treaty on behalf of the Indians of Long Island. Two weeks later, on April 23, 1643, Oratam signed a treaty agreement on behalf of another coalition consisting of communities from lands along both banks of the lower Hudson below the Highlands.

The killing of a settler by a Wappinger along the Hudson during the summer of 1643 was an indication that the treaties signed earlier that spring had not taken. The Dutch offense had been great, and the presents they gave too meager to condole bereaved survivors or erase the memory of lost kinsfolk. Many Indians were outraged by Kieft's offer of two hundred fathoms (four hundred yards) of wampum to sachems who killed what he called "madcaps" agitating for war. This time he found few takers. Pacham's change in attitude reflected the feelings of many River Indians. Just two years earlier he had called "the Swannekens ["Bitter" or "Salty People"; i.e., apparently humorless people from the other side of the salt ocean, a Delaware word for white men] . . . his best friends." Now he called for relentless war against them.

Indians were soon waylaying other settlers and burning outlying farms throughout the lower Hudson Valley. Warriors from nearly every Native community along the lower Hudson attacked with a ferocity and resolve that astonished colonists. One party destroyed De Vries's recently established replacement patroonship at Tappan. Another attacked Anne Hutchinson's newly built farm on the banks of the river that today bears her name in present-day Pelham, New York. Contemporary accounts report that Indians killed Hutchinson and five of her fifteen children on the homestead sometime in September 1643.

Reeling from these and other attacks, colonists throughout the outlying settlements abandoned their farms. Some took refuge in and around Fort Amsterdam. Others, including the now-ruined De Vries, finally gave up and left the colony altogether. Anxious to stem the flow of fleeing settlers, Kieft quickly moved to augment the meager forces available to him. He enlisted Underhill and fifty English colonists from Hempstead and the archipelago towns. He also authorized slave owners to arm their bondsmen and ordered the commander at Fort Orange to send some of its garrison downriver.

Kieft soon dispatched the scratch force he had managed to cobble together to attack Indians in Westchester and Staten Island. Both expeditions failed to engage Indians in battle. Easily detecting the oncoming columns, the Indians withdrew farther into the interior. Frustrated commanders contented themselves with killing or capturing the few stragglers they caught, burning crops, pillaging Indian houses, and rifling storage pits.

Yet the ability of colonial troops to move freely if clumsily through their territories had a sobering effect on many sachems. Leaders representing some of these communities met with Underhill at Stamford, Connecticut, during the first week of April 1644. Alarmed by the prospect of more lethal incursions, they asked Underhill to "appeal to the governor of New Netherland for peace." One week later, the Matinecock sachem made peace for his people and neighboring townsfolk. He promised that his people would not help Rockaways and other still-defiant Indians on Long Island.

Peace with the Matinecocks and their confederates further isolated Rockaways and others who refused to stop fighting. Kieft waited until the fall harvest was gathered in before ordering assaults on the still-belligerent communities. Led by Underhill, the force gathered for these attacks was stiffened with English veterans of the Pequot War. Their first incursion, made with 120 men, swept through western Long Island, reportedly killing more than 100 Indian people at Massapequa and an unnamed larger town.

The little army then sailed across Long Island Sound to the recently established English village at Greenwich, Connecticut, and headed inland. Slogging along snow-choked trails, the force, now numbering 130 men, managed to surprise a large Indian gathering at an unfortified town in the interior uplands of Westchester at the end of their first day's march. Employing the same strategy used at Mystic, Underhill ordered his men to burn the town along with its occupants. It was later reported that all but eight of the five hundred people trapped in the town died in the hail of bullets fired into the flaming houses. In contrast, Underhill lost one man killed and fifteen wounded in the attack.

Nearly six months passed before Indians around Manhattan began sending emissaries to make a lasting peace. In late May 1645, Massapequa sachem Tackapousha, accompanied by forty-seven warriors, came to Fort Amsterdam after Hempstead settlers murdered five of seven Indians they had captured to bring to the fort for interrogation. Evidently swept up in the murderous mood prevailing at the time, Dutch soldiers at the post wantonly killed the other two captives. Tackapousha, however, was more intent on ending the war than on bringing the latest murderers to justice. Telling Kieft that he had been sent to represent every Indian community on Long Island, he made peace on behalf of them all and offered warriors for service against Indians continuing to fight the Dutch.

News that 130 Dutch soldiers sent from Brazil had arrived in New Amsterdam in July compelled most of the remaining combatants to come to the conference table at Fort Amsterdam a month later. Exhausted after four years of war, all of the parties attending the August 30, 1645, treaty meeting accepted a restoration of the status quo ante bellum. The list of participants included most of the prominent Indian leaders from Long Island and the Hudson Valley. A number of the sachems who signed the treaty represented more than one Indian community. These were probably coalitions brought together by the war.

The earliest evidence showing how Indian communities organized themselves into coalitions led by influential sachems comes from deeds to lands in present-day Brooklyn signed between 1636 and 1639. These documents list both sachems of particular towns and "chiefs of the district" (like Penhawitz) who served as witnesses to the proceedings and gave their blessings to the bargains. Other considerable gatherings at Rockaway in 1643, and at the upland town above Stamford destroyed by Underhill's men a year later, suggest that many nations gathering at particular places could form even more populous combinations.

Lower River Indians formed at least four large-scale coalitions to combat the Dutch between 1640 and 1645: (1) the coalition of towns between Raritan Bay and the Falls of the Delaware, (2) the united western Long Island Indian communities, (3) the coalition of Lower River Indian communities on both banks of Hudson estuary, and (4) their closely related kinsfolk from the archipelago and the interior who were all but annihilated by Underhill's force. Although not identified as such in the August 30 treaty, the Long Island and lower Hudson Valley coalitions almost certainly constituted the major part of what Van der Donck later identified as the Manhattan speech community.

The presence of these coalitions—and the absence of emissaries representing Raritan Valley people, mid-Hudson Esopus communities, and upper Delaware Valley Minisinks—at the August 30 treaty shows that, terrible as it was, the crucible of Kieft's War failed to forge the closely connected but independent-minded people of Munsee country into a single, unified polity. Lingering hostility of Indians from central New Jersey toward Manhattans, attacks by western Long Islanders and Tankitekes on Raritan communities in 1641, and Tackapousha's promise to send warriors against those Indians still fighting the Dutch in 1645 represent only three examples of divisive enmities standing in the way of unity. Stronger pressures would be required before shared language and culture translated into social solidarity.

The immediate effects of the war are indicated by the fact that many Indian people and places near the center of Dutch colonization disappear from written records after 1645. Indian towns on Brooklyn lands purchased before the war and those burned during the fighting never again appear. Tankitekes and several other communities are not mentioned again. Shippan, Toquams, and other locales on lands bought by Englishmen along the archipelago disappear from colonial records after Underhill's men slaughtered their inhabitants in 1644. Penhawitz, Pacham, and a number of other sachems are also never again heard from.

As leaders since ancient times have done, the men who signed the August 30, 1645, treaty at Fort Amsterdam ending Kieft's War made a desolation and called it peace, to use the words of the Roman historian Tacitus. Company soldiers and militiamen had destroyed every Indian town within fifty miles of the fort's walls. Sparing not even women and children, they cut down standing crops, pillaged stored supplies, and burned what they could not take with them. By their own estimates, they killed between 800 and 1,200 Indian people. Unknown numbers of other Indians died of hunger, disease, or exposure, or were killed or carried off in internecine fighting or by Upper River raiders.

New Netherland also suffered. Nearly every outlying settlement around Manhattan had been attacked. Many colonists had been killed, and more than a few taken captive. Several disheartened colonists entirely abandoned the colony. Those farm families not killed or captured outright huddled miserably in New Amsterdam and the few towns stout enough to discourage attack. Their farms, breadbaskets of the colony, were nearly all destroyed. Fields lay fallow, livestock were killed, and the fur trade—the mainstay of the colony's economy and one of the main reasons it was established in the first place—ground to a halt.

The war also temporarily stopped colonial expansion into Indian territory. Indians signed only one deed during the three years following the end of the fighting. Settlers who elected to go back to their land had enough to do simply rebuilding what had been destroyed. Lower River Indians did not show much interest in parting with additional tracts of land.

Only a few Indians, mostly refugees in Raritan country, still believed they could use force to stop the Dutch from taking their lands. Most other Indians' hopes of recovering lost coastal lands held by colonists had to have withered in the face of harsh new realities symbolized by the 1645 treaty. They did not have home populations numbering in the millions, as the colonists did. Indians belonging to coastal communities had sustained immense losses during the late war. Settlers now held most of the best tidewater territories.

Diseases brought by European sailors and the first colonists had probably reduced the Indian population in Munsee country from 15,000 to 6,000 by 1634. According to colonists' own accounts, 1,000 people were killed during Kieft's War; assuming that twice that number either died or abandoned the region, only 4,000 Indians may have still lived in their homeland in 1645.

Whatever the actual numbers, Indian losses were nothing short of catastrophic. Entire lineages, along with their ability to maintain land-use rights, almost certainly were wiped out. Having neither families nor land to return to, many captives and most refugees driven from their shoreline homes probably chose to move into the interior farther from colonists, settling among new friends and relatives in safer locales. Following an evidently longstanding tradition observed nearly everywhere in Native America, Munsee country Indians had adopted colonists captured during the fighting to replace their lost loved ones.

Forced to give up these substitute relatives under the terms of the 1645 treaty ending Kieft's War, Indian families refusing to leave their coastal lands did not have sufficient numbers, resources, or time to reconstitute themselves on their remaining bits of ancestral territory directly in the path of colonial expansion.

Hopes that another Indian nation might come to their aid or push back colonists on the coast also dimmed at this time. The Indians of New England and the Five Nations had not yet recovered from small-pox epidemics that had ravaged their towns between 1631 and 1634. Mathematically at least, the impact of epidemic mortality is much more devastating on populations numbering in the thousands than on those whose home populations run in the tens of millions. Al-though high birthrates can allow even small populations to rebound quickly, devastating epidemic and war losses all but overwhelmed the Indians living in Munsee country.

Higher survival rates among colonists possessing acquired im-munity to epidemic diseases like smallpox further tipped the demo-graphic scales in favor of the settlers. People surviving smallpox tend to develop immunities that help them endure subsequent epidemics. Such survivors do not, however, transmit their acquired immunities to their children. In the grim arithmetic of mass death, larger popu-lations ensure higher numbers of survivors, even if the death rate is the same in both populations. Those survivors, in turn, can produce ever larger populations of descendants. Thus, while there is no clear evidence suggesting that Indians were inherently more vulnerable to epidemics like smallpox, their smaller numbers and lack of earlier ex-posure significantly increased their overall demographic susceptibility to Old World contagions brought by Europeans.

No amount of immunity protected people from wars like those that had just desolated much of Munsee country. Fighting swept up Indians throughout the region. New England Indians were still reeling from the Pequot bloodbath of 1637. To the north, Mohawks, Oneidas, and their Iroquois brethren—intent on avenging lost rela-tives and dominating the fur trade—seemed trapped in an endless round of bloody conflicts with all nations on their borders. Farther south, Powhatan warriors were making their last futile attempt to drive out Virginian colonists. Struggling for survival in their own homelands, few Indian nations anywhere in the Northeast, even if so inclined, could help Indians in Munsee country rebuild, much less migrate to or otherwise occupy new lands.

Only colonists possessed the resources and power to hold and occupy coastal lands in Munsee country during the desolate summer of 1645. Continued fighting and a series of epidemics would strike local Indian communities in quick succession over the next twenty years. Few people, either colonists or Indians, were untouched by the drumfire of devastation that rained down on the region by the time a career soldier named Petrus Stuyvesant, who replaced Kieft in 1647, finally surrendered New Netherland to an English fleet in 1664.

3

DRUMFIRE, 1645–1664

The seemingly endless succession of wars and rumors of wars that rolled across the Hudson and Delaware valleys during the final quarter century of Dutch rule raked the region like a smothering artillery barrage. More than a century later, in 1762, a New Jersey Indian named John Doubty living in exile in Ohio recounted his people's memory of this violent era to a visiting Quaker trader: "After the white people came the Dutch about New York shot an Indian for pulling peaches off his trees, which caused wars, and after peace, the Indians being settled thick in a town near the Dutch, in very deep snow, the Dutch taking the advantage killed the Indians[;] only one made his escape, who alarmed others so that two other wars and peaces ensued."

Dutch chronicles substantiate Doubty's story of the three wars in Munsee country. Doubty, however, conflated the signature incident of the second of these conflicts, namely, the 1655–57 Peach War, with the preceding Kieft's and the following Esopus wars. Thus, the terrors of these brutal wars burned themselves into a memory of seemingly continuous conflict. Fighting beyond the borders of New Netherland intensified the impact of interminable strife within the colony. Some, like the Dutch seizure in 1655 of the New Sweden settlements on the Delaware first established in 1638, were isolated incidents that did not lead to wider war. When the First Anglo-Dutch Naval War of 1652–54 broke out, Dutch and New England colonists agreed to a truce that largely confined the fighting to Europe. Although they armed Indian belligerents and plotted with and against one nation or another, Dutch and English colonists avoided formal involvement in the Five Nations' wars. Five Nations conflicts were indeed wide-ranging during these years, with conflicts against the Mahicans and other Northern Indians; against the French and their Huron, Erie, and other Indian allies on the St. Lawrence and around the Great Lakes; and against the Susquehannocks and other Indian nations.

Fear that these and other conflicts might spread to the Dutch and English settlements fueled rumors, alarms, and conspiracy theories. Killings, assaults, robberies, and insults joined disputes both foreign and domestic to create a tense atmosphere thick with retaliatory threats and talk of fighting. A continual series of local brushfire conflicts—the kind typically waged by more or less evenly matched opponents not strong enough to prevail over one another—sparked bouts of open warfare. Flaring and sputtering, such wars often seem to merge into one another to form memories of continuous conflict.

Fighting during Kieft's War conformed to this pattern, flaring into periods of intense violence followed by shaky truces, renewed raids, and inconclusive diplomacy. Even the Treaty of 1645 did not end the violence. The continuing hostility of Raritan people, and of bellicose Wiechquaesgeck and other refugees from the lower Hudson River living with them, made life hazardous for colonists traversing the lowlands between the Hudson and Delaware valleys years after the fighting ended. Unable to resolve these problems and blamed for all the troubles with the Indians, Kieft was relieved of his position and ordered to return to the Netherlands in 1647. The disgraced governor did not live to answer charges lodged against him. En route back to his home country, he drowned along with most of the crew and passengers of *de Prinses Amelia* when she sank off the coast of Ireland in a storm in the late summer of 1647.

It took Kieft's replacement, Petrus Stuyvesant, two years to finally get the holdouts in Raritan country to come to the conference table. Susquehannocks, who probably did not appreciate the way hostilities blocked their most direct trade route with Fort Amsterdam, helped convince the Indians living at Raritan that it was time to make peace. Meeting in Manhattan in early July 1649, sachems representing the Raritans and the Wiechquaesgecks still living with them put their marks alongside Stuyvesant's signature on a peace treaty resolving all outstanding differences. Stuyvesant took advantage of the opportunity to get the Wiechquaesgecks to sign over half of their home territory and promise sale of the remainder at a later date.

The peace agreement had not come too soon. Other troubles threatened when reports reached New Amsterdam the following spring that New Englanders planned to attack the Wappingers. This news came at a time when the Esopus, the Mahicans, and several New England Indian nations usually allied with the Wappingers had evidently promised the French that they would attack the Iroquois. Unwilling to risk Mohawk retaliation, the Wappingers refused to join the expedition. This angered the English, who threatened to attack their erstwhile allies. The Dutch feared that English conquest of the Wappingers, whose territories straddled the disputed border between New Netherland and New England, would allow the English to extend their boundary claims to the Hudson's shores. Such an unwelcome possibility helped persuade Stuyvesant to agree to a meeting with New Englanders to hammer out a mutually acceptable border in the late summer of 1650.

The resulting Fort Hope treaty did more than settle this boundary dispute for a time. Alarmed by growing Iroquois military ascendancy, Stuyvesant asked the New Englanders if they would consider joining in an alliance against them. The New Englanders took the proposal under advisement. Meanwhile, River Indians eager to get out from under Mohawk thumbs tried to prod things along by spreading rumors that Iroquois warriors planned to attack Dutch settlements. None of this came to anything, however. The outbreak of the First Anglo-Dutch Naval War prevented any union of Dutch and English colonists against anyone. River Indian hopes that settlers would enter into an alliance against the Iroquois were finally dashed when the governor of New France concluded peace treaties with each of the Five Nations in 1653.

Memories of the horrors of Indian war had hardly faded around the Hudson Valley when a party of Indian warriors said to number close to one thousand men in sixty-four canoes descended on New Amsterdam on September 15, 1655. They arrived while the city's garrison was away subjugating the Swedish settlements on the Delaware. Neither the identities nor the intentions of the Indians making up the force were clear to the colonists. Some said that Indians "living back of Onckeway [Fairfield, Connecticut] and Stamford" were in the flotilla. Others thought they recognized Indians from Westchester among them. Stuyvesant cast the net widely, including among them "Maquasas [Mohawks], Mahicanders, Indians from the Upper and Lower North River, from Paham's Land, Northern Indians and others." Years later, Wappinger and Esopus sachems affirmed that some of their warriors had been with the Indian army.

The Indians said they were on their way to fight Northern Indians, but the nervous colonists did not buy that story. Some thought Susquehannocks friendly with the Swedes had put the River Indians up to an attack. Still others alleged that the Indians were out to avenge themselves only on Dutch colonists and would leave alone the settlers of English, Finnish, and eighteen other nationalities then living in New Netherland. Shortly thereafter, the Indians' claim was supported when Tackapousha asked for Dutch help against an expected Narragansett attack from Rhode Island, just across Long Island Sound. Whatever the facts of the matter, shots were soon fired and people died. The conflict began when warriors who claimed they were searching for Northern Indians allegedly hiding in town shot and wounded one Hendrick van Dijck. Recently fired by Stuyvesant from his position as state attorney, Van Dijck had been one of Kieft's chief lieutenants during the last war. He was also evidently the colonist Indians believed had wantonly killed a woman picking peaches in his garden. The conflict following on the heels of this incident has since become known as the Peach War.

Leaving Manhattan, the warriors subsequently embarked on a three-day rampage across the region. Settlements at Pavonia and Staten Island were once again burned. Other attacks destroyed or

forced the evacuation of nearly every other outlying farmstead. Warriors reportedly killed between fifty and one hundred colonists and
captured one hundred more. Unable or unwilling to do further damage, the Indians then dispatched representatives demanding ransoms
for captives and the initiation of peace negotiations. Talks reached
an impasse when Dutch authorities refused to pay for the return of
the captured colonists. Both sides finally settled for a working disagreement in which Dutch authorities refused to give in to ransom
demands but presented Indian families with larger gifts than had been
demanded. In return, Indian families encouraged newly adopted captives to return to their homes.

Represented by his speaker Pennekeck, Hackensack sachem Oratam was a primary intermediary in these exchanges. Tackapousha
also again stepped forward. Meeting with Stuyvesant in March 1656,
Tackapousha promised that the Massapequas and the other Indians
on western Long Island who had recently acknowledged him as their
sachem would uphold any peace agreement so long as they could be
sure of Dutch protection. A dense cloud of stolid belligerence nevertheless settled over the region for another year until the last exchanges
of presents and prisoners finally restored some quiet along the lower
river.

Meanwhile, settlers from Fort Orange had begun buying farmlands
in Esopus country soon after they received news of the peace treaties
between the Five Nations and the French, signed in 1653. Shaken by
the news of the Indian attacks at and around Manhattan, most abandoned their farms and fled back upriver. Proof that they were wise
to do so soon emerged when it was found that the rampaging Indian
flotilla included many Esopus warriors.

Esopus families did not welcome the sixty or so settlers who returned to plant their fields in 1657 after the danger of attack faded.
The Indians' resentment was fueled by Fort Orange fur traders who
had continued sailing to their shores during the fighting. Most if not
all of these men engaged in sharp trading practices that left many of
their clients little more than drunk at the close of business. Relations
quickly went from bad to worse during the spring of 1658 when an

Indian shot down a trader on his yacht from the shore near Esopus. Other Indians burned two nearby farmhouses, killed and carried off livestock, and threatened further mayhem.

Hearing news of the troubles at Esopus, Stuyvesant sailed upriver with sixty-one soldiers during the last week of May to find out what was going on. After hearing out both sides, he ordered them to settle their differences. Sensing a not-so-thinly veiled threat in a sachem's statement that he could not control drink-befuddled young warriors who were spoiling for a fight, Stuyvesant replied that he "would match man with man, or twenty against thirty, yes even forty" of the Indians. Finding no one to take up the challenge, Stuyvesant told the sachems that he wanted to buy land for a fort on a bluff above Esopus Creek near the place where the Rondout Creek flows into the Hudson (present-day Kingston, New York). He then advised settlers to move inside the fort once it was completed. A stockade was erected by the end of June. Settlers moving behind its walls named the place Wiltwijck, "Indian town."

The situation moved closer to an open break when reports of further provocations and rumors of a secret meeting of perhaps as many as five hundred Indians caused Stuyvesant to travel back to Esopus on October 15. Blaming the unrest on the Indians, Stuyvesant demanded that the sachems pay a punishingly high indemnity of nearly one hundred strings of wampum and, in an unprecedented move, ordered them to give up their lands around Wiltwijck to cover the costs of fort construction, settlers' losses, and their expenses for moving into the fort. Promising to give them gifts if they gave up their land, he further urged the Indians to leave the region entirely if they wanted to avoid further difficulties. The stunned sachems tried to moderate Stuyvesant's demands. Failing that, they told him that they would come back in the spring to give up the demanded territory.

Spring passed into summer, and the Esopus still did not come to surrender their land. In August 1659, some Esopus sachems reminded settlers that Stuyvesant had not yet given them the presents promised the preceding spring. Then on September 4, a large delegation of Esopus sachems, accompanied by women and children, appeared at Wiltwijck. They began by telling the settlers that they had recently met with several sachems representing Iroquois, Susquehannock, and other nations who strongly urged them to keep the peace. Reminding their listeners that both sides were at fault in this dispute, they delivered seventy-five of the one hundred wampum strings demanded by Stuyvesant to show they were serious about wanting to live in peace with the settlers. No one, however, made any mention of vacating land.

Open fighting broke out before Stuyvesant could return upriver to settle matters. On the night of September 20, settlers fired into an Indian drinking party just beyond the fort walls, killing one man, wounding two, and seizing another. The next day a large body of Esopus warriors, estimated by terrified settlers at between four hundred and six hundred men, appeared before the walls of Wiltwijck. The disgusted fort commandant initially threatened to abandon the unruly settlers to Indian vengeance, but swallowed his anger and dispatched a messenger to inform Stuyvesant of developments. The messenger and the detachment of twelve men sent to protect him did not get far. The Indians captured the party near the fort. Sending the captives to a fortified Esopus town a day's march from Wiltwijck, the warriors settled down to lay siege to the Dutch village.

Word of the troubles reached New Amsterdam hard on the heels of reports that other Indians had killed some settlers at Maspeth, just across the East River from Manhattan. Settlers from outlying farms once again began fleeing to the protection of Fort Amsterdam. Gathering what men he could, Stuyvesant led a force made up of 150 soldiers, militiamen, conscripts, servants, and some Long Island Indians upriver. They landed on October 10, two days after news of their impending arrival had caused the Indians to lift their siege. Unwilling to send his small band out against an enemy of unknown strength, Stuyvesant ordered most of the soldiers and militiamen to join settlers defending the fort and returned with the rest to New Amsterdam.

As in earlier conflicts, Indian and colonial leaders quickly tried to stop hostilities before the fighting spread. During the last weeks of October, Mohawk and Mahican sachems set aside their own differences to work out a cease-fire agreement and secure the release of the two Dutch prisoners who were still alive. The resulting truce held through the winter, although the Esopus refused to meet with Stuyvesant when he again sailed upriver in late November.

Evidently angered by the snub and incensed by reports of continued Esopus defiance, Stuyvesant used the winter months to prepare quietly for war in the spring. Finding it difficult to recruit settlers, as they were reluctant to leave their families during dangerous times, Stuyvesant instead had to call on the West India Company to send reinforcements. Stuyvesant tried to ease some of the settlers' fears at a meeting with Tackapousha and other sachems from Long Island and the lower river held in March 1660. Stuyvesant accepted Tackapousha's explanation that the Maspeth killers had fled to Navesink and renewed friendship with the sachems. Three days later he received company permission to begin hostilities against the Esopus and a promise of men and supplies. Attending to the spiritual needs of his colonists, Stuyvesant appointed March 24 as a day of fasting, prayer, and meditation. Refusing a last-minute Esopus peace offer made through Wappinger intermediaries, Stuyvesant formally declared war and sent troops north.

Reinforced by twenty-five soldiers sent by Stuyvesant, the commander of the Wiltwijck garrison soon ordered his troops to form raiding parties and fan out across Esopus country. They struck during April and May, the hungry time when Indians living on the last of their winter stores concentrated on planting and the spring hunt. Dutch raiders killed and captured a number of Esopus men, women, and children; destroyed settlements and food caches; and reportedly killed eleven visiting Minisink Indians. Stuyvesant ordered eleven of the more defiant Esopus captives sent to Dutch Caribbean colony of Curaçao as slaves. Two or three others suspected of killing settlers were held for later punishment.

Intent on humbling the Esopus, Stuyvesant rebuffed repeated peace overtures. Keeping up the attacks, he further isolated the Esopus by securing neutrality pledges from their Wappinger and Lower River Indian allies. Stuyvesant finally agreed to a truce on June 3, after receiving word that his troops had captured and killed Preuwamakan, the oldest and most influential of the Esopus sachems. The Dutch governor subsequently met with the Esopus chiefs at Wiltwijck to conclude a general peace on July 15, 1660.

The chiefs attending this conference promised to give up their lands around the fort, return their prisoners, indemnify Dutch losses with substantial payments of corn, and keep the peace. Stuyvesant gave them gifts and returned three Indian prisoners, holding the eleven sent to Curaçao as hostages. The sachems put their marks on the treaty in the presence of chiefs from nearly every other Hudson Valley Indian nation, who promised to attack the Esopus in the event the latter renewed the war.

The absence of Indians from the Lower Bay at the July 15 treaty evidently was a deliberate omission. Stuyvesant had continued to receive reports of killings and other hostile acts allegedly committed by Indians from the Raritan country years after concluding peace with them in 1649. Stuyvesant had other problems in that area as well. An old land jobber, Cornelis Melijn, had become his most bitter political opponent. Former patroon partisan and political enemy of Kieft, Melijn had been sent back with the disgraced governor to the Netherlands aboard *de Princess Amelia*. Unlike Kieft, Melijn survived her sinking and returned to New Netherland two years later, buying a farm on Staten Island. Melijn's anti-authoritarian tendencies evidently soon embroiled him in disputes with Stuyvesant. Reports surfaced accusing Melijn of encouraging Indians to assassinate the governor. Melijn, it was said, had also hired more than one hundred musket-armed Raritan and Southern Indian bodyguards to defend him on his farm.

Still denied firearms by the governor, Indians were willing to do much for settlers willing to arm them. Guns were particularly important to Indians in Raritan country, who found themselves increasingly pressed from both sides of the lowland corridor between the Falls of the Delaware and Staten Island that lay at the heart of their territories. One report written in 1650 intimated that Susquehannocks armed with muskets had forced most Indians living along the corridor to temporarily abandon their homes and move elsewhere. At least some evidently moved to Melijn's farm on Staten Island. Others almost certainly relocated to Mattano's Nayack community at the westernmost end of Brooklyn.

Preoccupied with troubles at Esopus, Stuyvesant was unable to settle accounts with refractory Navesinks and Raritans allegedly armed by Melijn. Susquehannocks may also have helped alleged murderers of Dutch settlers taking refuge at Navesink slip farther from the governor's grasp. In April 1660, Stuyvesant received word from company employees on the Delaware that Mohawk ambassadors had urged Susquehannocks to offer asylum to Raritan or Navesink people living near Manhattan who feared Dutch attack. Susquehannocks, desperate to replenish their own dwindling numbers, apparently took the Mohawks up on their suggestion. They were mired in a seemingly interminable conflict with the westernmost Iroquois nations and faced the prospect of renewed war with Piscataway Indians in Maryland, whom they had been fighting since the late 1640s. Contemporary reports affirm that Indians from the Delaware River moved one hundred or so miles from their territories to the Susquehanna River and helped Susquehannocks fight these enemies. Navesink and Raritan people were probably among the one hundred Indians from the Delaware River who helped Susquehannocks withstand a Seneca siege of their main town on the Lower Susquehanna in the spring of 1663.

After receiving word of the July 15, 1660, Esopus peace treaty, company directors ordered Stuyvesant to either attack the Raritans and Navesinks or make peace with them. Their sachems rebuffed Stuyvesant's subsequent demands that they surrender all alleged murderers of Dutch settlers living among them. Instead they sent gifts in order "that the matter should be adjusted and forgotten." Stuyvesant rejected the presents. Unwilling to compromise and unable to attack, he had to settle for a stalemate in Raritan-Navesink country when renewed fighting at Esopus forced him to turn his attention northward.

Like so many others, the 1660 Esopus peace agreement proved to be more truce than treaty. Unwilling to admit defeat, many warriors at Esopus remained defiant. Stuyvesant's refusal to repatriate the eleven Esopus prisoners sent to Curaçao became a troublesome sticking point. Five Nations diplomats meeting with Stuyvesant during the following summer urged him to order the return of the men. Later that year, a concerned Stuyvesant wrote that the Indians at Esopus were losing patience and looking for an excuse to renew fighting. The winter of 1661–62 passed without incident, however. A relieved Stuyvesant wrote to his counterpart at Curaçao, ordering the return of two of the captives and directing that the remaining nine be told "that if they behaved well [they] too shall be released and sent back in due time."

Relations with the still-resentful Esopus took a turn for the worse during the spring of 1662. Ignoring Stuyvesant's warnings and Esopus threats, Wiltwijck settlers began to build what they named Nieuwdorp, "New Village." Now called Hurley, it was located a few miles west of Kingston on an upland overlooking broad fertile flats lining Esopus Creek. A year passed before alarmed residents threatened by angry Esopus neighbors wrote to Stuyvesant on May 10, 1663, asking that he send troops and preserve the peace by sending gifts to the Indians "at the first opportunity." Rebuffed by Stuyvesant, who refused to send soldiers or subsidize local expansion efforts, the settlers girded for an Esopus attack.

They did not have to wait long. Esopus warriors struck the two Dutch towns along Esopus Creek on the morning of June 7. Firing on farmers in the fields and burning houses within the villages, they quickly destroyed Nieuwdorp and nearly succeeded in burning Wiltwijck to the ground. They killed at least twenty settlers and captured another forty-five. Once again, Stuyvesant declared war, called for volunteers, and asked Mohawk and Mahican sachems to begin negotiating for the release of captives. He also met again with Oratam and other Lower River Indian chiefs known to be in sympathy with the Esopus to satisfy himself that their people would stay out of the fighting. Tackapousha once again pledged his support, this time more tangibly in the form of twenty warriors under the command of his brother Chopeycannows, sent to fight alongside seventeen Long Island Indians already helping protect colonists at Wiltwijck.

Stuyvesant sent a force of sixty men upriver under the command of a reliable captain-lieutenant named Marten Kregier. On July 26, Kregier led these men, reinforced with another one hundred from Wiltwijck and thirty-seven Long Island warriors, out against a fort reported to be the center of Esopus resistance. Guided by a Wappinger captive and a Dutch former prisoner who had escaped from the fort, the force reached the place only to find it empty. Kregier's troops spent the next few days burning crops and spoiling stores before putting the stockade to the torch and returning to Wiltwijck.

Distressed by the ease with which Kregier's force moved through their country, Esopus people scattered to friends and relatives among the Minisinks, Catskills, and Wappingers. Most busied themselves with planting new cornfields while their young people worked to erect a new fort farther from Wiltwijck. Meanwhile, Stuyvesant gathered intelligence about his Esopus enemies and worked to separate their friends from them.

In the meantime, Kregier kept up pressure by sending patrols out into the heart of Esopus country. On September 3, one of these patrols brought word of the new fort's location. Kregier immediately gathered fifty of his men and headed up the Wallkill River. Traveling with great stealth, they managed to surprise and take the fort two days later. Deep in Esopus territory and fearing counterattack, Kregier's men did not take time to burn the place. Instead, they plundered the houses and destroyed what they could not carry away. Withdrawing with nineteen prisoners and twenty-three liberated captives, they left the unburied corpses of at least thirty Esopus people behind.

The attack broke the back of Esopus resistance. Oratam and Mattano helped work out a truce with Esopus sachems, one of whom, a man named Sewackenamo who had taken refuge at Hackensack, emerged as the most visible Esopus pro-peace advocate. The truce they hammered out was a shaky one. Unknown Indians killed settlers at Communipaw and in Wappinger country during the winter and spring of 1663–64. Determined to maintain the cease-fire, both sides chose to regard the killings as isolated incidents. A renewed outbreak of fighting in the longstanding feud between the Mohawks and Mahicans and their Northern Indian allies in the fall of 1663 presented a more serious threat to peace. The Dutch dealt with the problem by brokering a truce between the adversaries at Fort Orange in December, persuading both to keep pressure on the Esopus to maintain their own cease-fire.

Representatives from nearly every Indian nation along the Hudson finally gathered at Fort Amsterdam to conclude a comprehensive peace on May 15, 1664. One day later, the assembled dignitaries signed the treaty document. In most respects, the terms resembled those of earlier treaties, calling for restoration of peace and repatriation of captives. Stuyvesant made a point of insisting that the Esopus finally turn over the lands near Wiltwijck that they had promised to give up four years earlier. Speaking for all Esopus sachems, Sewackenamo agreed to surrender all of the territory extending as far inland as the old and new forts. The Dutch allowed the Indians to harvest crops already planted around the forts before leaving. Both sides further pledged to meet yearly to air grievances and preserve peace. Treaty minutes do not mention exchanges of wampum, pelts, or gifts sealing the agreements. The former belligerents evidently believed they had already paid the price of peace in full.

Renewed epidemics of smallpox exacted a stiffer price than the agreed-upon treaty terms. First reported at New Amsterdam during the winter of 1660–61 the disease swiftly spread to every Indian and colonial community in and around Munsee country. An even more severe outbreak swept through the region two years later. The impact of these epidemics on Munsee communities can be assessed only indirectly. The 1663–64 epidemic may have played a greater role than Dutch military action in reducing Esopus ability to continue the war. Illness also may have kept three of the senior Esopus sachems away from the May 15 treaty meeting.

Whatever their immediate impact or proximate causes, the constant barrage of war, disease, and other calamities killed or drove away a substantial part of the total Indian population in the lower Hudson and upper Delaware valleys between the 1640s and 1660s. Death, destruction, and dispossession reached into the hearts of nearly every River Indian community. Epidemic contagion, wars, and rumors of war also desolated and demoralized colonists with unfeeling impartiality. Hundreds died in the nearly interminable fighting. More were carried off by epidemics. New immigrants from Europe would more than replenish colonists' losses. Indian population numbers, by contrast, plummeted. Many who survived the wars and epidemics accepted adoption into more powerful Indian nations like the Susquehannocks and Iroquois intent on recovering their own dwindling numbers. Others began leaving their lands for new homes farther from colonists and their diseases.

Overwhelming feelings of unappeasable anger and inconsolable grief would almost certainly have been the legacy of these calamities. The possibility of River Indians and colonists achieving levels of empathy needed to recognize each other's common humanity became increasingly remote as loss exacerbated feelings of indifference and outright hatred. Whatever their descendants may think, both sides could fall prey to these very human feelings. Although present-day writers rarely fail to condemn colonists for their overweeningly self-righteous, ethnocentric pride in their cultural superiority, there is no reason to assume that River Indians loved their own traditions and hated those who threatened them with passions any less intense or self-regarding.

Upheavals caused by war and disease widened economic disparities between Indians and colonists and rearranged worldviews at critical intervals. It was during such times that colonists felt strong enough to force River Indians to sign away their rights to particular pieces of territory, give up long-valued rights and privileges, and submit to colonial authority. Indian warriors and military leaders tried to reverse the sea change that threatened to overwhelm their people by killing and driving away settlers, and by fighting mourning wars to avenge lost loved ones. Their efforts only caused more grief.

Increasingly outnumbered and technologically outclassed, Indians in Munsee country finally began to accept the fact that war no longer represented a productive option for them. They had to find new ways to cope with ever-growing numbers of colonists flooding onto their lands. Accommodation, however, presented its own set of challenges. How, for example, could they secure protection without becoming slaves of their protectors? How could they obtain now-essential trade goods with fewer producers, less land, and dwindling resources? And, most perplexing, how could they slow or stop colonists from taking their land altogether and driving them away from their homes entirely?

4

DEALINGS, 1630–1664

Even if the settlers miraculously disappeared, the surviving Indians of Munsee country could never return to the life they had lived before the Europeans came. Whatever happened, they would have to put the past behind them and move forward. That meant trying to remember what might be most helpful and to forget everything else.

Everyone in Munsee country, settlers as well as Indians, had much to forget. Their relationships with one another had been neither harmonious nor uplifting. Epidemics had scythed ugly trails of death, disfigurement, and sorrow through both populations. Their wars were inglorious, ignoble, inconclusive, and brutally squalid affairs marked by massacre, pillage, and destruction in discouraging dimensions. Although the scourges of war, disease, death, and dispossession had fallen more heavily on the Indians, each side had sacrificed much and lost more. Everyone could point to offenses offered, outrages suffered, and sicknesses endured. Most almost certainly believed that these were punishments brought down by divine protectors somehow angered by sinful living or inadequate observance. It is equally certain that both Indians and colonists willingly paid the costs of spiritual renewal and moral rearmament as they poured energy and treasure into defense efforts.

Neither side could gain complete ascendancy. Forced to deal with each other, both had to give far more than they wanted to and get less than they thought they needed. Most settled for cobbled-together, creative working disagreements that both parties could blithely deny and easily forget when no longer necessary. Indians and colonists often conveniently forgot past concessions and mutually denied distasteful compromises. But their lives and histories had been joined. Stuck with each other, they had to live together—grudgingly, reluctantly— in the homeland they now shared.

Nowhere were the consequences of choices made by Indians and colonists compelled to live together on territory each wanted for their own more evident than in their land dealings with one another. These are chronicled in the more than six hundred deeds, signed by a comparatively limited number of sachems over the course of a century and a half between 1630 and 1779, that ultimately transformed all of the Munsee homeland into colonial property. The pattern shown on the maps in this book charting these sales is far from a confused hodgepodge of scattered tracts signed away by random Indians duped into putting their marks onto any paper colonists shoved in their faces. Instead, it more closely resembles a gradual and orderly process. Most deeds (at least during Dutch and early English times) conveyed small tracts and almost all shared borders with already sold lands. The resulting pattern is a systematic Indian withdrawal up river valleys from coastal centers of colonial power into the interior, overseen by a small number of sachems politically linked to colonial governments or interest groups over several generations.

Much more than simple surrender was at work here. Otherwise, why would the Europeans not simply have taken all the land they wanted from the Indians at one time? And why was the pattern of alienation so orderly? Despite obvious differences, Indian and European ideas about land and everything associated with it must have been similar enough to sustain a relationship corresponding to the size, orderliness, and duration of this documentary record.

One significant area of equivalence lay in the respect both peoples had for spiritual power. Everyone living in the Hudson and Delaware valleys not only believed in spirits but believed that they held their land in trust from them. Munsees believed that Kiisheelumukweenk,

"He Who Creates Us With His Thoughts," gave the land to their ancestors. Sachems representing families descended from these ancestors upheld customs protecting their ancient rights to these lands. Settlers similarly believed that their rulers and governments had God-given rights to lawfully claimed land. However they held the land, whether through statutory law or customary tradition, Indians and colonists clearly defined and resolutely guarded their rights to ground that held graves of ancestors whose numbers they would join when their own time came.

This is not to say there were not significant differences between the two cultures. Indian custom supported communal ownership. Sachems and councils charged with administering family lands used a custom called usufruct—the lawful right to something so long as it is being utilized—to allocate townsites, planting plots, fishing spots, hunting and foraging territories, and other places. Usufruct did not mean that Indians thought land was free, like air and water, open to anyone wishing to share it. Usufruct entitlements were available only to people with rights to land and only as long as they were willing to properly respect local customs and concerns. Land was not free to strangers from foreign places who did not have these rights or share these customs. Such people could obtain land only as a granted gift or through forced surrender.

European law, by contrast, defined all land under Crown or corporate control as private property and regarded land sales as final. Officials dispensed and protected fee simple ownership to purchasers who met ownership requirements and paid deed prices, survey costs, and title fees. Concepts like private versus communal ownership are neither cross-culturally incomprehensible nor necessarily absolute, however. Words used in land transactions—such as "give," "promise," and "forever"—mean much the same thing in most languages. Land tenure concepts, moreover, are neither simple nor unequivocal abstractions: all such ideas vary in meaning as well as substance, making them susceptible to interpretation and thus to manipulation.

Fee simple ownership, for example, grants owners rights to will their property to heirs and to sell or otherwise transfer it at will. It does not, however, completely privatize property. Covenants of one sort or another may limit ownership to various extents. Public necessity can trump private privilege through various forms of legal control and confiscation ranging from royal fiat to eminent domain and zoning regulations. Although there are no data documenting similar landownership customs among the Indian people of Munsee country, it is difficult to imagine that people intensely tied to particular places agreed that customs mandating communal sharing always outweighed personal needs or familial concerns. A colonist's failure to pay rents and taxes mandated by colonial law and an Indian's forgetting to give presents required by custom probably met with similar responses in both societies.

Other similarities suggest further common ground for cross-cultural comprehension. Much data exist, for example, showing that both Indians and colonists cared deeply about territorial integrity and paid close attention to land rights and boundaries. Both peoples also evidently took great care to grant particular persons resource rights to particular places for specified lengths of time. Both also accepted the fact that land could be militarily conquered as well as peaceably transferred. And both further felt that no transfer, whether forced or voluntary, was complete without the performance of appropriate rites and ceremonies—in this case, formal signing and sealing of a deed and a promised exchange of goods. Indians and colonists alike marked all stages of property transfer with rituals validated by presentations of goods that Indians might call gifts and colonists payments. Both peoples, moreover, kept records of their transactions. Indians used strings and woven belts of wampum, supplemented with notched or painted sticks, to jog memories. Europeans favored pen-and-ink writings on paper or parchment.

Some twenty years passed between the time Hudson sailed to the region in 1609 and 1630, the year the first deeds were signed. Evidently, by then Munsee Indians and colonists had settled on deeds as the instrument of choice in land dealings with one another. The fact that Indians accepted the European deed form shows that land transactions were not conducted on a completely level playing field.

Whereas a deed signed between two colonists merely transferred landownership, the deeds colonists used to obtain title to Indian land also secured European sovereignty over the property. The land Indians sold thus passed from Native to colonial jurisdiction under the rules and laws of the colonizing nation. Such a change in sovereignty would not happen when, for example, a Finn bought land from a Dutch landowner in New Netherland. Although title would pass to the Finn, the land would not become sovereign Finnish territory. Under international law, transfers of sovereignty in and among nations could be accomplished only through treaty agreement. In this respect, an Indian deed served as a kind of treaty between Native people and colonists.

Not all colonies used deeds to acquire Indian lands. Maryland, Virginia, and New France, for example, did not recognize private purchases from Indians. Officials in these provinces tended to acquire Indian land through seizure or treaty cessions. Modern-day Indian nations in the United States have the status of domestic dependent nations, and only the federal government has the right to have territorial dealings with them. Similarly, the French and English sovereigns issued charters designating territories in the New World as Crown lands, and colonial officials used treaties to claim Indian lands on their sovereign's behalf. Authorities always kept a tight leash on land affairs. The New England and Middle Atlantic provinces were the only colonies that regularly used deeds as instruments to obtain title to Indian land. Thus, what historian Francis Jennings called "deed game" shenanigans, in which rival colonists used privately obtained deeds to support contending land claims, arose only in those provinces.

Although rules changed from time to time, private individuals, corporations, and officials at every level of government from the municipality, town, and county to the province could conclude land deals with Indians in all colonies from Maine to Delaware Bay. Many thousands of documents recording these transactions lie in state and county archives scattered across this vast swath of territory. The sheer quantity of these documents bears witness to the complex nature of intercultural land dealings. Deeds, which drew their legitimacy among

Indians from customary laws, divided owners from nonowners. Statutory laws regulating provincial contractual agreements linked buyers and sellers alike to clan, Crown, corporate, or private interests.

As mentioned earlier, Indian deeds and the ideas behind them were susceptible to varying degrees of interpretation, manipulation, and worse. As legal instruments, however, their wording was usually clear and their structure simple and straightforward. For this reason, deeds were among the first forms printed on colonial presses. Their standardized structure, their easy-to-understand format, and the requirement that they be read aloud before signing helped both literate and unlettered people understand and endorse their contents. All deeds followed a rigid structure that began by specifying time and place of sale. Interested parties were then identified by name and affiliation, payments and other considerations were listed, and tract boundaries described. Each also contained wording describing the nature of the title that passed to the grantee and set out covenants obliging one or the other party to fulfill certain conditions. The document was then signed with signatures or marks and sealed by officials in the presence of witnesses. Endorsements added on the bottoms and reverse sides of deeds acknowledged payments paid and received, affirmed their registration in proper repositories, and included notations documenting subsequent divisions, transfers, and other actions affecting deeded land.

Even if all parties involved in a particular transaction did not precisely understand everything written or said, the rigidly repetitive structure of deed contents and the ceremonial readings and signings of deed documents composed what can be thought of as a ritual formula. Literate or illiterate, Indian or colonist, all people in colonial America were attuned to the nuances of social etiquette, political procedure, and religious ceremony. Respect for proper performance of reading and signing rituals during land deals went far in assuring all parties that appropriate ceremonies and forms were being observed. It seems unlikely that many would casually overlook or unquestioningly countenance omissions of particular parts of these rituals or alterations in their order of completion.

The uniform format followed in deed-signing rituals was mirrored in the strict order of administrative processes that provincial authorities used to convert communal Indian land into private property under colonial sovereignty. While specifics varied somewhat from colony to colony, jurisdiction to jurisdiction, and time to time, all prospective buyers were required to obtain permits or licenses to purchase Indian lands. A purchaser who obtained a signed Indian deed then had to follow the same basic steps to complete the land transfer: register the document; obtain a survey warrant; use the warrant to hire a surveyor; get the surveyor to lay out, describe, and map the tract boundaries; see to it that the appropriate authorities proved and filed the survey map; and secure a patent formalizing ownership of the surveyed property. All steps were papered over with records mostly filed in separate record groups. Although, like deeds, their forms were highly standardized, these documents nevertheless also remained susceptible to differing interpretations by those wishing to contest their contents or validity.

Purchasers had to pay a multitude of publicly posted and scheduled filing fees for every required license, warrant, and finished form at every stage in the complicated procedures colonists used to turn land into property. This made land purchase an expensive proposition in the provinces, where hard currency was in short supply. So scarce was money that settlers in Munsee country and elsewhere used Indian wampum beads as currency among themselves until well into the 1700s. Whether buyers paid in coin, wampum, or goods, the price they paid to Indians was only a part, and often only a small part, of the assets they laid out to acquire their land.

Endless complaints, accusations, and legal actions alleging bribery and corruption indicate that buyers also had to discreetly pay off strategically placed officials at every step of the process. Financial outlays, moreover, did not end when purchasers proved titles and received patents. People buying land in proprietary colonies like Pennsylvania and East and West Jersey were expected to pay annual fees known as quitrents. Those purchasing property in New Netherland and New York paid taxes on their property. The high cost of doing business and maintaining property ensured that would-be landowners had to be both well heeled and advantageously connected.

The low prices Indians usually accepted for their lands sustain the nearly universal belief that colonists duped them out of their territory. Most versions of the story fall into one of two camps. The first, and formerly the more prevalent, of these stories derives from the "barbarous savage" stereotype. In it, greedy Indian-givers are outdone by quick-witted settlers. The other, and currently more widely accepted, view repeats variations on the "noble savage" theme. Holders of this view tend to see Indians as guileless innocents whose sense of spirituality and wholesome communal cultural values did not allow them to fully grasp or willingly accept the selfish values of private property and exclusive landownership.

Of course, few narratives in either tradition are ever quite so simple. On one level or another, most writers acknowledge that all people weigh costs and benefits. By recognizing that similar choices can be based on different cultural calculations, one can appreciate how those negotiating across divides of language and custom nevertheless try to extract maximum benefits for minimal costs, howsoever people reckon them. Only by looking at the patterns left by all available records documenting individual transactions and comparing them with other land deals can investigators most fully appreciate the ways people belonging to different cultures adjusted wishful thinking to the hard realities of intercultural contact.

Just as the beliefs of Indians and Europeans involved in land negotiations did not differ to the point that neither could comprehend the other's concepts, buyers and sellers differed among themselves regarding what they wanted deeds to do. Whatever they thought they were doing, tangible things changed hands. Prices asked and given for things reflect notions of value. Although these fluctuate from one culture and situation to another, all people attach cultural values to things. Capitalist cultures tend to use mutually agreed upon market prices to establish value. More spiritually inclined traditional societies like the Munsees tend to express cultural values symbolically in terms of supernatural power and pollution. People holding such beliefs often exchange what they regard as ritually polluted but essential perishables for highly prized, spiritually pure, durable ritual objects. Skagit Indians in the Pacific Northwest, for example, gave away ritually polluted, perishable foods (which after consumption would ultimately pass through the body to become dung, sweat, and urine); in exchange, they received inedible but incorruptible, spiritually pure masks and dentalium shells. Sacrifices of such pure things were thought to please supernatural keepers of game and delight spirits of plants and animals, who might then give their fragile, corruptible bodies to people for food.

Similar logic may have guided exchanges of land for trade goods in the Northeast. It is entirely possible that Indians may have regarded places vulnerable to military and microbial assaults, denuded of game, and ruinously close to Europeans as ritually defiled land that had become, as one sachem put it, mere dirt. On the other hand, many sources clearly affirm that Indians considered glass beads, tobacco pipes, vermilion, and other European trade goods to be spiritually powerful like wampum. Archaeological evidence shows that copper, shells, and other objects had long been brought to Munsee country from distant places inhabited by foreign Indians; likewise, strange Europeans brought mysteriously produced exotic goods. Those who believed such goods were charged with alien spirit powers often also believed that such powers were not necessarily effective in foreign territory. Unlike local products, newly traded objects were untouched by local magic—still in their original boxes, so to speak—and could easily be considered spiritually pure objects unpolluted by everyday contact.

For all their ritual purity and practical appeal, wampum and trade goods were perishable, and thus not the same kind of thing as land in the Munsees' minds. Land was more than an imperishable resource base to Munsee people; it was a sacred trust from spirits and ancestors. Its value, both temporal and spiritual, exceeded the value of any object, except in cases where ancestors outraged by untended graves or spirits angered by lax thanksgiving observances brought sickness and death to undutiful descendants. Native enemies fearing vengeful ghosts and other spirits also accepted the fact that the levels of force used to take lives and separate people from their movable property could not by themselves pry territories in foreign lands away from those unwilling to abandon the graves of their ancestors or the shrines to their spirits. A Wiechquaesgeck sachem made this plain when he told colonists that the Mohawks "will not say they have any pretense to [Wiechquaesgeck] land, though being at war, they would destroy their persons and take away their beavers and goods."

Land was never just a commodity in Munsee country. Colonists drew up price lists specifying exact exchange rates for trade goods given for Indian peltry, but never did the same for land. The most generous distributions of trade goods could not equal the value of even the most grievously ritually polluted lands. It is hard to imagine that Indians would have willingly given up so much for so little in the way of material objects. The exchanges of goods for lands that are documented in deeds must therefore have met other, more compelling needs. One of the most compelling of these was protection, which both parties desired and expected deeds to provide.

Settlers wanted the protection of lawful title in an often inscrutably intimidating legal system controlled and manipulated by officials backed up by sheriffs, militiamen, and armies. They also used deeds as shields to protect themselves from Indian retribution that would surely follow outright seizure of their lands. Indians wanted legal protection of colonial administrators in peacetime and military protection in times of war. One deed contained wording explicitly expressing this expectation. In it, the Indian signatories stated that "to promote the good and general welfare of both nations, we think it fit and convenient to settle some of our lands [with] Englishmen who have from time to time and in times of greatest necessity been our benefactors." Although we cannot know for sure at this distance, Indian sachems placing their marks on colonial deeds probably hoped that their ancestors and spirits would look favorably on their efforts to protect the lives and lands of their people, even at the expense of giving up some of their ancestral domains.

And what of the low prices Indians accepted for their lands? A number of sources show that Indians in Munsee country soon learned that the prices they received for their land rarely matched what settlers were charged for the same parcel. The sachem Teedyuscung put this awareness into words at a treaty meeting at Easton, Pennsylvania, in 1756. Underscoring Indian resentment over land frauds perpetrated by Englishmen, he reminded his listeners, "I have sold great tracts of land at unreasonably low rates, to the English, far below what any person would allow to be their value." And in the dense, interlocking networks of a society where, as Penn wrote in the Quaker style, "wealth circulateth like the blood," information of such critical importance to so many people almost surely traveled fast and far.

Did awareness of this information make the Indians feel cheated? It probably did. Who would not want to get as much as possible for something they did not particularly want to part with in the first place? People forced to deal with vastly more powerful colonizers who insisted that they sell their lands had to put aside such thoughts. Indian efforts to drive up prices had very little effect on buyers facing the immediate prospect of vastly larger payouts before any benefit or profit could be expected from the land. How, then, could Indians use colonists' desire for their lands to get protections they needed?

Teedyuscung expressed Indian expectations succinctly in his Easton speech, saying that the "proprietor has purchased the lands so cheap, yet he sells them again too dear to the poor people, that they do not use the Indians well and think they owe us nothing." Teedyuscung expected colonists to feel obligated to give something more for receiving land at low prices. Scholars have a word for this sense of obligation. They call it reciprocity.

The late anthropologist Annette Weiner neatly defined reciprocity as a cultural process that "creates social relations, establishes friendships, validates alliances, sustains order in societies, and establishes political authority." Reciprocity exists in various forms. The best known of these is balanced reciprocity, which occurs when more or less politically equal parties give and receive commodities both regard as equivalent in value. Negative reciprocity occurs when one party accepts less for what both parties consider a more valuable commodity. This kind of reciprocity most often occurs in relationships between unequal parties significantly differing in population size, productive potential, and political power; it was characteristic of transactions between Indians and colonists in Munsee country.

Lacking sufficient power to completely refuse colonial demands, Indians accepted negatively reciprocal, asymmetrical value and exchange rates when parting with much more than they almost certainly wanted to give. Following a strategy often chosen by people compelled to accept unequal exchanges, they worked hard to make colonists promise to protect them militarily, give them just treatment in colonial courts, and take on other obligations settlers might not otherwise have accepted.

In this way, the treaty-like nature of Indian deeds tacitly sanctioned by Native custom and sealed according to colonial law allowed Indians to exchange land for a degree of protection and justice. Like all treaties, deeds established as well as renewed relationships. As long as these relationships existed, Indians in Munsee country constantly worked to oblige colonists to protect them. Sometimes they succeeded; other times they did not. And sometimes the price of protection was more than they wanted to pay. Evidence of their efforts to obtain protection is preserved in the records of assembly meetings, court proceedings, and governor's councils. These forums provided opportunities for Indians and colonists to air grievances, resolve disputes, and come to one another's assistance.

An example of the way Indians used deeds to extract promises of protection in exchange for land may be found in the 1639 deed to western Long Island. Agreeing to give up the land, Mechoswodt, the sachem who signed the deed, made sure that wording be entered into the document to the effect that he "be allowed, with his people and friends, to remain upon the aforesaid land, plant corn, fish, hunt and make a living there as well as they can, while he himself and his people place themselves under the protection of the [West India Company]."

This wording was open to many interpretations. What did alienation mean when Indians could continue to live on lands they had sold? What would happen when Indians and colonists wanted to use the same tracts in the same land? What did protection mean? Would failure to provide protection invalidate the agreement? In 1639, protection offered the prospect of survival in a region that stood on the brink of war. By the time the fighting stopped twenty-five years later, few if any Indians in Munsee country had any lingering illusions about the quality of colonial protection. The Dutch tried to force Lower River Indians to pay taxes for protection even before the ink had dried on the 1639 deed. All Natives soon realized that authorities protected them only when the Indians' interests coincided with colonial policy or squared with European notions of equity and justice. Justice was inconsistently and unequally applied in courts of law; for example, Indian testimony was allowed only when it suited provincial interests. Yet even that modicum of justice nevertheless helped keep the peace. And Indians sought peace to forestall seizure of the type forced on the Esopus, whose most productive territories were literally and figuratively taken by the sword.

Colonists were not the only people in Munsee country who believed military might could be used to regain lost lands. In 1641 warriors drove De Vries's settlers away from Staten Island, then in 1649, Indians from the same nation demanded that "there must be a new bargain made" if the settlers wanted to reoccupy the land. In 1655, during the Peach War, Indian warriors (some perhaps using arms provided by Melijn) retook the island. Two years later, local sachems negotiated a new deed returning the land to colonial control.

Still, no one could question who had the bigger swords in Munsee country. It is not for nothing that "Long Knives" was one of the expressions Northeastern Indians like Munsees used to identify the English. Sachems could neither ignore nor hide the corrosive effects of disease, defeat, and depopulation on their bargaining positions. This does not mean that they gave up hope that their political fortunes would improve or that the epidemics that threatened everyone in the region might at some point strike only colonists. But by mid-century, Indians throughout the region had to face the fact that, barring a raft of miracles, they could no longer effectively protect their lands and lives by going to war.

Losses suffered during the mid-century drumfire of wars also convinced settlers that the sword was a poor tool for prying land from Indians in Munsee country. After 1664 both peoples would use council chambers and courtrooms to wage their land battles. Then as now, Indians preferred to go straight to the top when dealing with officials. Governors, directors-general, and other high authorities served as agents of distant corporate, proprietary, or imperial interests. Men like Stuyvesant and his successors were often at odds with more self-seeking local colonists. Indians knew from long experience that high officials determined to keep the peace would make time to hear their complaints. They also learned that upper-level administrators often supported them when their interests did not conflict with official policy. Stuyvesant's successors soon found out that they could use Indian concerns as handy wedge issues in disputes with refractory provincials.

Although differing in form and content, custom and public opinion in Indian and colonial societies worked to restrain destructive self-interest and discourage acts that threatened the peace or outraged prevailing morality. Colonists added a further coercive layer of law to this regulatory mix. Colonial law did not at that time meddle in purely internal Indian matters. Authorities, however, made sure that Indians accepted colonial jurisdiction in all legal actions involving settlers. Colonial courts were normally places where Indians could appear only as defendants tried under provincial laws. Indians could neither serve on juries nor, in many cases, provide evidence or present testimony in any but the most serious capital cases.

Exceptions were actions involving longstanding sources of intercultural trouble like land disputes, liquor smuggling, and illicit firearms trading. In such cases, Indians could be called by plaintiffs as well as defendants, serve as witnesses, make depositions, testify in open court, and sometimes, as a significant symbolic gesture in signal instances, join juries.

Sachems soon saw how conflicting interpretations of words and meanings could embroil contending landowners in lengthy disputes that dragged on inconclusively for decades. The vast body of land-dispute documentation preserved in libraries and archives attests to the lengths Indians and colonists went to in exploiting differing word readings and less-than-exact boundary descriptions for their own ends.

Although the endlessly repetitive formal structure of deeds helped make them comprehensible, sections detailing property boundaries contained place-names and other information subject to differing interpretations. In the seventeenth century formally trained, licensed surveyors had not yet become a fixture of provincial life. Deed boundary descriptions and surveys made during these years were mostly amateur affairs. Many were notoriously inexact, often hazy, and sometimes just plain wrong. The impermanent character of boundary markers like winding streams, rock piles, and blazed trees caused further problems. The last practice provided particularly fertile soil for litigators exploiting boundary disagreements. Trees marked with numbers or letters carved into or painted onto trunks often could not be found when officials and Indians walked boundaries together at later dates. Other markers were no more dependable. Streams could change course and piles of stones disappear. And, most important to the Indians, locations and meanings of place-names recorded in their language were subject to their own interpretations.

No colonist formally accepted Indian interpretations as matters of law. On the other hand, colonial administrators could not afford to alienate Indians by simply ignoring their demands or rejecting their claims outright. Instead, both parties compromised. By hedging just a little, colonists could deny they were repurchasing any part of an already sold tract. Sachems doing the same thing could graciously allow colonists to settle on a little more land, accept generous gifts as signs of enduring friendship, and still retain rights to remaining territory.

Thus, the story of intercultural land relations in the ancestral Munsee homeland is not a mere cautionary tale of lamentable and easily dismissed folly, blunders, and missteps caused by failures of will, communication, and understanding. Cultural, linguistic, and temperamental differences certainly got in the way of perfect understanding. It is nevertheless difficult to imagine either Indians or colonists mistaking one another's intentions for long after they made the first deals or broke the first promises.

It seems instead that Indians and colonists arrived at working dis-agreements based on a form of creative misunderstanding. Providing a kind of plausible deniability, creative misunderstandings allowed people to conduct business otherwise discouraged by moral scruples or cultural prohibitions. Creative misunderstandings helped people establish relationships and make decisions that would otherwise have been unacceptable. Bending the truth but stopping short of breaking trust, people used the polite fictions of their creative misunderstand-ings and working disagreements to lessen the disruptive effects of all-too-human impulses like intolerance, greed, and resentment. By blending subtle tints of half-truths and white lies into weightier mixes capable of sustaining deed agreements and treaty pledges, people will-ing to reach across cultural divides could still find common ground. Discreet and courteous acceptance of readily denounceable untruths helped level the playing field, enabling people to work together in the face of otherwise overwhelming differences in beliefs, numbers, and political power. The system worked, however, only so long as it advanced everyone's interests.

The balance of power in Munsee country that led to such working disagreements had shifted in favor of the colonists by the time the En-glish took over New Netherland in 1664. Yet, although colonists now vastly outnumbered Indians, the fractious character of local provin-cial politics and nearly constant international tensions still prevented settlers from fully exploiting their numerical and technological ad-vantages. Company men vied with free traders; yeoman farmers with large landholders; townspeople with countryfolk; English settlers with Hollanders; and New Netherlanders both with New Englanders and French colonists to the north in New France, and with Marylanders and Virginians farther south. Allying with and competing against one another in a bewildering and ever-changing array of combinations, contending parties, factions, and communities at every level of society struggled for survival and advantage in a kaleidoscopically bewilder-ing political environment.

Differences between contending colonists created divisions that Indians could manipulate. Preoccupied Europeans inadvertently helped Indians exploit colonists' rivalries by conferring a unique sort of legal immunity upon those Natives who cooperated in investigations into land fraud, smuggling, liquor trading, gunrunning, fencing of stolen goods, and other illicit activities. Colonists encouraged trusted sachems to provide evidence against settlers who peddled guns and liquor to their people. Like all contraband, proscribed firearms and strong drink were always in great demand. These sachems were thus often able to hold the whip hand over smugglers all too aware that the Indians could turn in those who cheated them without fear of being prosecuted for buying or trying to buy highly desirable forbidden commodities. Adept culture brokers used their abilities to establish and maintain close relations with colonists and colonial governments to achieve degrees of prestige sufficient to attract and keep followers.

It is difficult to imagine that sachems were displeased when colonial authorities punished settlers and partisan rivals guilty of harassing, assaulting, or robbing them. They also welcomed gifts and promises of protection given in order to encourage their cooperation in suppressing contraband trade. They were more ambivalent about supporting prohibitions against alcohol, and they strongly opposed bans on munitions.

Conflicts like the Pequot War and Kieft's War provided unmistakable evidence of the decisive advantages firearms could confer in warfare. Lower River Indian sachems trying to get weapons looked with much misgiving on Dutch policies that banned the open sale of guns to their warriors and hunters while allowing Mahicans, Mohawks, and Susquehannocks to acquire muskets, lead, and powder. It is not surprising that they did not help Dutch West India Company officials prosecute settlers like Melijn who allegedly gave them guns and ammunition without authorization.

The thicket of laws, ordinances, and regulatory procedures mandated by authorities at home and enacted in the provinces presented a particularly productive environment encouraging emergence of

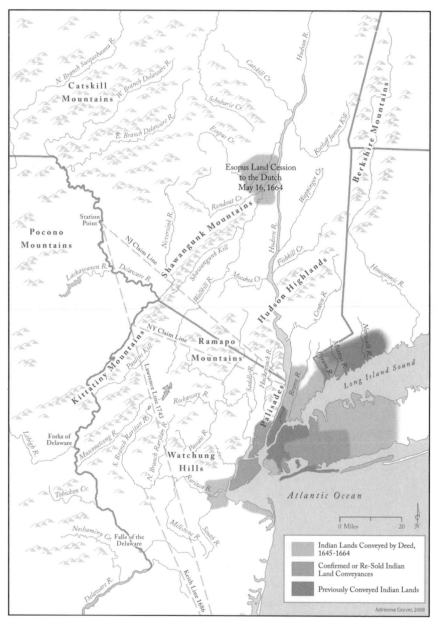

Map 3. Indian land sales to colonists in Munsee country, 1645–1664.

exploitable disputes. Lacking firearms needed to forcibly stop settlers from taking their lands, Indians in Munsee country could and did play off contending parties in land controversies against one another to slow, deflect, and even halt sales. Different figures and factions alternately worked with and against Indian interests with baffling unpredictability. Embattled Indians, however, could usually expect support from one side or another in most land disputes. Some rifts, like corporate struggles between patroons and company officials, were private affairs discreetly worked out in boardrooms and council chambers. Others, like Melijn's very public feuds with Kieft and Stuyvesant, and the often poor relations between Dutch and English settlers in the colony, were common knowledge and easily visible to anyone taking the trouble to look for them. Such public disagreements were tailor-made for Indian exploitation.

Records documenting land controversies large and small in Munsee country show how Indians exploited colonial differences to further their own interests. Three well-documented examples, from Brooklyn, the Matinecock lands, and Navesink-Raritan country, will have to stand for the many occurrences showing how Indians tried to protect their land and people by playing off contending colonists during the Dutch regime.

One of the longest-lasting land disputes in Munsee country occurred at Matinecock in the present-day Long Island towns of Hempstead, Huntington, and Oyster Bay. Much of this dispute centered on contested meanings of deed provisions and locations of deeded boundaries. Dutch officials, who had an entire colony to worry about, tended to take more nuanced views of such ambiguities than local townsfolk did. They could afford to see these deeds as preliminary agreements requiring future negotiation of the finer details. Poorer, preoccupied, and the ones on Long Island who had to pay for Indian land, townsfolk usually favored strictly literal, conclusive interpretations. Hempstead settlers in particular chose to regard their 1643 deed as a final sale. They did not feel that it was their job to keep paying off Indians to maintain peace in New Netherland. They only wanted them gone as soon as possible.

The Indians, however, refused to go. Frustrated townsfolk dispatched a delegation to meet with Stuyvesant at Fort Amsterdam on August 23, 1647, seeking to get the Dutch to drive the Indians out. Hoping to appeal to Stuyvesant's reportedly suspicious nature, they told him that the Massapequas were plotting the colonists' destruction. Stuyvesant did not rise to the bait, being even more suspicious of the townsfolk. He regarded the Hempstead settlers as subversives loyal to New England. Unlike the English at Gravesend and other towns nearer New Amsterdam, the Hempstead settlers openly maintained contact with New Englanders just across Long Island Sound. Neither Stuyvesant nor, as it turned out, the West India Company directors were inclined to indulge them at the expense of one of the colony's more dependable Indian allies.

Massapequa and Matinecock sachems managed to sow further dissension among their English neighbors by subsequently selling adjoining, unclearly bounded tracts to rival townsfolk. In 1653, for example, Suscaneman's predecessor Asharoken sold tracts of land to English buyers where the Fort Hope Treaty line separated New Netherland from New England on Long Island. These lands became the nuclei of the contending towns of Oyster Bay and Huntington. Five years later, Tackapousha signed deeds conveying land on the western border between Oyster Bay and Hempstead. Arguments over both sets of sales would embroil settlers for decades.

Settlers were not the only Long Islanders tangled up in these land wrangles. Having earlier inserted himself into arguments over Indian title to lands west of Secatogue, Montaukett sachem Wyandanch used the Oyster Bay, Hempstead, and Huntington border disputes to further his efforts to exert influence over Indian affairs in western Long Island. In a codicil to a March 17, 1658, deed, he promised Oyster Bay settlers that he would support them against Huntington's claims to land sold earlier by Tackapousha. Wyandanch dispatched an adviser to mark out the boundary, which was described in a subsequent deed signed two months later.

For a time it looked like Wyandanch's efforts to sidestep Tackapousha would succeed. A year later, death—perhaps with a little help from what one settler said was poison—put an end to Wyandanch's machinations. His attempts to involve himself in land matters in western Long Island had represented a major threat to Massapequa and Matinecock autonomy. His involvement in their affairs would have ended any chances they had to deal independently with colonists. What was worse, this involvement would have made it possible for Wyandanch to sell their lands out from under them, leaving them with the choice of moving wherever they were told to go or abandoning Long Island entirely.

Mattano similarly tried to manipulate suspicions that divided rival claimants in Brooklyn. His first efforts to exploit such rivalries met with limited success. The Dutch claimed what amounted to nearly all his people's lands under the terms of both Tackapousha's broad conveyance of November 13, 1643, and another, later cancelled, September 10, 1645, deed to the most westerly portion of lands within the bounds covered by the 1643 deed. A small patch in this latter area was also claimed by yet another group of New England exiles led by Lady Deborah Moody, who settled at Gravesend with Dutch permission during Kieft's War. After the war, these English settlers secured their claim in a sale, again arranged with Dutch approval, concluded with Mattano's father, Emerus, on November 1, 1650.

Mattano made his first move as unsettling news of the killings of three colonists by unknown Indians at nearby Hellgate reached New Amsterdam in the spring of 1652. On June 17, a group of Nayack sachems offered to sell land at Flatbush, which they said the West India Company had not yet paid for, to an agent of Utrecht merchant and would-be patroon Cornelis van Werckhoven. Stuyvesant did not welcome the offer. He was first concerned by what he regarded as the unusually high price offered to the Indians for the land by Van Werckhoven's agent. He also worried that the Indians would see any deal as a concession to the recent killings. Stuyvesant put his concerns into a letter to the directors, asking if it was wise "to encourage and embolden the Indians" by repurchasing "the same lands which they previously have, of their own good will, sold, given, ceded and received payment for, and which since have been partly occupied."

Stuyvesant was convinced that paying twice for any vacant plots within tracts sold earlier by the most prominent sachems in the region would set a dangerous precedent. Even a small payment for a minimally productive plot could constitute "an inducement to murder more Christians, imagining them to be fainthearted, and [to] threaten a massacre so that later on they may again obtain money and goods for another piece of wild and waste land." He was right. When Melijn circulated a rumor that the Dutch were plotting to join with the New Englanders at Gravesend to kill his people, an alarmed Mattano threatened war if colonists took the land without paying for it. Although Stuyvesant doubted that the Indians had a greater "claim to the wild and waste bush, upon which God and nature had grown trees, than any other Christian people," he nevertheless recommended that the Indians be given a gift to prevent "blame and new troubles."

Mattano and the Nayacks immediately took advantage of Stuyvesant's offer to make new gifts to the Indians by concluding two deals for land at Flatbush with contending colonists. Mattano's manipulations helped him secure de facto recognition of his rights to lands included in earlier purchases. They did not, however, prevent Van Werckhoven's agent from inserting what amounted to an order of eviction into the Nayack deed. Even though deed conditions required that Mattano and his people move to nearby Staten Island, Indians were seen living at Nayack twenty-five years later.

Mattano and his kinsmen (see figure 3) had more success manipulating land rivalries across the Narrows in Staten Island and in the nearby Raritan-Navesink country. On March 28, 1651, and December 26, 1652, Mattano sold two tracts of land along the southern shores of Raritan Bay to another of Van Werckhoven's silent partners. His father, Emerus, had sold land along the Navesink Highlands in 1650 to the agent of another prospective patroon named Hendrick Van der Capellen toe Ryssel. Van der Capellen was a well-connected nobleman whose agents had been buying up Indian land around the Lower Bay in partnership with Cornelis Melijn since the 1640s.

All three purchases were made along the same political fault lines that Mattano and Emerus had tried to exploit in Brooklyn. Stuyvesant openly hated Melijn and made no pretense of hiding his dislike for aspiring absentee patroons like Van Werckhoven and Van der Capellen. He knew that their possession of feudal manorial privileges would openly infringe on his authority. Determined to protect his prerogatives, Stuyvesant demanded and received company authorization to invalidate private purchases of Indian land made without his authorization.

This had the effect of stymieing the would-be patroons. Unable to find settlers willing to move to a dangerous place like Navesink, Van Werckhoven gave in as gracefully as he could. Stuyvesant allowed Van Werckhoven to exchange the claim to his erstwhile patroonship for title to land purchased as a private citizen at New Utrecht. Van Werckhoven's manager there, Jacques Corteljou, abandoned further efforts to turn the lands into a patroonship of his own after his employer died in 1655. The outbreak of the Peach War that year put an end to all efforts to acquire Indian lands until the fighting ended.

Van der Capellen was less easily deterred. He was one of the first colonists to resume Indian land acquisitions after peace returned to New Netherland in 1657. On July 10 of that year, his agent negotiated a new deed to Staten Island. The deed was signed by Mattano and a consortium of other Hackensack and Lower Bay sachems. Oratam added his prestige to the deal by signing on as a witness. Stuyvesant was alarmed by Van der Capellen's continuing efforts to establish a patroonship by sidestepping his authority. He particularly resented the latter's private, unsanctioned acquisition of land first purchased from Indians nearly thirty years earlier. Refusing to accommodate the ambitious Van der Capellen, Stuyvesant again asked for and received company permission to annul his Indian purchases. The company ordered Stuyvesant to negotiate a new deal with the Indians. Company directors tried to sweeten the pill for the influential Van der Capellen by advising Stuyvesant to resell the land to him under the same terms offered all free settlers.

Having received the company's blessing to protect its land interests, Stuyvesant moved to forestall further acquisitions by Melijn and Van der Capellen by negotiating a new deed with Indians for land at

Pavonia on January 30, 1658. He need not have bothered. Van der Capellen died a year later. His heirs subsequently sold his land rights to the company for three thousand guilders.

Van der Capellen's death did not stop efforts to acquire Indian lands at Raritan and Navesink. Stuyvesant received word that colonists from Gravesend were negotiating for Navesink land just as rumors that an English fleet was sailing to seize the colony made both Indians and English settlers more willing to defy company authority. Determined to stop the Gravesend settlers from getting the land at Navesink, Stuyvesant hurriedly dispatched Marten Kregier to look into the matter. Kregier had just returned to New Amsterdam after the arrival of winter closed campaigning season in Esopus country.

A concerned Stuyvesant authorized Kregier to promise the openly unfriendly Raritan and Navesink people "that all former acts and claims shall be forgotten and forgiven, if [they agree to] sell the land to nobody but the director-general and council." The sachems could not miss the note of desperation evident in this offer to overturn earlier purchases. They were already negotiating a sale to Brooklyn buyer Jacques Corteljou at their town of Ramenesing, south of the Navesink Highlands. Meanwhile, Kregier arrived at the mouth of the Raritan. Finding he was unable to sail his ship upstream, he had to cool his heels while one of his guides went inland to meet with the chiefs. The guide returned with several Raritan and Navesink Indians who promised to sell some lands in the area to the Dutch. On December 12, 1663, Stuyvesant extracted a promissory note framed in the form of a deed for land at the Navesink Highlands from Mattano and several other men representing Mattano's brother, the Navesink sachem Peropay. The goods listed in the deed evidently represented a pledge of earnest money rather than a final payment for the land. Even more intriguingly, Corteljou signed the deed as a witness and an interpreter.

Two weeks later, the Navesink sachems sent a message to Stuyvesant setting their price for the territory in question. They demanded an additional payment of goods worth four thousand guilders. A stunned Stuyvesant responded by ordering troops to Navesink to prevent

Gravesend settlers from entering the country. The men needed to garrison such a post were then on duty at Wiltwijck, however, and could not be spared. In the end it did not matter. On February 16, 1664, Stuyvesant heard that Peropay had been in Brooklyn. While there, he told the Gravesend men that he preferred to sell the Navesink land to them.

Things quieted down until March 25, 1664, when a Navesink messenger carrying a demand to Stuyvesant for immediate payment of the four-thousand-guilder price suddenly burst into a meeting at New Amsterdam with Lower River chiefs negotiating the release of prisoners held by the Esopus. Putting his business with the sachems on hold, Stuyvesant told the messenger that he could not "make a contract for the land and put up a house there . . . as long as we were engaged in a war and had no stable peace." He asked Peropay to put off the Gravesend men and promised to travel to Navesink to seal the deal "when the corn planting began."

Stuyvesant could do nothing else. He had to devote the months running up to corn planting time to restoring peace along the wartorn Hudson. The Navesink people did not wait. Peropay signed over the land at Navesink to the Gravesend settlers the same day his messenger spoke with Stuyvesant. Stuyvesant may have vented his spleen by preventing Raritan and Navesink representatives from attending the May 15, 1664, treaty meeting ending the Esopus War. There may be another explanation for the Indians' absence, however. The fact that extensive preparations were being made in England for the conquest of New Netherland could no longer be concealed. Raritan and Navesink people surely heard the rumors circulating through Gravesend and other English communities. Their nonappearance at the treaty meeting may therefore also reflect a certain reluctance to show any attachment to a regime whose days were evidently numbered.

By playing off rivals in the ways these examples illustrate, sachems managed to maintain strong bargaining positions. This allowed them to continue accepting gifts and receiving payments for their testimony for or against various rivals in subsequent provincial town meetings, courts, and council chambers. They could also still pick and choose land buyers. Even after large tracts were sold, they could still slow occupation by selling small and often unclearly bounded tracts in, between, or near already purchased lands to unsure, unscrupulous, or uninformed settlers. Pursuing such strategies, a number of sachems ultimately signed a very large number of deeds over a long period of time. In Oyster Bay alone, a township containing 160 square miles, Matinecock and Massapequa leaders managed to conclude 138 real estate deals with townsfolk before descendants of the Indians who first sold a neck of land on Long Island Sound in 1658 put their marks on the last Indian land sale in the town—a confirmation deed signed in 1711.

This delaying strategy was a makeshift stopgap measure built on desperate hopes. By grudgingly giving up portions of ancestral land to different and often mutually hostile purchasers, sachems bought time during which they could hope the balance of power might shift in their favor. If they were patient and lucky, they might stop settlement, take back lost lands, and maybe even oversee a revival that could restore their nation into a populous power capable of turning the tables on colonists.

Despite their best efforts, sachems had surrendered very nearly all of their remaining coastal and tidewater lands in the Munsee homeland to colonists by 1664 (see map 3). The amount of lost land came to a bit more than 10 percent of the total ancestral Munsee estate. At first glance, that percentage does not seem very high. Formal conveyances to settlers, moreover, did not necessarily mean that sold lands were immediately vacated by Indians or settled by colonists. Speculators like the would-be patroons Van Werckhoven and Van der Capellen often could not attract settlers. Most smaller purchasers were cash poor and could afford to take up, clear, fence, and occupy only a fraction of the lands they acquired. Both colonists and Indians regarded unfenced lands as commons open for hunting, foraging, running livestock, and fishing upon. Indians did not hesitate to exercise their reserved rights to camp; plant; cut timber for fuel and canoes; gather berries and herbs; and harvest bark, grass, and reeds for house-mats and baskets on lands already deeded to colonists. The fact that they often had to ask permission to enter sold land reduced, but did not end, their ability to extract resources from these territories.

The 10 percent deeded over to settlers by 1664 did however include a good part of the most productive lands in the Munsee homeland. Restricted access to these territories significantly reduced the Indians' ability to maintain themselves on the large but generally less productive interior lands to which they still held title. Compelled to substitute inland products for lost coastal resources, they increasingly relied on bark slabs and cattail reeds instead of sedge grasses for house walls and bedding; deer, bear, and other woodland animals instead of fish, oysters, and waterfowl; and shallow forest-clearing soils rather than deep deposits at river mouths for planting corn, beans, and squash. Although they continued to camp on vacant beaches and unfenced marshlands, they would never again enjoy unchallenged access to wetlands, mudflats, and stretches of shoreline where they formerly freely harvested clams for wampum and secured vast quantities of meat from migrating bird flocks and teeming schools of spawning fish.

Pushed back into the less productive and more remote lands in the interior, many Indians in Munsee country found themselves increasingly distant from commercial centers at New Amsterdam and Wiltwijck that they were now dependent on for goods and services. On the positive side of the ledger, they still held sole title and unchallenged ownership to 90 percent of their ancestral homeland. The remaining readily habitable portions of this territory consisted mostly of small stretches of level land tucked into narrow valleys surrounded by rocky uplands, swampy meadows, or sandy pinelands. Colonists would soon press them to sell the best pieces of these inland tracts. Struggling to learn how to live on ever-shrinking and increasingly separated parcels of good terrain, Munsee people would have to find additional ways to further slow, and perhaps even stop, colonial takeover of their remaining productive lands if they were to survive as a sovereign people on their ancestral home territories.

5

CONTENTIONS, 1664–1674

In the spring of 1664, King Charles II presented a proprietary grant
for a vast new territory to his younger brother, James, Duke of York
and Albany and the future James II of England. The new proprietary
took in all of Munsee country and included the whole of the Dutch
colony of New Netherland as well as Nantucket, Martha's Vineyard,
and a sizable chunk of Maine. The king made the grant while his nation was enjoying friendly relations with the Netherlands. Just as
Stuyvesant's seizure of New Sweden in 1655 had not otherwise disturbed world peace, Charles II's decision to press the Crown's claim
to land in faraway New Netherland (based on John Cabot's 1497 voyage to the Gulf of St. Lawrence) held by a Dutch trading company did
not necessarily mean wider war between the two mother countries.

Determined to swiftly reduce the Dutch outpost, the Duke of
York put together a small but formidable force of three hundred
men and placed it under the command of Colonel Richard Nicolls.
Nicolls was an experienced soldier, loyal to the king, and a retainer
of the duke's household. York promised him governorship of lands
he was able to take from the West India Company. Nicolls and the
three frigates carrying his men and supplies sailed from Portsmouth,
England, in the early summer of 1664. News of their arrival off the
Lower Bay reached New Amsterdam by the end of August. The arrival of another one hundred New Englanders under the command

of Connecticut governor John Winthrop, Jr., stiffened Nicolls's little force.

Small as this combined army was, Stuyvesant was unable to marshal forces sufficient to resist it. On September 6, 1664, the director-general surrendered New Amsterdam. Fort Orange capitulated two weeks later, and the Delaware River settlements a month after that. During this time, both the Indians of Munsee country and the more than nine thousand settlers living in New Netherland came to grips with the fact that the English now controlled the whole of the Atlantic coastline from Virginia to New England.

The English invasion probably caused little surprise among Indians already aware of the politics that preoccupied colonists. Sachems and settlers watching Nicolls's ships darkly lolling in the quiet waters off Gravesend Bay could only take their coming as a reminder, if one was needed, that they now had to contend with ever-broadening forces and events. Indians in the region, survivors of wars and epidemics, could still believe that storms brewed in other men's worlds might yet be dealt with locally. Once the commotion died down, more astute sachems found that the nearly bloodless English takeover simply added new levels of complexity to the already contentious maelstrom of interests pitting colonists against one another. Many quietly began looking for ways to take advantage of opportunities presented by the new competitions that almost immediately arose between colonists and conquerors.

Nicolls did his best to bring order to the contending colonial factions as he moved to reconcile fractious colonists and suspicious Indians to proprietary rule. He enacted new laws, appointed new officials, and fixed new names onto old places. In his role as the new province's governor, Nicolls met in assembly with representatives from the predominantly English towns in Long Island and Westchester during the summer of 1665 to announce a fresh set of regulatory ordinances. These came to be known as the Duke's Laws. The code trod lightly on existing rights, respecting established religions; guaranteeing jury trials; and permitting elections of sheriffs, justices, and other minor officials. The code did not, however, provide for elected representation

or a regularly convened legislative assembly. Although the laws recognized existing land titles granted by Dutch authorities, the code ordered owners to acquire new patents from the proprietor by April 1,
1667. Larger landowners were required to pay a registration fee of two
shillings, six pence for every one hundred acres of property.

Names as well as laws changed as New Netherland became New
York, and New Amsterdam was transformed into the city of New
York. The areas of predominantly English settlement on Long Island,
Staten Island, and much of what later became Westchester (point-
edly known among the Dutch as their Oostdorp, "East Village") be-
came the east, west, and north ridings of the newly formed provincial
county of Yorkshire. Fort Amsterdam was renamed Fort James, Fort
Orange became Fort Albany, and Wiltwijck was christened Kingston.
Nicolls gave the name Albania to the land between the Hudson and
Delaware today known as New Jersey.

Everyone in the region knew that Nicolls would need more than
his three-hundred-man army if he was to secure his conquest for
the duke. English settlers already living in New York could not be
counted on for support. Nearly all were Puritan expatriates who still
passionately hated the restored royal regime. Proprietary demands for
new payments on already purchased lands increased their reluctance
to come to the aid of the new government. Many settlers living east
of Manhattan, moreover, preferred to consider themselves citizens of
Connecticut. Few would willingly support Nicolls if any challenge to
his administration arose.

Luckily for Nicolls, New York was enjoying a rare season of peace
during the first months of proprietary rule. As far as any of the locals knew, England and the Netherlands were still at peace. The bold
English move to take a Dutch possession during peacetime was,
however, a clear indication of strained relations. England's mercantile squabbles with the Netherlands and France had flared into open
warfare in the past. Every indication suggested that the then-quiet
economic cold war would soon turn hot again.

No one could know how complicated the region's already volatile
political situation was about to become. The prospect of new invasions

loomed when news of the outbreak of the Second Anglo-Dutch Naval War reached New York during the spring of 1665. A year later, France unexpectedly joined the fighting against England. Suddenly, Nicolls and his meager garrisons faced the twin possibilities of a Dutch counterattack from the sea and an overland invasion from the north by newly reinforced French forces already at war with the Five Nations.

The king himself made Nicolls's position even more difficult. More in need of money and political support than policy coherence or undivided family loyalty, Charles split his brother York's yet-to-be-conquered proprietary in half. In two royal grants made while Nicolls's fleet was still en route to New Netherland, Charles gave land already renamed Albania in anticipation of the expedition's success to two of his more loyal stalwarts. One of these men, Sir George Carteret, named the new colony New Jersey in honor of his native island. He dispatched a distant cousin, Captain Philip Carteret, to govern the new proprietary. Cousin Carteret arrived in New York, commission in hand, in late July 1665.

Sachems of mainland Indian communities across from Manhattan quickly realized that Carteret's arrival signaled the emergence of exploitable new divisions at the very epicenter of colonization in their country. They also shared the opinion held by many settlers that wars against various Indian nations had weakened the divided and often poorly provisioned Dutch colony, making New Netherland easy prey for the English takeover. Still embroiled in their own war with the Five Nations, Lower River Indians knew that ongoing Iroquois conflicts with the Susquehannocks, Mahicans, Northern Indians in New England, and others elsewhere threatened catastrophically wider and potentially more divisive involvements. Most could plainly see that the disunited English would, at the very least, need to establish peace with and among Indians, especially with those living in the heart of their settlements, if they were to hold on to their newly won territories.

Lower River Indian and Five Nations leaders moved quickly to make their peace with Nicolls's new government. Their price remained the same: a relationship they called friendship based on justice in legal disputes, fair dealing in trade, and military protection in war. Nicolls pledged to meet these demands in a series of treaties signed during the first two years of his administration. Colonel George Cartwright, one of a group of royal commissioners dispatched to assist Nicolls, negotiated the first of these treaties shortly after taking Fort Orange. Meeting at freshly rechristened Fort Albany with Mohawk and other Five Nations leaders at the end of September 1664, Cartwright promised the sachems equal protection under English law and assured them that trade would continue as before. Aware that the River Indians and their allies were then at war with the Mohawks, Cartwright affirmed that the English would remain neutral. They would not support moves against the Iroquois made by Wappingers, Esopus, or any Indians "as have submitted themselves under the protection of his majesty . . . in these articles of agreement and peace."

A year later, Nicolls himself traveled upriver to persuade the Esopus sachems to submit to the same articles of peace and agreement accepted by the Five Nations. He met with their civil sachems and a group of war captains representing the humbled but still-defiant younger warriors at Kingston on October 7, 1665. After settling several unresolved land disputes and adjusting boundaries of lands ceded in the peace treaty with the Dutch, concluded just before the English takeover, Nicolls got the sachems to accept a general treaty of friendship. In it, both the Indians and the English agreed to work together to keep the peace. The Indians also agreed to accept the jurisdiction of English courts in actions involving settlers. Thanking the governor for the substantial gifts given to seal their new accord, the sachems pledged to "come once every year and bring some of their young people to acknowledge every part of this agreement . . . to the end that it may be kept in perpetual memory."

The October 7, 1665, agreement became known as the Nicolls Treaty. Meetings initially held annually for a few years after the signing and more irregularly thereafter helped maintain peace between the Esopus nation and the English for the next hundred years. Neither it nor Cartwright's earlier treaty, however, put an end to the threat of widening hostilities posed by the wars carried on by the Five Nations.

An opportunity for a comprehensive peace unexpectedly presented itself a few months later in the form of a French army. Governor of New France Daniel Remy, Sieur de Courcelles, led a force large enough to threaten the Mohawk towns south to the New York frontier during the winter of 1665–66. The army got lost in the snow. Reaching the Mohawk Valley, the troops found that they had missed their mark by some fifty miles. They came out of the forest near the newly established Albany suburb of Schenectady. Some settlers there gave food and blankets to the hungry, freezing soldiers while others sent word of their coming to the Mohawks. Having lost the element of surprise, the French column returned to Canada, harried all the way by Mohawk warriors.

Courcelles's superior, the French viceroy to North America, Alexandre de Prouville, Sieur de Tracy, led a second expedition the following summer. This time the French did not lose their way. Unable to stop so powerful a force from marching into their country, the Mohawks evacuated every one of their towns. Tracy's men had to content themselves with plundering the empty villages before marching away.

Sobered by the successful summer attack, the Five Nations quickly made peace with the French. Chastened Mohawks also began negotiations aimed at ending their chronic warfare with the Mahicans and their Indian allies in Munsee country and New England. They persuaded their Oneida and Onondaga confederates to accept an offer made by Connecticut governor Winthrop to broker a peace conference. Sachems representing the belligerent nations subsequently signed a peace treaty at Albany on September 10, 1666, in the presence of representatives from New York, Connecticut, and Massachusetts Bay.

The treaty was signed just as France joined the Dutch in their war against England. Happily for the colonists, the hard-won peace agreements hammered out during the late summer of 1666 discouraged further military adventures in the region for the present. Unwilling to involve themselves in a war largely being fought elsewhere unless ordered to do so by their home governments, settlers in New France and

New York quietly pursued their long-standing and profitable clandestine smuggling trade. As they had done during the First Anglo-Dutch Naval War, and as they would continue to do in other conflicts whose primary theaters of operations lay elsewhere, everyone along the frontier observed an informal truce until diplomats in Europe made peace. The agreement this time, known as the Treaty of Breda, formally ended the war on July 21, 1667. Exhausted by the struggle, treaty signatories at Breda largely accepted the existing situation in the colonies. The English gave a little by recognizing the recent Dutch conquest of Surinam. The Dutch reciprocated by letting the English keep New York.

Unlike the Breda treaty, which was more like a truce than anything else, Nicolls's treaty with the Esopus effected a long-lasting settlement. At their yearly meetings in Kingston and, as the years passed, at less frequent get-togethers more often held at Albany or New York City, sachems and settlers ritually reaffirmed friendship. The cordial atmosphere created by ceremonial exchanges of pelts, presents, and pleasantries helped participants iron out most problems on meeting agendas. So quickly did peace finally return that Kingston magistrates ordered the watch at the town fort to stand down permanently just seven years after the Nicolls Treaty was signed.

In contrast, the hard-hammered agreement restoring peace between the Iroquois Confederacy and the Lower River Indians and their Mahican and Northern Indian allies, made at Albany in September 1666, did not hold. Old enmities died hard, and many Indians in Munsee country continued to help Susquehannock allies still at war with the Five Nations. The fighting sputtered on largely unnoticed by colonists until word reached New York during the winter of 1668–69 that Esopus and Navesink sachems were among Susquehannock emissaries offering to make peace with the Mohawks. The Mohawks evidently received the proposal favorably. They felt a particular closeness toward the Susquehannocks because both nations acknowledged a common ancestry. Mohawks were not, however, interested in ending their war against Mahicans, Wappingers, and Wiechquaesgecks closely allied with Northern Indians who were also again fighting against them. The diplomats settled for what they could achieve. In early August 1669, Hackensack sachem Pierwim showed New York governor Francis Lovelace (who had succeeded Nicolls in 1668) a belt from the Mohawks affirming that they had made a separate peace with the Lower River Indians.

A few weeks later, reports reached New York that Indians from the upper Hudson river had joined a three-hundred-man-strong party of Northern Indian warriors invading Mohawk country. Led by the Massachusett war chief Chickataubit, the force laid siege to the easternmost Mohawk castle at Caughnawaga for several days. A large force gathered from the Western Iroquois nations relieved the town after the brief siege. Five Nations warriors soon trapped and defeated the retreating invaders at Kinaquariones near Schenectady. Most of the invading force was killed on the field. The few warriors taken prisoner were later mostly put to death.

Indians throughout the Hudson Valley fled from their homes when news of the defeat reached their towns. Some moved far to the west around the lower Great Lakes. Others, like the Wiechquaesgecks, sought shelter closer to home. For the second time in less than a quarter of a century, they abandoned their home territory to take refuge among sympathetic relatives, this time in the Housatonic Valley. In February 1671, one of the Wiechquaesgeck sachems offered to redeem the promise made in 1649 to sell the remaining half of his homeland to the English and move away permanently. It was at this meeting that their sachem affirmed that Mohawks who drove them from their homeland had no rights to the land.

The proffered sale never came off. Shortly afterwards, New York, Massachusetts Bay, and Connecticut merchants, determined to end fighting that suppressed the Indian trade, managed to cobble together another peace agreement. Meeting in Albany on November 8, 1671, a conclave of sachems including several from River Indian communities once again put their marks to yet another treaty meant to end the long-festering blood feud.

Meanwhile, the English still struggled to consolidate a measure of control over their ramshackle domain in New York. Lovelace would need more and better cooperation from both settlers and Indians if he was to secure the English conquest. Colonists living in the new New York did not seem to be in a particularly cooperative frame of mind. Far from settling existing squabbles, the transition to English control sparked new and increasingly rancorous boundary disputes and power struggles. As they had in the past, contending colonists continued to use promises and presents to get Indians from Munsee country to support their sides in the many disputes. Needing the Five Nations to be at peace in order to safeguard the border, the English were in more need than ever of good relations with River Indians in the heart of their colony.

Only Manhattan, home to a largely Dutch majority at least outwardly willing enough to accept English rule, seemed secure. Farther east on the mainland, Connecticut colonists pressed claims to territories farther west, using charter bounds that awarded their province all land from the Atlantic to the Pacific oceans lying between their north and south borderlines. On Long Island, Hempstead, Huntington, and Oyster Bay settlers seemed more interested in their ongoing boundary disputes than in provincial security.

Philip Carteret, who had assumed control of New Jersey shortly after his arrival, was soon at odds with local settlers and New York officials. Puritan colonists from western Long Island, whose recent purchases of Indian lands in the former Albania were secured by patents issued by the New York government, had begun building houses in and around the soon-to-be-named town of Elizabeth before anyone in the region knew about Charles's division of the duke's province. They preferred to remain within the New York government and flatly refused to acknowledge Carteret's authority over them.

In New York, town governments in the county of Yorkshire scrambled to secure new patent applications by the April 1, 1667, deadline specified in the Duke's Laws. Anxious to get new deeds patented and old patents grandfathered in under the code, settlers rushed to make deals with Indians everywhere around Manhattan.

As Stuyvesant had done after the Peach War, the first English governors worked hard to settle land disputes amid the flurry of new purchases. Matinecock now became the site of one of the most intractable of these. Tackapousha, who had signed the first deeds to land in the area, distrusted all Englishmen, especially those who allied themselves with his Northern Indian enemies from across Long Island Sound. He also took seriously the many treaties of peace and friendship he had signed with the Dutch. Honoring his Dutch alliance and unconvinced that they would not return, Tackapousha remained aloof. Staying quietly at home, he was among the few sachems who did not formally welcome Nicolls to Munsee country at the time of the English takeover.

Tackapousha would soon have to change his position. Emboldened English settlers at Hempstead made increasingly strident demands, ordering Indian people to leave lands they denied selling. Their efforts forced the sachem to swallow his pride and ask the new governor for help. Nicolls responded by ordering both parties to present their cases for his consideration in New York in late February 1665. The meeting solved nothing. Hempstead settlers subsequently presented a deposition complaining that twenty armed Massapequa Indians had forcibly stopped a survey of land at Matinecock. Shortly thereafter, Nicolls wrote to the Hempstead magistrates, advising them to settle the matter by giving Tackapousha a small gift and, if this did not work, to allow Nicolls to treat with the Massapequa sachem on their behalf. The magistrates rejected both proposals.

A now-frustrated Nicolls ordered the antagonists to come to Fort James in October 1666. Frustration turned into anger after both parties refused to accept Nicolls's compromise that would have allowed colonists already living in the disputed territory to remain so long as they paid the Indians and allowed them to have a small planting ground. To explain why he rejected the compromise offer, Tackapousha subsequently produced a map showing where lands now claimed by Hempstead settlers exceeded the original purchase boundaries. Nicolls later learned that settlers there claimed they had already paid the Hempstead magistrates for the land at Matinecock and had suggested that the magistrates should be ordered to give their purchase money to the Indians.

In the middle of this, the Matinecock sachem Asharoken and several of his associates (including the young Suscaneman) stepped in to support Tackapousha and undermine the Hempstead settlers by firming up their ties with the rival Oyster Bay settlers through land sales. In a series of ten deeds, they conveyed several small tracts and an island to prominent townsmen between 1667 and 1669. This marked the beginning of the Matinecock practice of selling large numbers of small plots to influential neighbors over brief spaces of time.

There the matter lay until early June 1669, when Lovelace ordered the Hempstead magistrates to produce proof that they had paid the Indians for the Matinecock lands. A little more than a year later, the governor gave Oyster Bay settlers permission to buy the land after Hempstead authorities evidently failed to provide the requested evidence. Tackapousha, however, refused to sell the land to anyone; then he did not show up when ordered to appear at Fort James on June 26, 1671, to meet with Lovelace to discuss a sale. Patience exhausted, Lovelace ordered up a session of the province's Court of Assizes and put the issue before them. The court directed Tackapousha to sell the disputed land to whomever would pay for it. Bowing to the court order, Tackapousha demanded that the governor make the purchase. Lovelace agreed and promised to sell the property to Hempstead.

On Long Island broad stretches of sandy shoreline left places like Matinecock open to intruders; west of Manhattan, less tractable geography discouraged outsiders' incursions into those parts of the Munsee homeland. Ice floes in winter, and high winds and strong tidal crosscurrents the year round, made the watery high road of the Hudson River especially treacherous for anyone crossing in small boats or canoes. The steep cliffs of the Palisades rising above its western banks presented an unbroken rock wall that stretched more than thirty miles from the Hudson Highlands south to Pavonia. In and around Newark Bay, Mattano, Oratam, and other sachems guarded the marshland approaches to their home territories around Hackensack using the same play-off strategies employed by their Long Island brethren. Farther south, Raritan and Navesink warriors cultivated a reputation for implacable hostility that kept all but the boldest colonists away from the otherwise attractive lowlands.

The lowlands across from Staten Island presented the widest avenue of approach into the interior. Stuyvesant had tried to get Oratam to surrender the key to this area in 1663, a year before the English conquest, by asking him to convey land on the west bank of Newark Bay. Oratam refused to sell. Like the Navesink sachem Peropay, Oratam felt that all signs indicated that Stuyvesant's days as director-general of a Dutch colony were numbered. He put Stuyvesant off, saying that his old men, fearing that they would be robbed by Indians in the interior if they moved away, did not wish to part with the land. Oratam went on to tell Stuyvesant that he could not move discussions forward until the young men returned from their hunting. Transparently flimsy as the excuses were, the much-harried Stuyvesant had to accept them with as good a grace as possible. The colony fell before talks went further.

Oratam's 1663 politic demurral was one last act of defiance toward the end of a long career. Worn down by war and disease, neither Oratam nor his people could put off the colonists any longer. Settlers finally got their chance to breach the meadowland barrier guarding the heart of Hackensack country less than one month after Stuyvesant surrendered New Amsterdam. On October 1, 1664, Nicolls issued a license to purchase land on the west bank of Newark Bay to some English settlers from the town of Jamaica. Three weeks later, three of them secured a deed from three Indians representing owners who lived nearby on Staten Island. It was later stated that Oratam gave his blessing to the deal. Nicolls acted quickly, issuing a patent for the tract the following December without waiting for a survey. The patent affirmed that the Indians had signed over an unprecedentedly large expanse of five hundred thousand acres, extending seventeen miles north to south between the mouths of the Raritan and Passaic, and reaching twice that distance into the interior, almost to the east bank of the Delaware River.

The October 28, 1664, deed patented by Nicolls later became known as the Elizabethtown Purchase (see map 4). Other Long

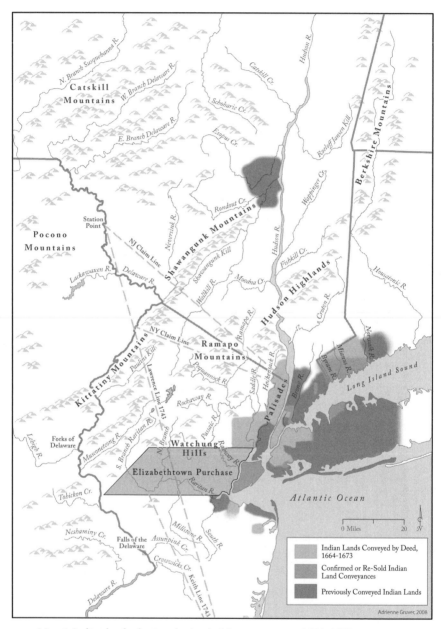

Map 4. Indian land sales to colonists in Munsee country, 1664–1673.

Islanders obtained another license from Nicolls and made another substantial purchase at Navesink, called the Monmouth Patent. Both places were intended to be keystones in Nicolls's plan to consolidate control over Albania by settling colonists willing to accept his authority on untenanted lands close to Fort James. The plan did not work. What was meant to unite settlers under a strong central government instead became a source of dissension between what became the bitterly divided colonies of New York and New Jersey.

Elizabethtown, in particular, became disputed territory immediately after Carteret announced that he was taking over the lands covered by Nicolls's patents in Albania for his proprietary masters in England. Among Carteret's first acts as governor of New Jersey was to issue an order requiring that settlers holding patents from New York obtain new patents from his government. The Elizabethtown Associates, as the New York patent holders between the Raritan and Passaic soon came to be known, refused to obey the order. For much of the next century, they faced off against proprietors in a seemingly interminable legal battle that occasionally flared into open violence. Proprietary authorities determined to collect quitrents from Elizabethtown Associates living in this very sizable chunk of their charter territory ultimately challenged the validity of every aspect of the original Elizabethtown deed. They focused their most penetrating questions on the deed's boundaries, and disputed both the rights and identities of the Indians who signed the document.

The proprietors soon pointed to several apparent irregularities in the deed to show that the associates' purchase was fraudulent. Several noted that Oratam did not sign the 1664 conveyance. Others branded Mattano and the two other Staten Island Indians who signed the deed as foreign Indians lacking the right to sell the tract. The names of the other two Indians listed in the body of the deed did not match those on the document's dotted line.

As the centerpiece of their defiant refusal to accept Carteret's demand for new patents requiring quitrents, the associates took special care to chronicle all aspects of the 1664 deed transaction. Copies of many of these documents survive. A number of other records penned by colonists uninvolved in the controversy help to identify the Indians who signed the deed and provide insights into how they used the sale to hold on to their remaining lands in Hackensack country.

Although old and ailing, Oratam was not necessarily inactive, in spite of his decision not to sign the Elizabethtown deed. Less than one month after the English takeover, Oratam sold Hackensack Neck in present-day Kearny, New Jersey, to one of Nicolls's ship captains. A few years later, Sarah Kierstede, a former captive of the Indians and sometime interpreter, claimed that Oratam made her a present of 2,300 acres of land at Overpeck Creek at about the same time for her past services to him as an interpreter.

There are no records that Oratam came down with the smallpox then running rampant throughout the region. His public announcement designating Pierwim as his successor at a February 1664 meeting with Stuyvesant, however, clearly shows that he had mortality on his mind. Pierwim evidently also grew close to Sewackenamo while the Esopus leader took refuge at Hackensack during the late war. He took the Esopus sachem's name, identifying himself as Sewackenamo in the Elizabethtown deed and several later documents. In order to minimize possible confusion, he carefully noted his alias, Hans, when using the Esopus sachem's name.

Both Pierwim and Oratam maintained their connections with the seat of power on Manhattan after Nicolls took over New Amsterdam. Pierwim's participation in the sale of Elizabethtown to settlers bearing Nicolls's license signaled his acceptance of New York's authority over land affairs in Albania. Oratam likewise limited his final land sales to purchasers bearing New York licenses.

Neither Oratam nor Pierwim formally welcomed Carteret. The new governor was made to feel even less welcome after he published his commission in the new settlement he soon named Elizabethtown. In spite of this, Carteret did what he could to secure the colony for his proprietary backers. In late May 1666 he reached out to Oratam with an offer to officially establish friendly relations. The offer, made shortly after the sachem reportedly had been poorly treated while visiting New York, was accompanied by a request to buy land at present-day Newark. Oratam did not respond on the record to the governor's clumsily self-serving offer of friendship and respect. Off the record, Pierwim later stated that the reluctant elder Hackensack sachem quietly gave him permission to sell the tract to Carteret.

Other local sachems, including two of the Elizabethtown signatories, subsequently closely aligned themselves with the New Jersey proprietors. Pierwim stubbornly remained loyal to New York. In August 1669 he headed an Indian delegation welcoming the newly installed Governor Lovelace to Fort James. Lovelace evidently had been told to expect Oratam to greet him. When Lovelace asked whether they accepted Pierwim as their sachem, "the Indians then present (in owning him so to be) held up their hands."

This was the first and last time anyone would raise their hands in public to acknowledge Pierwim as the Hackensack sachem. His refusal to switch loyalties from New York to New Jersey revealed an inflexibility at this point in his life that probably made him a liability in the eyes of his followers. His people needed a wilier leader willing to quietly play off contending colonists. Pierwim evidently did not then possess such qualities, and his followers apparently quickly deserted him. For a time, Hackensacks failed even to mention his name when dealing with New Jersey authorities. He would not, however, disappear from public life. Casting his lot with the New Yorkers, he moved north, closer to the duke's proprietary lands.

Staten Island turned out to be another persistent trouble spot even after Stuyvesant repurchased it from the local Indians on behalf of the West India Company in 1657. Both New York and New Jersey proprietors contended that Staten Island lay within the boundaries of their provinces. Lovelace saw his chance to kill two birds with one stone when reports of new troubles on the island reached him at Fort James in February 1670. Settlers on the troubled island complained that Indians who refused to move away were threatening to kill livestock trampling and eating their crops. Determined to evict the Indians and affirm New York's title to the island once and for all, he ordered sachems to bring in or secure representation from every Indian who still claimed land on Staten Island.

The list of Indians demanding payment included several sachems and four children, who in fact had not yet been born when the second deed had been signed thirteen years earlier. On April 13, 1670, Pierwim and other sachems finally signed the third and final deed to Staten Island. The document helped Lovelace address his most pressing concerns in the area. It satisfied the last Indian claimants to the island, removed a lingering source of discontent, and helped establish New York's authority over the place. It did not, however, put a complete end to Indian occupation. Locals needing help on their farms and in their fields and homes continued to hire Indians as farmhands, laborers, and servants. Some allowed families and friends of Indian workers to set up campsites in vacant, out-of-the-way parts of their properties. For the next hundred years, Indians continued to come to the island to work, fish, collect shells and shellfish, and gather wood and grasses for baskets and brooms.

Having finally secured Staten Island, provincial officials turned their attention back to the adjacent mainland. Seven years after the English conquest, the lush valley drained by the Hackensack and Passaic rivers still lay tantalizingly out of settlers' reach, despite the Elizabethtown Purchase. The area must have seemed like a fertile crescent, as alluring and as unattainable then as another half a world away would later be. Then as now, internal dissension, diplomatic disarray, poor planning, and problems of supply and geography stymied outlanders even after they secured the watery approaches to the beckoning meadowland valley drained by the two rivers.

Trying to build new communities in a political atmosphere riven by local disputes and cross-provincial rivalries, still-struggling settlers who now controlled the approaches to the meadowlands had little time to pressure Hackensacks for more territory. Hackensack country was further protected by the Palisades. The line of formidable cliffs was not an insurmountable barrier, however. Inroads into the valley beyond could be made along a dried-up section of former Hudson riverbed that cut through the cliff walls at the Sparkill Gap at Old Tappan Landing (present-day Piermont, New Jersey). Just north of Old Tappan, around Nyack, the cliffs drew back from the river, forming a

CONTENTIONS, 1664–1674   103

concave cordon ringing a broad, low-lying basin. More daring colonists like De Vries (forced by the Indians from his farms on Staten Island at the beginning of Kieft's War) had earlier tried to establish settlements on the small wedge of isolated flatland at Tappan. Huddled between towering cliffs and the fast-moving river, outposts there were easily swept away during troubled times.

Like Nicolls before him, Lovelace was determined to give a boost to his province's lagging rate of expansion. And like his predecessor, Lovelace believed that Munsee lands to the west of Manhattan in Carteret's rival province were just the place for expansive development. He accordingly issued an order allowing private citizens in New York to purchase territory, especially on the mainland, directly from Indians. Two groups of New Yorkers soon obtained two deeds from the Indians taking in the whole of the Palisades. Both sets of buyers promptly registered their new purchases in Manhattan, filing documents written in Dutch.

As they had in Staten Island a year earlier, New Yorkers coyly referred to the lands purchased through both deeds as "under the jurisdiction of the province of New Jersey," but not necessarily within its charter borders. With patience and perhaps some well-placed payoffs, Lovelace hoped to extend New York's sovereignty over the desired land. New Yorkers certainly seemed to have the support of the Indians. The list of sachems who signed the deeds included leaders from every major Indian community between the lower Hudson and upper Delaware rivers below the Highlands.

One of the younger signatories, Towakhachi, better known among the settlers as Claes de Wilt or Claes the Indian, was probably originally from Wiechquaesgeck country on the east side of the Hudson. Whatever his origins, he soon became prominent in land affairs on the west bank of the river. Claes was listed by various spellings of his Indian name in the bodies of both Palisades deeds and signed each as a translator using his European nickname. Translators had been especially needed for this transaction. The negotiations involved Indians and settlers who mostly did not understand each other's languages. Both deeds were originally written down in Dutch. Only the second deed was translated into English before insertion into New York records.

The two Palisades transactions brought together uncommonly large gatherings of local leaders from the region, unusual in peacetime and all but unprecedented for land deals up to that point. Inclusion of every major sachem and many local leaders in the proceedings indicates that the Indians had formed themselves into an unusually large coalition for the purpose. The great strategic importance of these land sales almost certainly motivated the sachems to gather at a corresponding level of organization and complexity. The buyers probably encouraged Indians to include all possible claimants in order to maximally secure their titles as they girded for what seemed an almost inevitable land battle with New Jersey proprietary authorities.

The expected battle did not take place. Although the deals openly challenged Carteret's authority, he could do little about them. A revolt led by rebellious deputies in the New Jersey assembly demanded all of his attention. New Jersey's laws, unlike those of New York at the time, gave settlers the right to elect a general assembly of twelve deputies to serve in the legislature with the governor and his council. In 1668, settlers elected an anti-proprietary slate. The new deputies declined to take the oath of allegiance to the proprietors. Openly defiant, they refused to acknowledge the proprietors' right to require new patents, did not pay demanded quitrents or fees, and promptly arrested provincial officials trying to collect the resented imposts.

A movement that began as a rent strike soon grew into an insurrection known as the Rebellion of 1672. Carteret had to flee the province, sailing for England on July 1. Alarmed by Carteret's report, the Crown quickly confirmed the proprietary rights granted six years earlier. Fortified by this confirmation, the proprietors published a declaration on the following December 6, ordering settlers to submit to their authority or be declared rebels. In the event, resolution of the issue had to be put on hold. On the morning of July 30, 1673, proprietary partisans and rebellious associates both awoke to an incredible sight. Just off Sandy Hook, a fleet of twenty-three warships under Dutch command was preparing to sail into New York Harbor.

This fleet arrived sixteen months into the conflict today known as the Third Anglo-Dutch Naval War. The war started pretty much where the last one had left off five years earlier. As in the preceding Anglo-Dutch wars, most of the fighting was done elsewhere. Colonists with little appetite for involving themselves in a European war promptly surrendered Manhattan. The new Dutch conquerors interfered very little in the province's affairs, aside from replacing some officials, administering loyalty oaths, and changing a few other names (New York became New Orange, Kingston became Swaenenburgh, and Fort James was renamed Fort Willem Hendrijck). Their interest in the region instead focused on commerce raiding and the capture of small, isolated, and they hoped, fur-laden outposts farther north like the French fort at Pentagoet in present-day Castine, Maine.

The Dutch commanders held numerous meetings with locals at Fort Willem Hendrijck during the weeks immediately following the English surrender. They were careful to politely welcome, discreetly impress, and generously give gifts to Indian delegations coming to greet them. One group of unnamed Hackensack chiefs accompanied by twenty of their people arrived at the fort in September 1673 to present a speech and exchange presents formally affirming their nation's friendship. Other nations were more distrustful. A Mohawk delegation appeared five days later, counted the number of troops, and took a good look at the fleet before decorously welcoming the Dutch. They then returned upriver to "make a report thereon." Like most River Indian communities, who did not send delegates to New Orange, the Mohawks and their confederates decided to bide their time before formally acknowledging the Dutch reconquest.

In the meantime, after remaining in Manhattan only briefly, the fleet sailed off in search of fresh conquests. They left one of the expedition's officers, a man named Anthony Colve, in charge to complete the reduction of the English colony and manage affairs till the outcome of the war was decided. Colve did not wish to add troubles with the Indians to his list of problems. Reminding settlers that this was wartime, he told them that he would deal harshly with anyone who cheated Indians and declared a virtual moratorium on new purchases of Indian lands. The effectiveness of these actions is imperfectly known. Few records document Indian relations during Colve's tenure in New Orange.

Neither Colve nor anyone else along the Hudson knew that the colony had already been returned to England by diplomats signing the Treaty of Westminster, which ended the war on February 4, 1674. The journey across the ocean still took many weeks. And the wheels of bureaucracy ground as slowly then as they do today. Several months passed before Charles II appointed a new man to govern the province. More passed before the new governor set foot on New York shores in late October, carrying instructions authorizing sweeping changes in the way things were done in the region.

Over the decade between 1664 and 1674, canny sachems had been able to use the confusion and uncertainty created by colonists' preoccupation with invasions and fears of invasion to parry some of the more worrying colonial thrusts into their territories. Many could, if they chose to, reflect on the preceding ten years with some relief and more than a small sense of achievement. They had passed on much of their people's remaining birthright more or less intact. Some important lands had been lost in the process. Still, the sachems had done their best to sow confusion, cloud title, and slow settlement at more vulnerable points like Elizabethtown, Navesink, and the Palisades. Mohawks, although still warring on River Indians, had not attacked their towns along the Hudson or their refugee camps in New England. More important, they had been spared further outbreaks of the epidemic contagions that had ravaged their communities ten years earlier.

Freely available, high-quality, cheap imports always drive out pricier domestic products whose higher costs lead their makers to compromise quality and produce shoddier and less appealing manufactures. European-made textiles, glass beads, and tools and weapons of iron, steel, copper, lead, and brass were drying up age-old Indian demand for domestically produced, painstakingly handcrafted goods. What the Indians lost in autonomy, however, they gained in convenience and, in the case of high-tech items like firearms, in quality. For the last time in their history, Indians in the Munsee homeland looking for the right tool for a particular job could choose from the best of both worlds.

A healthy new generation was growing up on poorer but still productive interior parts of their homeland. Many of those who survived the early epidemics now possessed antibodies that afforded the same degree of immunization from further outbreaks as the settlers enjoyed. The final decades of Dutch rule also were a time of plenty for Indian people in Munsee country. Game driven from lands cleared by colonists flocked to inland forests dotted by Indian farmsteads located on good soils near clean, fresh water. Locally, the beaver were gone and Indians hoping to trap or trade for their pelts had to travel farther into the interior. Susquehannocks helped Munsees bypass powerful interior Indian nations like the Five Nations barring access to the fur country beyond the Appalachians. Many among the Susquehannocks were grateful for River Indian assistance in their ongoing wars with the Iroquois. They reciprocated by allowing River Indians to pass through their territory to trap and trade in the Far country around the Great Lakes.

The decade between 1664 and 1674 had turned out to be a quiet recuperative interval. Although the serious problems challenging the Indians' continuing survival in their ancestral homeland had not disappeared, ten years of health and peace had given the people of Munsee country an important respite. More reflective souls among them must have suspected that they were only passing through the quiet eye of the colonial storm. The leading edge of that storm had brought death and devastation on an almost mythical scale. They could do no more than prepare as well as possible for the trailing edge that was sure to follow.

6

RESPITE, 1674–1679

The coming to Munsee country of Sir Edmund Andros, appointed captain-governor of New York when the English regained it from the Dutch, did not in and of itself signal a return to tumultuous times. The Duke of York wanted his turbulent province placed on a paying basis. The strong-willed new captain-governor, a stormy figure cast in the mold of Stuyvesant, was expected to accomplish the task by reining in troublemakers judged as placing private self-interest above public well-being. Powers that be in England gave him several tools to do the job. Andros brought a new charter from the king that rejoined New Jersey to New York. Many thousands of Indians and more than twenty thousand colonists, slave and free, now lived within his charter bounds. Andros chose to rule over the whole of the duke's proprietary as well as former Dutch lands west of the Delaware also claimed by Maryland. Erstwhile New Jersey governor Philip Carteret, who had returned on the same ship as Andros, had to make do as his deputy in New Jersey until that fractious colony could again be brought into some order.

Although he did not know it yet, Andros was also supported back home by a new bureaucracy specially designed to streamline administration, reduce waste, and maximize profit. In March 1675, the king established a powerful and professionalized Board of Trade. He ordered the twenty-four privy councilors selected as his Lords of Trade on the board to make English commerce more profitable by integrating all foreign trade, colonial and otherwise, into the domestic economy. Their tools of choice were supplied by the Navigation Acts. These gave them the power to regularize customs duty collection; suppress illicit trade, smuggling, and piracy; and, in North America, regulate all trade with Indians. They expected colonial governors like Andros to treat their directives as royal orders and felt certain that he would impress this fact on Indians and everyone else placed under his authority.

Those who came to know him would learn that Andros was cultured, well born, and fluent in both Dutch and French. He was also well connected, with extensive experience in European courts. He was on particularly good terms with Dutch stadtholder Willem Hendrijck of Orange, his enemy during the late war but also the man who would marry York's daughter and, in 1689, become King William III of England. More readily in evidence were the leadership qualities that made Andros a good choice to oversee a smooth, complete transition back to proprietary rule. An energetic, passionate man, Andros was careful to conduct himself decorously in public. He civilly offered the king's protection to those pledging loyalty to the new government and gave those who chose to depart time to get their affairs in order before he formally accepted the Dutch surrender on November 10, 1674.

Andros had come to a colony controlled and still largely populated by strangers, more than a few of whom owned slaves from lands considered even stranger by many. After 150 years of contact and more than a half century of colonization, settlers in the region were still largely pinned to a narrow winding ribbon of tidewater wedged between the coastal uplands and the sea. They were held in place by a combination of still-strange geography and still-powerful Indian nations. York had ordered his man to make this strange land and its refractory inhabitants accept new borders and work together in ways that may have seemed even stranger to old hands in the region.

Vast parts of Andros's New York were still sovereign territory of powerful Indian nations. Although the total Indian population in the Northeast had dropped considerably by this time, it was still

substantial; a little more than thirty thousand Native people probably continued to live in lands claimed by the English Crown between
Chesapeake Bay and the Bay of Fundy in 1674. Furthermore, the colonists still mostly lived concentrated in a few towns on or near the tidal
reaches of the region's major waterways. Indians vastly outnumbered
settlers in the places where numbers counted: along the frontier where
small, scattered settlements were often far from towns and cities. The
number of warriors Five Nations sachems alone could call on equaled
the entire force of two thousand soldiers and militia then available to
Andros. Most of these Indian men, moreover, were more experienced
and far more skilled in forest warfare than their colonial counterparts.

Haltingly at first, River Indian delegations started coming to the
once-again renamed towns of New York, Kingston, and Albany to
welcome Andros as he undertook the customary provincial grand
tour made by all newly arrived governors. They soon queued up in a
constant procession once it became plain that a Dutch counterattack
was not immediately in the offing. Claes the Indian spoke words of
welcome for the Tappans during the first Indian state visit, in early
December 1674, to the fort at the southern tip of Manhattan rechristened Fort James. Tackapousha paid the next courtesy call in January,
performing the greeting ritual on behalf of all the Long Island Indians.
One month later, a party of Mahican sachems performed the same
ceremony at Fort Albany. Meeting with local magistrates in Albany
in February, the Mahicans announced that they were now confeder-
ated with the Wappinger, Wiechquaesgeck, and Esopus Indians. They
asked Albany men to protect them in the event their shaky truce with
the Mohawks collapsed. They promised, in turn, to maintain their
friendship with New York on behalf of the new confederacy. It was a
short-lived coalition; no other record of it survives.

Two months later, a delegation of thirty Navesink Indians officially
greeted Andros and Carteret in New York. The size of this retinue
doubtless reflected the sense of apprehension the Lower Bay Indians must have felt at the time. Bad news from Raritan country had
reached the city before them. The body of an Indian who drank himself to death near Raritan Bay, and two corpses of settlers found on

the banks of the Millstone River, had only just been interred. Four wampum belts presented to the governor clearly conveyed Navesink concerns. Holding up three belts, the Indian speaker reminded Andros that they were allies, lamented the recent deaths, and promised that they would not harbor anyone hostile to the English. Their sachem Metapis then held up the fourth belt and asked if they might give asylum to seventeen Susquehannocks then being held captive by the Mohawks.

Metapis's unexpected request must have brought Andros and his council up short. Even at that late date, the Susquehannocks were still one of the most powerful Indian nations in the region. River Indians had long-standing ties with the Susquehannocks that had almost always been marked by some degree of deference to them. This request signaled an important political shift. How was it that Navesink people could suddenly reverse roles and offer asylum to Susquehannocks? As far as the English knew, the Susquehannocks were still a powerful, populous, and well-armed nation. Their farmers were known to till some of the most productive soils in the Northeast, and their traders still controlled a vast western fur empire.

The answers to this question lay far from Susquehannock country. Competition for control of western trapping grounds and trade markets had long been one of many bones of contention feeding the maw of the endless war embroiling the Susquehannocks and the Five Nations. French arms and aid had helped keep the Susquehannocks in the fight. Now the French had signed peace treaties with the Five Nations. Even more remarkable, Iroquois Confederacy diplomats were managing to convince the French that they should shift their support to them. Although still formidable, Susquehannock strength was sapped by war and disease. The French were realists. It might not take much to get them to look the other way if their longtime Susquehannock allies started looking like losers.

After several years of undocumented but clearly careful negotiations, the Five Nations concluded a peace and trade agreement with the people of Ottawa country out west around the Great Lakes in 1673. Five Nations sachems knew that the Susquehannocks would have to find a way to break up this new meeting of minds if they wanted to maintain access to vital western trade markets and trapping grounds. Susquehannocks meanwhile knew that they ran the risk of making enemies of the French if they openly attacked the latter's allies in the Ottawa country. The Five Nations raised the stakes by promising to carry any furs obtained from the Ottawas east to Montreal instead of to Albany. Intimating that the Susquehannocks might be an unnecessary impediment to this new flow of furs, they asked the French for help against a people they characterized as "the sole enemies remaining on their hands."

Susquehannocks quickly found out about the Iroquois maneuvers. Refusing to openly respond to the provocation, they evidently got River Indians to do the dirty work for them. Reports reached colonial capitals that Esopus trappers had killed eight or nine Indians while visiting Ottawa country. Iroquois Confederacy diplomats used the incident to try to detach the Esopus from their Susquehannock allies. In April 1675, Mohawk emissaries carried a note to Albany from the governor of New France, demanding compensation and cessation of further Esopus attacks. Ruffled Albany magistrates ordered Kingston authorities to straighten out the mess. Coming to Kingston later in the month, Sewackenamo and the other Esopus sachems told assembled officials that their warriors had not yet returned. Although they claimed to know nothing about the incident, they acknowledged past trouble with people they called French Indians. The sachems promised they would look into the matter, presented four strings of wampum to satisfy Mohawk honor and condole families and friends of the dead, and promised substantially larger payments if they confirmed that their men did the killings.

Little more than a month later, an embassy of Wappingers dropped in on Andros. They carried with them an extraordinarily large amount of wampum: some twenty-four belts and another band woven into a circle. They told Andros that these belts carried a major Mohawk offer to the Susquehannocks, proposing that they put the past sixteen years of war behind them, make their peace with the living and the dead, and move among the Mohawks.

Peace was something the Susquehannocks very much needed. They were stuck in the fight of their lives. The fight was not, as almost universally thought, with the Five Nations, however. Sometime in February 1675, the entire Susquehannock nation showed up in St. Mary's City looking for a new home in Maryland. On the face of it, they were simply accepting an invitation made by the Maryland government. More probably, Marylanders had issued them an order they dared not refuse. Unwilling to wage an almost surely suicidal war on two fronts, they agreed to move where the Marylanders put them. Their new home would be the site of a fort of their old Piscataway Indian enemies where Piscataway Creek flows into the Potomac River just south of Washington, D.C.

Isolated on a hostile frontier and surrounded by old adversaries, the Susquehannocks soon found themselves in serious trouble. Their problems began during the early summer of 1675 when several of their people evidently were inadvertently caught in the line of fire of Maryland settlers shooting it out with local Doeg Indians over yet another theft of hogs that had taken a deadly turn. No one condoled the deaths, and grieving Susquehannock relatives soon began avenging their dead kinsfolk in the age-old way.

Concerned authorities in Maryland and Virginia put together a combined force of nearly one thousand militiamen and a contingent of Piscataway warriors over the next few months. Once again, unruly militiamen took matters into their own hands. Arriving at the Susquehannock town on September 26, they decided to murder the five chiefs sent out to parley with them. This began a siege that ended six weeks later, after the fort's occupants managed to slip away unnoticed.

The Susquehannocks scattered for a time. Many gathered near the Occaneechi towns along the Roanoke River just north of the present-day Virginia–North Carolina border. Some took up the Mohawk offer and moved among the Five Nations. Most, however, were not willing to live with their ancient antagonists just yet. Unable to return to their homeland, they did the next best thing and accepted a Unami invitation to live with them on lands around Delaware Bay.

Those Susquehannocks moving among the Occaneechis and Five Nations managed to escape the Virginians. Those coming to Delaware Bay, however, still had to contend with Maryland. That province's leaders had claimed the Delaware Valley as their territory since the colony's founding in 1634. Susquehannock opposition had long played a major role in frustrating Maryland's territorial ambitions there. Maryland had finally removed that obstacle when they got the Susquehannocks to move to the Potomac. Suddenly, distant, distracted New York stood as the only significant impediment to Maryland's long-hoped-for expansion into the Delaware Valley.

Although recent troubles had strained relations with New Yorkers, neither the Unami-speaking people living along the lower Delaware River nor the Northern Unami– or Munsee-speaking townsfolk living farther upriver wanted to fall under Maryland's control. They much preferred dealing with faraway New York. Mattano's kinsman Ockanickon, from the Falls of the Delaware, and Ockanickon's brother Mamarikickon, who was then living on the Millstone River, publicly strengthened ties with the latter province at a meeting with Andros in September 1675. Everyone present used the get-together as an occasion to forget all past differences, including the several recent deaths, and to ostentatiously display solidarity.

Andros took advantage of the sachems' anxieties over the recent killings of settlers in their territory to press for further land cessions. He managed to purchase a considerable tract of land running eight or nine miles north and south of the falls on the west bank of the Delaware. This tract was on land claimed by New York but not officially included in the duke's patent. Andros's offer to the chiefs included 120 yards of wampum, many axes and knives, and most notably, six guns and a considerable amount of powder and lead—items still denied by law to Indians living around Manhattan. The governor's unusually generous offer was clearly meant to buy more than land. His meaning could not have been lost on the chiefs. Their acceptance of the presents therefore had the dual effect of stiffening New York's hold over the region and discouraging bolder interlopers from Maryland.

The arrival of the Susquehannock main body in Unami country during the following summer threatened to undo Andros's efforts to keep Maryland away from the Delaware Valley. The presence of their Susquehannock enemies on Delaware Bay gave Maryland authorities a clear excuse to occupy and annex land of strategic importance to the Crown by claiming that it was obviously being improperly defended by ineffective caretakers in New York. Distressed by the prospect of such a seizure, Andros wanted the Susquehannocks gone as quickly as possible. He told them as much at a meeting with two of their sachems in Albany the following June. Reminding them of the Mohawk invitation made the previous year, Andros urged them to make the move.

The Susquehannocks politely demurred. Two months later, Andros learned that they preferred to remain an independent people rather than become part of the Mohawk nation. Few would risk returning to the Susquehanna Valley, however. Most instead planned to take refuge in the Minisink country along the nearby Northern Unami–Munsee borderlands above the Falls of the Delaware, shielded from attack by the mountainous terrain of the Poconos and New Jersey Highlands.

In the meantime, Northern Indians in New England became locked in a struggle for survival with neighboring colonists. The conflict became known as King Philip's War, after the English name of the prominent Wampanoag sachem Metacom, who came to embody the Indian cause in the minds of colonists and their descendants. Unlike the Susquehannock troubles, which have been largely forgotten, King Philip's War is one of the nation's best-remembered Indian conflicts. The war reached into every corner of Indian New England, spreading into what is present-day Maine before the fighting finally sputtered out in 1677, after more than three thousand Indians and at least six hundred colonists were killed.

Indians in Munsee country greeted news of the war with varying degrees of dread and enthusiasm. Most living along the coast had little sympathy for Indians locked in the struggle. There had been bad blood with the Pequots and, after 1637, with Narragansetts and Niantics taking up where the Pequots left off. Indians everywhere on Long Island suffered from their attacks, and most sullenly paid the wampum tribute Northern Indians demanded to forestall further assaults.

Other Indians at Esopus and various locales in and around the mid–Hudson Valley must have felt a strong obligation to help kindred Northern Indian allies. The Esopus and Northern Indians had fought together for decades against the Mohawks, and had given one another food and shelter when fighting went against them. These experiences doubtless strengthened bonds of kinship and friendship forged in battles that took little notice of colonial province lines.

Whatever their feelings, hardheaded Lower River Indian sachems shared Andros's belief that there was little to be gained by plunging headlong into someone else's fight. Most therefore did what they could to work with the governor to prevent the spread of hostilities into New York. Andros had the easier task. He could order his soldiers to stand down and remain in their quarters. Sachems could thwart ambitious war captains through the simple expedient of not turning control over to them. They could not, however, order warriors to stay out of the fighting. Their task of persuasion was made all the harder by the light in which many warriors regarded the war. They saw battle as a chance to settle old scores, curry a bit of favor with their clansfolk, and with some luck, perhaps win a name for themselves. Sachems who denied warriors their chance to win glory by helping embattled friends and kin could easily lose followers.

Tackapousha and other sachems on Long Island managed to keep both their followers and their warriors at home by working out a face-saving arrangement with Andros. Warriors could not go into battle unarmed. Wanting to make sure that no belligerents could use their involvement as an excuse to widen the war, and willing to promise them protection, Andros wanted the Long Island Indians disarmed. Protesting loudly, but not too loudly, Tackapousha and like-minded elders made a show of reluctantly obeying Andros's order to surrender their people's guns as the governor progressed through their towns in his tour of the island during the spring of 1675.

Other sachems from Munsee country soon trooped to Manhattan in groups of twos and threes to assure Andros that their people also would remain neutral and would support the English if fighting was in prospect. Andros thanked them and gave the sachems presents to show his gratitude. He also demanded and impounded guns owned by Wiechquaesgecks and Wappingers known to have ties to Northern Indians. To keep them out of harm's way, he invited both nations to move closer to Manhattan and gave their sachems passes authorizing safe conduct in nervous times. Andros also put a stop to all trade of guns, lead, and powder to Indians—to all Indians, that is, except the Five Nations. The governor, of course, knew about the long-standing war between the Mohawks and the Northern Indians. Although he did not want the Mohawks crossing over into New England just yet, he let them know that he expected them to use their guns to kill or capture any Northern Indians entering his province.

Although no one knew it yet, the tide of the war was turning. Buoyed by their warm-weather successes against the New Englanders, many Northern Indians withdrew inland to sit out the winter of 1675–76. Although safe from New Englanders' attacks, like the one that destroyed the main Narragansett fort in December, they were not far enough away to escape detection and assault from other quarters. On February 25, 1676, an exhausted Massachusetts settler stumbled into Albany. He told the magistrates he had just slipped away from captors camping on the Hoosic River some forty miles to the north. The man said there were more than two thousand, mostly young Indian men, including five hundred or six hundred "French Indians with straws in their noses" planning spring operations at the encampment. Although the numbers sounded incredible to the Albanians, they were not all that far from the mark. Just then, two bodies of Northern Indian warriors totaling nine hundred men were camping with Mahican friends somewhere along the Hoosic. Metacom was there, helping to conduct negotiations with French Indians bringing guns and ammunition from Canada.

This was an opportunity Andros decided to take advantage of. He quietly invited the Mohawks to camp around Albany, gave food and shelter to their families, and provisioned their warriors. An overwhelming force of Mohawk warriors soon fell on the Hoosic encampment, killing and capturing many and scattering the survivors. Sending their captives back to New York, the Mohawks pressed eastward, attacking Northern Indians wherever they found them. Reeling from the assaults and unable to break through what in effect became a Mohawk blockade, the Northern Indians could not bring in supplies or reinforcements from Canada. Cut off from their lines of retreat and losing operational mobility, the Northern Indians were forced to turn and face their colonial antagonists in New England. Increasingly disorganized and pinned between Mohawk warriors and vengeful settlers, Northern Indian resistance in New England collapsed by the end of the year.

Catastrophes north and south of the duke's province dislocated lives everywhere in English America. Colonists ruined by war flocked to the unravaged Hudson Valley during and after the troubles of 1675–76. Some English refugees moved north from Chesapeake Bay. Most, however, came from New England. Like other immigrants before them, the majority initially settled in and around Manhattan. More enterprising individuals, many joining together into partnerships and syndicates, began buying mostly smallholdings directly from Indians or from local town authorities. Land jobbers started purchasing larger tracts from sachems in hopes of reselling parcels to newcomers at marked-up prices. As in the past, Indians in Munsee country could not stop colonists from pressing them for lands. They could and did, however, continue to find ways to limit expansion into their territory. Most did so by contesting past deeds or restricting numbers of new sales. Uncertainty caused by civil unrest, English surrender and reconquest, and changes in proprietary governance encouraged Indians and settlers to test the effectiveness of a variety of mutually accommodative strategies.

Uncertain conditions in New Jersey provided particularly fertile ground for accommodative strategies. Although reunited politically with New York under Andros, New Jersey uneasily retained its proprietary administrative framework. Infighting and financial troubles continued to dog investors for decades, causing proprietary authorities to divide their holdings in two in 1676. Across from New York, Philip Carteret became governor of what became known as the province of East Jersey. He planned to move the province's capital to the mouth of the Raritan River (soon to be the site of Perth Amboy), where he hoped to build a port capable of drawing trade away from New York. Ensuing arguments over who had control over revenue and governance caused a falling-out between Andros and Carteret that led to the latter's arrest, trial, and release in New York in 1680, and the former's recall to England a year later.

At the same time, Quaker investors established their West Jersey proprietary. Locating their capital at Burlington on the east bank of the Delaware River, they claimed land west of a diagonal boundary line separating their province from East Jersey at a point starting at Little Egg Harbor. The hazily defined line ran north-northwest through unsurveyed Indian territory to a place where it crossed the uppermost reaches of the Delaware River. Arguments over the exact location of this and other provincial boundaries would embroil the Jerseys and their neighbors in land disputes that Indians tried to manipulate for decades to come.

This confused state of affairs was further complicated by uncertainty over the extent of earlier-granted patent lands. Most sachems in East Jersey who sold land to settlers along the lower reaches of the Hackensack and Passaic valleys moved upriver of the purchased properties. Those selling land in what had become the Monmouth Patent followed a different course of action. Most chose to remain in their towns within the purchase bounds. Rather than evict them, settlers instead moved past and around them. Navesink Indians saw little reason to give up their towns. Settlers dreaded the prospect of having to call on meddlesome provincial authorities for help in ousting recalcitrant Indians. Middletown and Shrewsbury township magistrates instead quietly worked out another working disagreement with the Indians. As other disputants had done elsewhere, both sides tacitly treated the original 1665 deed less like a final sale and more like a preemptive option warranty legally required to obtain the necessary patent. Township elders subsequently authorized purchases of tracts claimed by Navesink Indians within previously patented town bounds. Colonists ultimately obtained title to much of this land in a series of twenty-four deeds signed by Navesink sachem Peropay and the other local sachems between 1674 and 1680.

At the same time, Tackapousha also continued to look for opportunities to slow colonial expansion into his people's remaining lands across the Great South Bay on western Long Island. In the summer of 1675, he entered yet another complaint that Hempstead settlers had failed to pay for their lands at Merrick in present-day Nassau County. The settlers admitted never making the payment, saying they did not have to because the Dutch had bought the land for them. Besides, they insisted, Wyandanch, whom they believed was Tackapousha's overlord, had confirmed the colonists' rights to the lands in question by right of conquest during Kieft's War.

The dispute dragged on through Andros's administration. No matter how much he threatened, cajoled, or tried to reason with the aggrieved parties, no one gave ground. As with other disputes between similarly stubborn opponents, the outlines of a final settlement had emerged years earlier, in this case two government-guaranteed reservation tracts on the banks of Hempstead Harbor on the north side of the island and a small tract farther south at Fort Neck along the Great South Bay. Many years of acrimonious dispute would pass before everyone settled for a compromise along these lines.

Around this time Andros began offering sanctuary to Indians from foreign parts willing to submit to his province's protection. In April 1676, Andros asked Wiechquaesgeck sachems to send messengers to New England offering protection and land to Northern Indians who would agree to move to New York. Hackensacks, Tappans, and Mahicans soon joined Wiechquaesgecks sweeping through New England looking for Northern Indians interested in starting new lives in the Hudson Valley.

Later that month, one of the Wiechquaesgeck sachems returned with fifty Indians from a place along the uppermost reaches of the Housatonic River he called Wayattano. Speaking for the party, he affirmed their desire to live in friendship and politely told Andros they would consider a move to New York. A few months later, Connecticut authorities advised Andros to attack "some hundreds" of Northern Indians fleeing from what was almost certainly the Wayattano locale toward Esopus. One month later, the same authorities suggested to

Andros that he take the same course of action against another group of one hundred or so Northern Indians making the same journey. Connecticut troops attacking the first group reportedly killed or captured about one-third of the 150 people in the party. The destination of both groups was identified as Paquiage, a Mahican town in the present-day Catskill Creek village of Leeds, New York.

Andros neither delivered up Northern Indian refugees claiming his protection nor allowed Connecticut troops or Mohawk warriors to attack them once they crossed into New York. Instead, he offered asylum to any Northern Indians who had stayed out of the fighting. Directed to avoid asking too many questions (because the governor could not give sanctuary to admitted killers of colonists), Andros's agents relocated asylum-seekers at a new village established for them by the New York government. It was located on the Hoosic River along the province's northeastern frontier with New England near the site of the Northern Indian encampment recently attacked by the Mohawks. The place was called Schaghticoke, not to be confused with the Connecticut town of the same name on the upper Housatonic River. Schaghticoke on the Hoosic soon became a major frontier settlement astride the main river and road route between New York and New France.

Only a few of the one hundred to three hundred people who moved to Schaghticoke during the first years of its existence were originally from the Hudson Valley. This, however, did not stop people from referring to everyone living at the place as Mahicans or lumping them together with people they collectively called the Upper River Indian Nation. At the same time, colonists began regularly referring to all Native people living below Albany as Lower River Indians.

Growing numbers of Susquehannocks evidently also took up Andros's offer to move to the Duke of York's province. Several sources report their movements into the Mohawk and Delaware river valleys at this time. Few, however, document their presence in any particular place. This is due in part to the fact that no one in New York had much interest in admitting that Mohawks and Delaware River Indians were sheltering open enemies of Maryland, Virginia, and the Five Nations. Susquehannocks also had a strong interest in maintaining a low profile. They almost certainly avoided gathering in numbers anywhere that might attract unwelcome attention.

Changing consumption and production patterns make it difficult to archaeologically distinguish different Indian communities living together at particular places at this time. By the third quarter of the seventeenth century, European manufactures had largely replaced stylistically distinct, domestically produced clay pots and pipes that had acted as markers identifying ethnicities of particular communities or locales everywhere in the Northeast. Although archaeologists can discern differences between European goods produced in different places at different times, the same traders often traded similar brass kettles, glass beads, gun barrels, and other goods to several neighboring Indian nations, limiting the ability to use trade goods for purposes of identification. Contemporary maps and descriptions, moreover, clearly show that members of different Indian nations were then living together in many places.

River Indians and Mohawks had been negotiating diplomatic agreements intended to help them live together with colonists for more than half a century when Andros arrived in New York. During this time, Indians and Europeans had adopted aspects of each other's diplomatic styles. Europeans came to use Indian metaphors for diplomatic alliances, first describing them as ropes and later as iron chains. They understood that blood, liquor, and tears rusted and weakened these figurative iron links, commonly referred to as the Covenant Chain. So they worked together with Indians to do what they could to make sure that frequent meetings and constant exchanges of presents and pleasantries burnished and brightened the links that bound them together. Francis Jennings characterized the functional expression of the particular figurative Covenant Chain between New York, the Five Nations, and the River Indians as "an organization of peers, unequal in power and status, but equal in the right of each to govern itself." Evolving over time to encompass English provinces and Indian nations throughout the region, the alliance provided a framework for mobilizing allies in times of war and maintaining forums for airing grievances and discussing trade arrangements.

Andros ushered in a series of what Jennings called constitutional changes to Covenant Chain relationships. In keeping with his mandate to centralize royal authority, the governor instituted a series of ground rules in Covenant Chain procedures that would profoundly, although not immediately, change how Indians in Munsee country and every other Native community in the Northeast did business with the English. These came into being during talks carried on during the spring and summer of 1677 that established a more substantial Covenant Chain figuratively forged from gold or silver, significantly farther-reaching and thought by Indians and colonists alike to be less brittle than the iron chain it replaced.

Andros worked to anneal his metaphorical precious-metal chain into a broad bond binding every Indian nation and English province in the Northeast to the Crown's interests. He was not an altruist, however. Andros did everything he could to ensure that his patron, the Duke of York, and his patron's province would be dominant in this new arrangement. He started by making sure Mohawks and River Indians supported his insistence that Albany be the central meeting place for Covenant Chain conferences. Andros buttressed Albany's position by giving the city's magistrates control over the new Schaghticoke settlement. The Five Nations further secured New York's pride of place by giving Andros and subsequent New York governors the ceremonial title "Corlaer," the name of Arendt van Curler, a recently deceased Dutch trader remembered as a faithful friend and reliable culture broker.

Jennings makes a good case for the idea that Andros established his new Covenant Chain during a subsequent series of meetings. Andros began by gathering River Indians and emissaries from Connecticut and Massachusetts together in Albany to air grievances and put the sorrows of the recent fighting behind them. He then went south to Kingston, where he sat in on a meeting renewing the Nicolls Treaty with the Esopus Indians. After helping to mediate lingering payment and boundary disputes there, Andros returned to Fort James, where he spent much of May haggling over talking points to be discussed at meetings scheduled for the summer with representatives from the New England and Chesapeake Bay colonies.

Mohawk emissaries met with Andros and New Englanders at the first of these meetings in Albany during the first week of June. Making sure that everyone stayed on script, the New York governor oversaw the ritual renewals of friendship and sat quietly by as everyone pledged to settle future disagreements at the Albany fort. He also saw to it that participants accepted a nonaggression pact that protected Northern Indians at Schaghticoke from Puritan vengeance. It was at this meeting that Mohawks, lamenting the loss of the "Old Corlaer," gave his name to Andros in hopes that the governor and his successors would embody similar qualities of reliability and devotion to duty.

One month later, Andros returned to Albany, this time in the company of commissioners from Maryland and Virginia. There they met with embassies from each of the Five Nations (and from Indian communities throughout the Hudson and Delaware valleys) between July 20 and August 24. Explaining that they could not recall war parties that had already left for the south, the Indians asked that Marylanders and Virginians overlook losses of farm animals or produce that might disappear when hungry warriors hunting down their mutual Susquehannock enemies were nearby. Promising to make good any losses caused by their warriors, they pledged that they would thereafter act peaceably toward settlers and friendly Indians alike when traveling through both provinces. As the Mohawks had done with the New Englanders, all of the Five Nations and the Hudson and Delaware valley Indians agreed to make Albany the site for future meetings with Marylanders and Virginians as well.

These negotiations did much to establish Albany as a central meeting place for colonists and Indians. The Albany magistrates that Andros appointed to oversee Indian affairs there and at Schaghticoke ultimately became the Board of Indian Commissioners. Within a few years, this local committee of magistrates would become a formally constituted board serving as an instrument of imperial power. For the present, however, the Albany magistrates and the newly arrived mayor's secretary Robert Livingston did what they could to make frontier diplomats welcome in their city. Their immediate work centered on finding means to safeguard the security of Northern

Indian refugees at Schaghticoke and those Susquehannocks taking shelter in territory claimed by New York along the Delaware River.

Five Nations warriors did not, however, stop killing and carrying off Indians who ran afoul of raiding parties that continued to range along the northern borders of New England or across the western frontiers of the other English colonies. Authorities in other colonies also did not stop trying to make separate deals with Five Nations sachems that bypassed Andros and Albany. And Lower River Indians living nearer settled towns still mostly preferred to travel to Kingston, Elizabethtown, and New York City to affirm old treaties and transact new business.

At one of these meetings, in July 1679 at Fort James, River Indians informed Andros that they had decided to divide themselves into Upper and Lower nations. Joris, a young Esopus sachem (sometimes also identified as a Mahican leader), told Andros that he had been chosen sachem of the Indians living on the river below Albany two years earlier. Speaking for all River Indians, he went on to inform the governor that the Mahicans and Northern Indians at Schaghticoke had consolidated into a single nation. He finished by asking that one of the leaders there be appointed sachem of those "that live above the river at Albany, as Joris was below."

The July meeting was also the place where Joris made what appears to have been an extraordinary declaration. He told Andros "that heretofore they were brethren to the English but now they are their children." Here, for the first time, a sachem from Munsee country ceremonially referred to his people in council as children. Up until that time, colonial officials trying to rhetorically subordinate Indians in the Munsee homeland by metaphorically referring to them in that way were firmly countered by circumspect sachems using such terms as "brothers," "cousins," or "friends." The metaphors had little effect; whatever word they used to distinguish themselves from one another, the harsh realities of war and disease soon returned to impartially devastate every community in Munsee country.

7

DEVASTATION, 1679–1685

The future must have looked bright for the people of Munsee country as the new year dawned in 1679. The luck of sachems and metewak blessed by spirit powers seemed to be holding. Their towns were still free from epidemics like the influenza outbreak that had struck the Senecas three years earlier and the smallpox that continued periodically to ravage port cities throughout the English colonies. Their sachems kept them out of wars farther north and south and continued to limit land loss. Potential reinforcements in the form of refugee Indians from nearby regions presented new possibilities for renewal and recovery.

Many people living in the Munsee homeland looked inward for the best ways to assimilate the hundreds of refugees now living among them. Others looked outward to suddenly open roads leading to distant trapping and trading grounds. To be sure, the Five Nations still stood in the way. River Indians, however, no longer had to depend on Susquehannock forbearance to help them safely travel farther south and west. Closer links with Northern Indians through friends and kinsfolk at Schaghticoke and the Upper River Mahican towns further cleared paths to Canada and the Great Lakes. New prospects beckoned.

A slaughter of innocents of biblical proportions, what Germans call a *Kindermord*, abruptly dashed all bright hopes. It arrived in the form of a smallpox epidemic that struck the port of New York sometime in August 1679. The disease progressed rapidly, striking the Five Nations in September and reaching Quebec one month later. The epidemic virus sickened people everywhere. The fifteen-year respite enjoyed by everyone in the Hudson and Delaware valleys made small-pox particularly deadly to young people who had not had the chance to develop immunity to the disease. In one awful stroke, smallpox carried off much of the coming Munsee generation.

Desolated survivors lived in the kind of society where spirits were thought to cause everything and where nothing happened by chance. Despite the fact that no records document the fact, the people of Mun-see country must surely have turned to their spiritual leaders to iden-tify the malevolent spirits that had attacked them and find out why they had done so. Indians in Munsee country almost certainly focused their grief and anger on foreigners thought to have unleashed evil spir-its against them.

The most likely culprits in their eyes could not be their overwhelm-ingly powerful colonial neighbors, who did not need the help of spirits to crush them in a single blow. The evildoers must instead be unrec-onciled relatives of dead enemies whose restless spirits remained un-appeased by treaty wampum, condolence gifts, and soothing words. In the time-honored ways of mourning war, grieving warriors set out to avenge their dead by attacking people belonging to suspect nations. They killed or captured strangers waylaid on their travels and took whatever possessions they could carry away, while hunting, trapping, and trading wherever they went.

Colonial records were soon full of reports of Indians venturing far from their homelands. Most duly noted that they were travel-ing to avenge past injuries and get furs. In March 1680, Danckaerts heard that a large party of Indians from the Albany area "had gone south to make war against the Indians of Carolina, beyond Virginia." Noting that they had lost many people to smallpox, he went on to observe that their now-essential pelt inventories had run low and needed replenishment. A year later, Minisink sachem Tomachkapay furnished evidence indicating that his people had joined the expedi-tion. Speaking to Anthony Brockholls, then acting governor of New

York following Andros's recall, Tomachkapay said that his warriors had just killed six Indians and brought back another five as captives from another nation far to the south. He went on to explain that they had done this to avenge the deaths of two Minisinks killed by what he called "angry people" from that nation during a recent hunting trip "as far as the Spanish Indians" (see map 5).

The identities of some of these southerners were revealed when Maryland and Virginian commissioners came to the Covenant Chain meeting place in Albany in June 1682. They complained that a party of "Maquase and Mahikanders" had attacked their Piscataway friends somewhere in the more westerly parts of their provinces. They demanded compensation, called for the return of any prisoners still living, and insisted that the sachems promise to restrain their warriors and stop further attacks.

The following July, sachems representing the Mahicans, Catskills, and Esopus gathered at Albany to hear the complaints against them. Sachems at this meeting, whose numbers included Joris (identified as a "Mahikander") and the prominent female Esopus leader Mamanuchqua (identified as a "squae"; see figure 4), politely responded on the following day. Presenting two wampum belts, they renewed their Covenant Chain bonds and apologized for all offenses offered and damages done. They also presented a beaver pelt in token of a promise to travel farther westward beyond Maryland and Virginia when again "going out a hunting beaver."

These were not the only Indians from Munsee country traveling far in search of beaver. In February 1681 the French explorer René-Robert Cavalier, Sieur de la Salle, came upon others in company with thirty or so hunters he called Loups ("Wolves," the general term the French used when talking about Eastern Algonquians) and their families near the mouth of the St. Joseph River. This 215-mile-long stream runs across the base of Michigan's Lower Peninsula before emptying into Lake Michigan near the city bearing the river's name. It was then an important communication and trade route that, with a short portage, bypassed more northerly French posts like Michilimackinac to link Lakes Erie and Michigan.

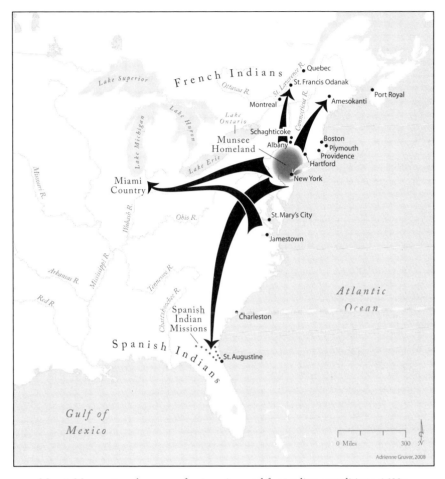

Map 5. Munsee travels on war, fur-trapping, and fur-trading expeditions, 1680s.

La Salle wrote that members of this party had been living in the region for at least two years before his arrival. He identified them as Indians who had left homes in the east between New England and Virginia "partly because the beaver had become very scarce and partly because of the hate they bore the English." Speaking through an Indian interpreter from Boston whom La Salle identified as Ouiouilamet, the Loups told the Frenchman that they were there to hunt up

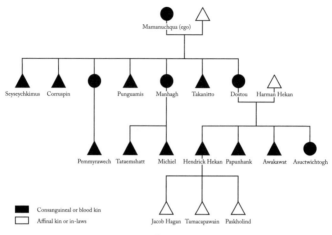

Figure 4. Mamanuchqua and her kin.

enough beaver to buy their way into the Iroquois Confederacy or any other nation willing to offer them lands and fields far from the English. La Salle identified Mahicans, Minisinks, and Esopus, as well as Wampanoags, Narragansetts, and Mohegans from New England, and Piscataways, Conoys, or Powhatans from Chesapeake Bay, among the Loup party. The list reads like a comprehensive directory of Eastern Algonquian nations between Boston and Virginia. It is tempting to speculate that the group represented a deliberately organized expedition formed to explore possibilities for a general emigration.

The Indian from Boston whom La Salle called Ouiouilamet may have been Wawanolewat, the Anglophobic pro-French Northern Indian war leader better known among colonists as Grey Lock. Other prominent figures in the group included "Nanangoucy from Menissen," a man who subsequently served as La Salle's intermediary, and a "Mahigane [i.e., Mahican] Indian" named Klas. Nanangoucy was almost certainly the Delaware Valley sachem Nanacuttin, later noted as an uncle of one of Ockanickon's sons. Klas, for his part, may have been Claes de Wilt, the already mentioned Hudson Valley culture broker. Europeans described both Klas and Claes as adventurous and as skilled linguists, lending credence to the speculation they were one and the same man. Chroniclers along the Hudson and Delaware valleys include neither Claes's nor Nanacuttin's names among Indians dealing with colonists in or around the Munsee homeland at the time La Salle wrote about them. Whether or not they were the men who met with La Salle, other records place both Claes and Nanacuttin back east by 1682.

Munsee Indians remaining in their homeland were still reeling from the epidemic that had carried off so many of their young people and inexplicably spared so many elders (Colonists mention many elders in their records after this time, affirms that many survived.) We may therefore assume that immunities acquired during previous contagions probably protected older survivors of earlier epidemics. In the seventeenth century, though, the elders would have credited spiritual help rather than antibodies for their survival.

They and their grieving families must have wondered why the spirits allowed so many of their children to die. As Indian interments throughout the Northeast attest, European manufactures tended to constitute the largest share of offerings placed in children's graves during this period. Such goods were intended to equip the dead in the afterlife. Grieving parents evidently placed European goods in graves of children who had not lived long enough to enjoy them in this world. To obtain these colonial wares, traders and trappers could bring home only the small amounts of furs they were able to fit in backpacks and canoes. War parties could bring back prisoners for adoption or sacrifice to avenge deaths and mollify restless spirits. Threats of retaliation might also discourage enemies from casting spells, though this could only be a forlorn hope. Neither warriors nor traders, however, could get the vast quantities of furs needed to acquire sufficient quantities of European goods to appropriately outfit the heartbreakingly large number of children for their journeys to the next world. Only land sales could provide the requisite amounts.

The worries of colonists mourning their own losses were multiplied by increasingly sure knowledge that disruptive and potentially expensive administrative and political changes were in the wind. Andros had been recalled to England in seeming disgrace in 1681, facing charges of mismanagement and worse. His return appeared doubtful and no one knew who his permanent successor would be or what he would do. Regime change meant at the very least that those officials fortunate enough to keep their jobs would have to pay steep fees for new commissions. Other fees for sale, survey, and registration of new deeds and confirmation of old patents would require further outlays. Some of these could be considerable. The entire province of East Jersey was up for sale. Quakers who had already bought West Jersey soon showed great interest in acquiring the rest of the duke's domains beyond the Hudson.

They and nearly everyone else in and around the region were ready to trade the goods Indians needed for titles to land they wanted. East Jersey was being administered in the name of Elizabeth, Lady Carteret after her husband died deep in debt on January 14, 1680. Working with trustees appointed under the terms of her husband's will, she immediately began looking for buyers interested in taking the unprofitable and troublesome colony off her hands. Determined to remove legal impediments that might put off prospective purchasers, she and her trustees ordered their governor to clear Indian title to as much land in the province as possible without delay.

Indians living along the Raritan and Hackensack rivers knew something was up. Alert to all rumors floating through the region, they may have heard that New York might be giving up its claim to the Jerseys, ending opportunities to exploit uncertainties that had helped them slow settlement for nearly a generation. Whatever they suspected, they could not have anticipated the relentless persistence of Lady Carteret's agents, who started swooping down on their towns in earnest in the late spring of 1681.

Several sachems surrendered the whole of the long-denied main stem of the Raritan River in a series of nine deeds signed between May 1681 and April 1682. Others conveyed two tracts in Hackensack country around the same time. Pressure ended only after the governor received a letter from Lady Carteret and her trustees, directing him "not to purchase any Indian lands, make patents, or suffer any settlements to be made until further orders," because buyers willing to pay a bargain price for the province had been found.

Farther east, Suscaneman was running a fire sale of his own. Concerned Oyster Bay town fathers embroiled in generations-old land disputes with Indians and neighboring townsfolk worried about what the coming of a new governor would mean to their patents. They laid siege to Suscaneman, who signed twenty-seven deeds to small lots in the heart of the town within the space of little more than a year's time. Farther north, other sachems signed a number of deeds for settlers wishing to shore up their own titles to lands in present-day Westchester County. Claes and several local sachems signed four deeds giving over rights to lands along the east bank of the Hudson to the New York merchant Frederick Philipse I, who used them to establish a grand manor in the style of the former patroons. Other sachems sold smaller nearby tracts to less imposing merchant princes.

To the east, local sachems signed over two deeds to Rye settlers for tracts on the still-uncertain border with Connecticut. Katonah, a young survivor of the recent epidemic originally from Connecticut's Pequannock Valley, was first mentioned in colonial records chronicling another transaction nearby. Like Taphow—another man originally from Pequannock who rose to the rank of "commander in chief" of the Indians of Northern New Jersey, evidently after marrying into a prominent Ramapo Valley family—Katonah probably made a similarly advantageous marriage that helped him become an influential sachem along the borderlands between New York's Westchester County and Fairfield County in Connecticut.

Meanwhile, Andros successfully defended himself against the charges that caused his recall; the duke decided to replace him anyway. New York's new governor, Thomas Dongan, arrived in New York in early August 1683 to replace caretaker Brockholls. An Irishman and the only Catholic to hold New York's highest office in colonial times, Dongan had orders to consolidate Crown authority, more closely regulate commerce, and, by so doing, finally put the province on a paying basis.

Dongan was the first politician to divide New York into administrative counties. He then used newly constituted county courts run by placemen on his payroll to consolidate his power over the province's land and people. County courts asserting supremacy over local governments within their jurisdictional bounds represented concentrations of power that terrified formerly all-but-autonomous town fathers. Farmers and merchants in the increasingly well-to-do Long Island towns near Manhattan could be certain that the revenue-hungry governor would use his new county courts to extract money and land from them. They braced for orders requiring them to prove the validity of existing titles and take out expensive new patents for their towns. Perhaps most worrying of all, they dreaded the prospect that court officials appointed by the importunate governor would order them to show cause why they should not surrender to the Crown unpurchased Indian lands within town boundaries. Goaded by a sense of urgency bordering on desperation, they deluged their Indian neighbors with demands for new deeds and confirmations of earlier sales.

Deed frenzy reached its peak in Oyster Bay. Having been colonized by New Englanders hoping for union with Connecticut, the openly seditious town was an ideal target for Dongan's placemen. Dongan's new county courts could make short work of titles based on hazily worded and unclearly bounded Indian deeds that already mired the town in seemingly endless squabbles with Indians, neighboring towns, and provincial authorities. Few outside of Long Island would care if decisions putting an end to these protracted and distracting disputes went against Oyster Bay.

Concerned townsfolk desperate to shore up shaky titles promptly hunted up their reliable deed signer Suscaneman. In Oyster Bay they had him put his mark on documents affirming that Tackapousha gave him permission to sell or confirm earlier deeds to land on behalf of himself and his relatives. They also secured letters confirming Suscaneman's understanding that he would equitably share land sale proceeds with all Indians with interests in the properties. Relatives serving as sureties for this promise put their marks next to his name on thirty-five deeds conveying most unsold land in the town between 1683 and 1686.

Similar goings-on were occurring elsewhere in the duke's province. During the spring of 1684, for example, Suscaneman, Tackapousha, and several of their sons, heirs, and retainers confirmed earlier sales for anxious town fathers in Flushing. Reserving only the right to cut bulrushes for themselves and their posterity, they pledged not to make further claims on the town. A few months later, several sachems confirmed sales of land in the town of Gravesend, signing the last Indian deed to land in Brooklyn in the newly founded county of Kings. That fall, Katonah and his kinsfolk sold land in and around White Plains to Rye town fathers intent on acquiring all remaining unsold Indian lands within their town's charter boundaries.

Private citizens were also busy amassing enormous personal holdings of their own on the shores of the lower Hudson. Dongan's instructions empowered him to grant manors, English equivalents of the earlier Dutch patroonships, to colonists wealthy enough to purchase and patent large expanses of Indian territory. One of these men, Albany Board of Indian Commissioners secretary Robert Livingston, obtained a license to purchase Indian lands for a manor in present-day Columbia County from the governor in 1685.

Wealthy merchants based in New York City also began amassing lands in hopes of securing estates of their own at this time. In February 1685 a very young and very ambitious Lewis Morris obtained an Indian deed confirming an earlier purchase in the Bronx made by his father, Robert Morris, of a tract he renamed Morrisania, which included land originally bought by Swedish ship captain Jonas Bronck. Witnessed by Claes, the confirmation document was signed by several other signatories claiming to be descendants of the original sellers.

Just to the north, New York merchant Frederick Philipse I finished acquiring the last pieces of the vast ninety-two-thousand-acre Manor of Philipsburg that ultimately stretched between the Hudson and Bronx rivers from Spuyten Duyvil in the Bronx north to the Croton River. Nearby, a number of Lower River Indian sachems signed or witnessed several deeds to lands on both sides of the Hudson at and above the Highlands, purchased by Stephanus van Cortlandt and other prominent merchants.

Dongan acquired an even more massive estate for himself on the west side of the river above the Highlands in two deeds signed between late 1684 and the following spring. Together, these deeds put an unprecedented three hundred thousand acres of Lower River Indian land into the hands of an individual purchaser.

Sachems along the lower river did not stop with these sales. Sensing an opportunity, they let Dongan know that they had not been paid for their shares in the section of the Palisades astride the still-contended border between New York and New Jersey sold fifteen years earlier. Dongan was determined to secure the property for New York. He allowed a sharp-dealing merchant named Nicholas Depui and one of his partners to obtain a New York deed to the same land from local Indians tracing descent to the original sellers.

Names and numbers of Indians mentioned in these and other contemporary records began to change as age and infirmity began removing experienced sachems from public life between 1680 and 1686. Many of the men and women whose names disappeared during these years had been leaders since Dutch times. More than a few were probably well on in years. Although they never openly worked together in one body, their individual efforts as family, town, and coalition leaders had seen their people through wars, epidemics, and relentlessly intensifying pressure to sell land and move away. Their very survival indicated to followers that they were backed by powerful spirits as much as by skill and good connections. They maintained influence by making new ways of doing things work with old ways of thinking. This was the key to their effectiveness, and it helped them grapple with developments that could and did overwhelm larger and more powerful Indian nations.

Indications that something was dreadfully wrong first appeared when news reached New York in late January 1684 that sickness had compelled a delegation of Wiechquaesgeck sachems to miss their appointed meeting in that city. Two years later, a Schaghticoke man visiting Albany told magistrates that "all the Indians upon the North

River were dead" and that "the Indians that live upon [the Hoosic] River are few in number." Something of an overstatement, it nevertheless did not fall far short of the grim reality. The disease that struck these people was probably malaria. Although the word "malaria" did not exist at the time, the shaking and fever identified as ague in 1684 bore all the classic hallmarks of the disease. The fever that struck in 1684 may have been either a deadlier, recently mutated, or newly introduced variety or a familiar form that struck at a time when there were many elders vulnerable to attack.

From whatever cause, nearly two generations of the most experienced Indian leaders in Munsee country vanished from colonial records in just the two years before and after the 1684 fever. Rates of disappearance were the same nearly everywhere the disease struck. A similar rate of disappearance would never again occur during the remaining years of the colonial era. Much vanished with these elders. They were parents, diplomats, religious leaders, breadwinners, storytellers, and craftspeople. Their memories held stores of knowledge and tradition. The smallpox that killed so many young people in 1679 carried off most of their more promising pupils. Those who survived were few in number and mostly untested, because their elders had little time to pass on lessons learned before they too joined their ancestors.

8

SOLDIERING ON, 1686–1701

Devastating as it was, the epidemic of 1686 did not wipe out the entire Munsee leadership cadre. Tackapousha, Suscaneman, and other sachems soldiered on in the face of demographic catastrophe and land loss. New sachems like Taphow and Weequehela joined young leaders like Katonah in making up some of the losses. It is not known if these survivors tried to revitalize old religions that had failed to protect their most dedicated adherents. Awareness that colonists also suffered from the same diseases, combined with general colonial disinterest in missionary enterprises, probably explains why few Indians in the region felt the need to seek the help of Christian spirit power. All, however, needed more substantial material assistance available only from Christians. Loss of so many sachems, metewak, captains, hunters, and warriors made them vulnerable as never before. Loss of experienced artisans capable of crafting stone and bone tools and fashioning clay pots and pipes made them even more dependent on European metal implements, glassware, and other manufactures. They had also lost all of their most productive lands fronting on the Hudson River and tidal stretches of the Delaware. These losses forced further movements inland to less productive territories.

Deeds signed at this time did more than force Indians to move inland. They also pumped goods into Munsee communities. Agreements that listed payout amounts (most did not) show that Indians received a combined total of £1,000 in specified goods and money. Even when what was drunk away, used to pay debts, or simply unpaid is subtracted, the total wealth transfer listed in these deeds is considerable. Much higher quantities of goods and money than most Indians in the Munsee homeland were used to were suddenly available for sharing among much smaller numbers of people.

What happened to all this wealth? As mentioned earlier, a sizable proportion of European manufactures were placed in the graves of children. Much also probably wound up in Iroquois towns like the Seneca site preserved in present-day Ganondagan State Historic Site. Archaeologists working at this and contemporary townsites elsewhere in Iroquoia have unearthed substantial amounts of European wares. Also as earlier mentioned, the occupants of these towns extracted tribute in the forms of trade goods, wampum, and peltry from River Indians and other nations.

Trade goods did more than accompany the dead or pay off tribute takers. New leaders got their chances to show respect, skill, and good sense at funerals and other get-togethers where gifts were offered and exchanged. As in the past, those placing goods in the right hands won friends and followers. Munsee leaders, in particular, needed all the support they could muster as they made decisions that affected their people's future. Should they stay or leave? Move farther inland or relocate entirely to Canada or to the Far country? Whatever they did or wherever they lived, what would they do and with whom would they do it?

Decisions of sachems in Munsee country now affected smaller numbers of followers. It is not certain, however, that this made consensus any easier to achieve. Survivors facing difficult decisions almost certainly felt exposed, unsure, and unsafe. These kinds of feelings often make people more willing to tolerate leaders who concentrate power and authority in their hands, a process that evidently occurred in Munsee country. In earlier times, colonists often used the word "king" to describe any sachem. After 1686, settlers increasingly familiar with Indian customs largely limited use of that term to particularly influential leaders like Taphow and Weequehela. Although these Indian kings could not in any way be considered despots, they tended to act more forcefully than their predecessors. The fact that they retained authority among people still able to vote with their feet indicates that many people tolerated more authoritative sachems. Whatever their positions in life, all Munsees had to learn new ways of relating to each other and the outside world if they expected to keep their suddenly smaller, more scattered, and increasingly isolated communities intact.

Indians in Munsee country were not the only people weighing costs and benefits of increased concentrations of authority during these years. Settlers were also looking for ways to deal with governors and other officials implementing policies meant to bring their provinces closer into the imperial fold and bind them more tightly to royal interests. Colonial administrators charged with these tasks were expected to enact laws and negotiate treaties aimed at maintaining peaceful relations with Indians, especially with Indians like those in Munsee country who lived, as the expression went, within the bowels of the settlements. Past promises were repeated and new assurances given. Indians were to be equitably treated in courts, council chambers, and boardrooms; be protected from those who would enslave them or abuse them with alcohol; and be fairly dealt with in trade and land matters.

They were also expected to limit their trading to specifically designated places like Albany and were prohibited from sheltering Indians from foreign parts or strangers of any sort without first notifying local authorities. Local communities still played major roles in Indian relations. Towns continued to form committees to buy Indian land. Many also kept up the practice of appointing overseers to manage relations with Indian neighbors. The trend, however, was toward increased centralization. Dealings with River Indians and others were quickly taken over by formal organizations vested with greater powers and wider areas of responsibility. One of the most important of these was Albany's Board of Commissioners of Indian Affairs.

Ships making the two- to three-month Atlantic crossing in growing numbers at this time carried minutes of commissioners' meetings and other reports on Indian affairs to London. Many passed other vessels sailing in the opposite direction, carrying news of fast-breaking developments in Europe. Among the bigger stories was the death of Charles II on February 2, 1685. His brother York was crowned King James II of England that April. The new King James moved quickly to further the process of consolidation of royal power in the colonies begun by his elder brother. He started by upholding the late king's 1684 revocation of Massachusetts Bay's charter. Determined to bring all of New England's provinces into line, James joined Massachusetts Bay with Plymouth, Rhode Island, Connecticut, and New Haven to form a single royal colony. In June 1686, the king appointed Sir Edmund Andros as royal governor of this new Dominion of New England.

New York also became a royal colony when its proprietor ascended to the throne. Now Royal Governor Dongan finally felt secure enough to implement policies crafted to extract the maximum amount of revenue from balky colonists. Dongan began by issuing long-dreaded orders directing town governments to prove existing titles within their bounds and take out expensive new patents. As expected, he chose for his first targets the towns on Long Island. Each had to pay fees of several hundred pounds for new New York patents. On the plus side, these Dongan Patents, as they are still known, helped establish clearer boundaries that more firmly secured titles held by existing landholders.

Specific provisions inserted into all new patents required towns to select boards of trustees made up of freeholders to administer commons and unpurchased town lands for the public good. Although new trustees had to pay the governor for their commissions, their appointments ended fears that Dongan or his minions might seize vacant or unpurchased town lands for their own purposes and profits. In order to make the new patents more palatable, trustees also were given first rights to purchase all common and public lands in town bounds on the condition that they pay an annual fee. Although fee structures and reporting obligations have changed over time, boards of trustees and freeholders, and their authority to manage open lands and waters in Long Island, remain intact today in the same basic form as when first instituted more than three hundred years ago.

Dongan also used his revenue-raising efforts on Long Island to convince Indians and settlers alike that it was finally time to put an end to their land wrangles. Hempstead, Huntington, and Oyster Bay settlers, determined to leave as little as possible for royal authorities to confiscate, had already acquired or confirmed purchase of almost all remaining Indian lands in their towns by early 1687. No one in Hempstead raised a voice in opposition when Dongan granted a 150-acre reservation on the east side of Cow Neck to Tackapousha on June 24 of that year. Taking the power to sell reservation land out of the Indians' hands, the deed stipulated that Tackapousha and his heirs pay "yearly and every year forever unto his sacred treaty . . . one shilling current money." Three days later, Dongan granted Suscaneman the two-hundred-acre Matinecock Reservation for his people in the town of Oyster Bay, just across Hempstead Harbor from Cow Neck, on the same terms (see map 6).

These tiny reservations must have felt uncomfortably cramped to people used to having the run of the country. Tackapousha and his relatives subsequently spent increasing amounts of their time farther south in the still uncircumscribed bayside Indian towns at Fort Neck, Merrick, and Rockaway. Far from colonial settlements, these out-of-the-way places lay in small clearings deep within marshlands that bordered bays sheltered from the Atlantic by narrow sand spits. Suscaneman himself moved westward for a time, settling among friends and relatives maintaining ancestral rights to territory claimed by the two Jersies.

Ten years had passed since Jersey proprietors had agreed to split their province in two. During that time, they had not managed to agree on a mutually satisfactory border. A 1686 meeting between the governors of New York and the Jersey provinces failed to resolve the issue. Taking matters into their own hands, East Jersey proprietors had their surveyor-general, George Keith, run a partial line from Little Egg Harbor on the south to the South Branch of the Raritan River between April and May 1687. The Keith's Line blatantly favored East Jersey and was promptly rejected by the other province. It was at this delicate point in proceedings that word reached the West Jersey

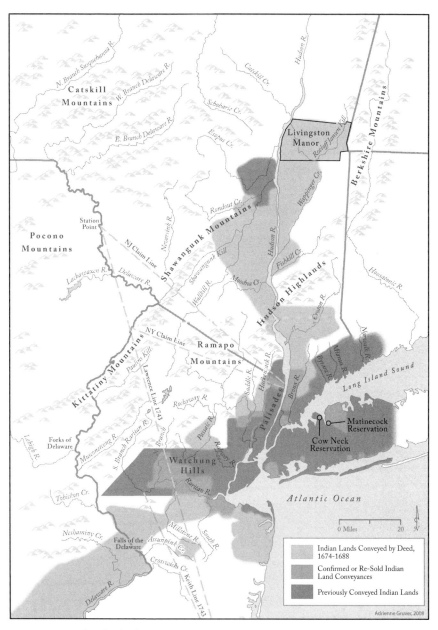

Map 6. Indian land sales in Munsee country, and Indian reservations established on Long Island, 1674–1688.

Indian Lands Conveyed by Deed, 1674-1688

Confirmed or Re-Sold Indian Land Conveyances

Previously Conveyed Indian Lands

Adrienne Gruver, 2008

capital at Burlington that the province had once again changed hands. Daniel Coxe, physician to Charles II and a naturalist intensely interested in the Americas, had purchased the right to govern West Jersey the previous February. The new governor, who, like most absentee proprietors, never managed to visit his province, chose to maintain the proprietary's Quaker-dominated government, although he himself was not a Friend.

Wealthy and powerful, Coxe was determined to become the largest landowner in West Jersey. Along with the proprietary shares he bought, he acquired more than 120,000 acres to gain the controlling interest he needed to get himself appointed governor of the province. Working through local land agents, Coxe ultimately amassed an estate of more than 1,000,000 acres. His agent's first purchases took in large blocks of land above and around the Falls of the Delaware that did more than simply add to the new governor's growing holdings. The purchases finally opened the long-desired direct route between Raritan Bay and the Delaware River. For the first time, deepwater ports at the East Jersey provincial capital of Perth Amboy and the West Jersey capital at Burlington were joined by a secure overland passage.

As with most other purchases, the prices the Indians received for these lands were small compared with the vastly larger outlay Coxe paid to royal authorities for the right to govern the province. Like Dongan in New York, Coxe and his fellow proprietors in Pennsylvania (acquired by William Penn in 1681) and East Jersey soon looked west for trade profits as they sought more reliable ways to extract revenue from refractory settlers for themselves and their monarch (whose recent Indulgence Declaration protected Penn and other Quakers from persecution). Coxe and the other governors also made it their business to follow royal instructions ordering them to preserve good relations with Indians who could lead them to western wealth and whose grievances could quickly cloud title and clog cash flow. Indians bringing news of furs in the Ottawa country were quickly heard, as were complaints about surveys taking in too much land and settlers failing to pay for their land purchases. Grievances found to be valid, and there were many, were quickly heard.

Proprietary land reform in Pennsylvania and the Jerseys ordered by the new royal government presented already closely linked Indian sachems and provincial authorities with abundant opportunities to rake in revenues. Settlers unable to produce Indian deeds were directed to pay the original signatories or their descendants for new copies and to pony up fees for new surveys and patents. Proprietors were reluctant to drive away potential rate payers, so they gave settlers possessing unregistered titles issued by Nicolls and titles privately obtained from Indians the opportunity to settle accounts and buy new patents. At Navesink, many established Quakers and more than a few of the many new Scottish families now flooding into the province decided to obtain proprietary titles to long-encumbered lands. More refractory Puritans in Elizabethtown were less forthcoming. They refused to ask proprietors belonging to sects many detested for dispensations to lands they considered their own. They had used their own money to buy their land from its Indian owners, and had paid for patents and all other paperwork required by a lawful English governor before the Jerseys even existed. No one offered to reimburse them for their past expenses. Instead, the new proprietors made it clear that they intended to milk settlers for quitrents, fees, and any other cash they could safely extract under color of law.

Policies designed to concentrate power in fewer hands would put an end to arrangements that allowed the weak to play powerful factions off against one another. Functionaries unfettered by all but absolute authority could enforce laws and regulations made by distant masters. Individuals, communities, and even entire nations or nationalities might be disenfranchised, arbitrarily moved about, or driven away. Consolidation would at a minimum rearrange matters in favor of the privileged few who possessed the largest estates and the best connections. Prospects for the less well off in both colonial and Indian communities, on the other hand, only grew dimmer.

More experienced Indian leaders in the Munsee homeland must have seen both threats and opportunities in the king's consolidation efforts. The few remaining elder sachems with close relations to merchants and officials could reasonably expect continued dispensations.

The majority of Indian leaders after 1686 were much younger and less well connected than their predecessors had been. These new men and women must have looked to the future with less assurance. Like their equally apprehensive colonial neighbors dealing with King James's appointees, they almost certainly wondered what would happen if the faraway English monarch succeeded in bringing all of their country under his complete control.

People in nearby New England were already getting a taste of life under imperial rule. Andros, who long cherished dreams of consolidating Crown authority, arrived in Boston with more than a mandate to dissolve the existing freestanding chartered governments into a single dominion. He also carried orders directing him to combine separate provincial militias into a single military force under his sole command. Andros tried to reassure suspicious colonists that the king had issued the order only to prepare for war with France. Whether Andros knew it or not, as he made this assurance James was quietly negotiating a secret alliance with the French king.

James further gave Andros the power to put an end to town meetings; to impose new duties, fees, and taxes; and to treat sachems' signatures on Indian deeds as little more than what the governor characterized as "scratches of bear's paws." Unsurprisingly, Andros's exercise of such powers fueled widespread unrest. Connecticut officials refused to surrender their charter, famously claiming that they hid it instead in the hollow of a tree since known as the Charter Oak. Other acts of defiance followed. None of this stopped James from issuing still more edicts. Armed with a second royal commission sent from London in the spring of 1688, Andros personally led a force that compelled Dongan to give over governance of New York province to the Dominion of New England on September 11, 1688. Leaving career officer Francis Nicholson behind on Manhattan as his lieutenant governor, Andros went on to receive equally sullen submissions from the Jersey proprietary governments a week later.

James's dream of a consolidated dominion under his complete control came to a sudden end when a massive force of English expatriates carried by an armada of Dutch warships appeared off the south

English coast in November 1688. The force encountered no effective opposition and quickly forced James to flee to France. Dutch stadtholder Willem Hendrijck of Orange, Andros's old friend and James's son-in-law, was subsequently crowned King William III and his wife, Queen Mary II on February 13, 1689.

News of William and Mary's ascension reached North America a few months later. Colonists in the English provinces rushed to proclaim themselves loyal subjects of the new sovereigns. James's detested dominion was promptly dismantled and Andros was arrested in Boston. In New York City, Nicholson escaped before five hundred armed colonists led by a militia captain named Jacob Leisler seized Fort James. Acting on his own initiative, Leisler renamed the place Fort William Henry and set up a temporary government to hold the province for the Crown until duly constituted authorities arrived from London.

In the meantime, William and Mary declared war on France in May 1689. The hostilities soon developed into a wide-ranging conflict known in the colonies as King William's War. Like the arbitrary borders erected by royal decrees and disputed by colonists, the formal commencement of hostilities was little noticed by River Indian and other Covenant Chain allies who were already fighting against the French. Regime change, however, was another thing. Sachems could not help noticing that a mob carried Leisler to power. They also noticed that magistrates at Albany and other places rejected Leisler's initial efforts to make them submit to his authority. As they had during uncertain power transitions in the past, they did what they could to keep colonists guessing and their own options open. Sachems delayed as long as possible before performing rituals that recognized Leisler as their acting governor. They may have also helped spread rumors that they loyally planned to help Andros retake the government if and when he returned to New York.

In the meantime, men from the Upper and Lower River Indian towns were among the 1,500 warriors under Five Nations command that fell on the French village of Lachine just outside Montreal on a quiet morning in late July 1689. They burned the village, killed more than 200 of its inhabitants, and carried off another 120 as prisoners. Confident that their attack had crippled the Canadians, Covenant Chain war captains did not see the need to send out large scouting parties to screen the frontier with New France during the snowy winter of 1689–90. Thus, no one was standing guard when 210 soldiers and warriors coming from Canada poured out of the snow-filled forest through the open gates of Schenectady during the night of February 8, 1690. The attackers killed more than sixty townsfolk, took another eighty prisoner, and burned down the town.

Other French counterattacks along the Acadian frontier shocked the divided and uncertain colonists into realizing that they needed to focus their energies on the French rather than on each other. Just seventeen miles east of Schenectady, Albany magistrates finally accepted Leisler as their caretaker commander after his chief lieutenant arrived with 160 men to reinforce the city garrison in the first week of April 1690. The Lower River Indians dispatched eighteen warriors to join a second group of reinforcements after reluctantly acknowledging Leisler as their Corlaer. They promised to send another sixty to Albany later, when the nine hundred militiamen pledged by Leisler and the governors of neighboring provinces assembled there for a concerted assault on Montreal, planned for the coming summer.

A motley assemblage of several hundred militiamen and another one hundred or so Mohawk and River Indian warriors gradually straggled into Albany during the next few months. The little army finally marched to the lower end of Lake Champlain in July. The force fell apart as smallpox ravaged the camp. Returning warriors and militiamen spread the sickness wherever they went. Thousands fell ill, and hundreds reportedly died.

The impact of this epidemic on Indian communities in the Munsee homeland is unknown. Several elder Lower River Indian sachems were last mentioned in 1690. Most had been in close contact with authorities in New York at the time they disappeared from the records. Unlike their colleagues in more remote locales, they had sent warriors to Albany, and it was returning men who spread contagion to their hometowns. Their ages and locations also made them vulnerable to an outbreak, so it is quite possible that most fell victim to the epidemic contagion.

A company of royal troops led by Major Richard Ingoldsby arrived at the tip of lower Manhattan in front of Fort William Henry in February 1691. Ingoldsby's ship had been separated from the vessel carrying both his credentials and the newly appointed royal governor, Colonel Henry Sloughter. Leisler decided to wait until the governor arrived before giving up the colony to someone not carrying the proper papers. Sloughter's ship sailed into the harbor a month later. In the meantime, several men were killed in fighting that broke out between Leisler's and Ingoldsby's troops. Combining their forces, Sloughter and Ingoldsby (helped by a local ship captain named William Kidd) soon compelled Leisler to surrender Fort William Henry. Resenting Leisler's resistance and knowing that the king had not formally recognized the caretaker government, Sloughter gave his ear to the many enemies Leisler had made during his brief stewardship. The new governor acted quickly, trying, convicting, and ordering the execution of Leisler and eight of his closest supporters for treason. Although Sloughter commuted the sentences of six of the condemned men, he had Leisler and his chief lieutenant hanged, drawn, and quartered on May 26, 1691.

Whether they succumbed to disease or fell from favor for supporting Leisler, many Munsee leaders last mentioned in documents in 1686 did not return to colonial notice after 1691. Tackapousha, who never formally recognized the now-disgraced caretaker's authority, quickly stepped forward to welcome Sloughter to his new province. Sachems from the Highlands and Schaghticoke soon followed. Unfortunately for Sloughter, he did not live to enjoy the privilege long. He died suddenly in July 1691, and Ingoldsby stepped in as interim governor pending the arrival of a permanent replacement.

Around this time the first delegation of French-allied Indians from the fur-rich Far country around the Great Lakes traveled to New York. Hoping to pull out of the fighting and open a way to Albany, they asked River Indian friends to help them make a separate peace with their English and Iroquois enemies. They arrived just as men returning from the abortive Montreal expedition spread smallpox across the Hudson Valley. The entire delegation came down with the disease and died.

This did not stop the New Yorkers from sending a delegation of their own. In early October 1691, Ingoldsby gave Albany and Esopus magistrates permission to each dispatch six men west in the company of no more than twenty-five Indians. Led by Arent Schuyler, younger brother of Albany mayor and frontier diplomat Pieter, the party stayed away for nearly a year. On August 14, 1692, the younger Schuyler sent word to Ingoldsby announcing his arrival back east at Minisink with a party of Shawnees. The message included the minutes of a meeting with Shawnees and Minisinks he attended in the Far country the previous May. At the meeting, a Minisink man named Mattaseet, who had been living among the Shawnees for the past nine years, offered the Shawnees land above the Delaware Water Gap and promised that Governor Ingoldsby would make peace with the Five Nations on their behalf so they could move there safely.

The Shawnees were a much-scattered people who were probably living somewhere along the upper Ohio Valley when Europeans first came to Munsee country. They had been living with River Indian and other Eastern Algonquian expatriates at various spots in present-day Ohio, Michigan, and Illinois for nearly twenty years when King William's War broke out. Meeting at Fort William Henry with the Shawnees brought east by Schuyler and Mattaseet a week after they arrived at Minisink, Ingoldsby assured them that they would be safe from Iroquois attack, and would be welcome if their people moved to New York. Four days later, Ingoldsby ordered that Schuyler escort the ambassadors on their return journey to bring their people back "to settle among our Indians with their peltry."

A letter from Arent's older brother temporarily halted proceedings. The elder Schuyler reminded Ingoldsby that the Shawnees were still formally at war with the Five Nations. He went on to suggest that the governor ask "ten or twelve of the most important Schowaenos" to stay behind in Albany while his brother accompanied five or six prominent men from each of the Five Nations to conclude a formal peace treaty with the Shawnees. Ingoldsby had barely responded to Schuyler's letter when his replacement, Colonel Benjamin Fletcher, arrived to take up the governorship of New York in early September 1692. Fletcher wasted little time. Meeting with the Shawnees in the presence of their Minisink sponsors two weeks after his arrival, he promised to help make peace with the Five Nations on their behalf and asked them to hurry back with their people.

Fletcher made a slight change in personnel before sending the party back to the Far country. He replaced Arent Schuyler with the far more experienced frontier diplomat Aernout Viele, who, together with Mattaseet and the Shawnee ambassadors, soon returned to Illinois where most of the Shawnee main body was encamped. Meanwhile, at his first Covenant Chain meeting with them, Fletcher managed to secure Five Nations approval for a Shawnee relocation and a promise that they would make peace with the Far Indians. For the next year or so, the English heard little but vague rumors concerning the progress made by their western embassy.

Fletcher arrived in New York with explicit orders to reconcile divided colonists, strengthen the frayed Covenant Chain alliance, root out any lingering opposition, and form a united front against the French. He hardly had time to get the lay of the land before word of yet another unexpected midwinter attack reached New York. On February 6, 1693, six hundred French and Indian troops suddenly appeared in the Mohawk Valley. The surprised Mohawks barely had enough time to escape before the raiders marched in and burned all three of their towns. In less than a week they destroyed most of the Mohawks' winter stores and captured more than three hundred of their people. Only the army's determination to lay waste to the whole of Mohawk country gave the Covenant Chain allies time to respond. A force of nearly six hundred Englishmen, Mohawks, Oneidas, and Schaghticokes led by Pieter Schuyler caught up with the heavily encumbered column, slowed by prisoners and a sudden thaw, as it was withdrawing north to New France. In a running battle Schuyler's men killed between thirty and eighty of the raiders and liberated most of their prisoners.

Fletcher reacted to news of the attack with a swiftness that surprised those used to more dilatory responses from their governors. Although he arrived in Albany too late to help local forces chase the French back to Canada, he impressed returning soldiers, militiamen, and warriors by personally accompanying the several hundred soldiers sent to buck up the city's defenses. Mohawk sachems sat quietly while he chided them for allowing the French to surprise their towns. They listened politely as he praised their courage during the counterattack, and brightened considerably when he ordered Schuyler to find shelter for their families in the town and to replenish their corn stores. Pleased to meet a governor whom they hoped would do more than fight the French, to the last Mohawk, they pledged continued loyalty, announced plans to rebuild their towns closer to Albany, and conferred the title Cayenquiragoe, "Swift Arrow," on a man whose name they knew meant "arrow maker" in his own tongue.

When the roads cleared the following spring, Fletcher traveled throughout his new province, replacing undependable officials with obedient placemen. He, like Andros before him, was determined to forge the provinces into a united front against the French. Fletcher was a hard-bitten campaigner rather than a cultured staff officer like Andros. He spared few feelings and personally looked at all reports, tolerating few fools. The governor lost little time quieting fears sparked by an improbable report that 350 Lower River Indians from Tappan and Hackensack were preparing to avenge Leisler, and he swiftly squelched similarly false rumors of French and Indian attacks.

Fletcher kept a careful ear open for news of real threats. He got an earful from a delegation of Indians from the upper part of the Delaware River later that spring. He was then in Philadelphia to take over the government of Pennsylvania. Quakers had not sent men to fight against the French and were suspected to be secret supporters of the ousted James. As a result, a wary William and Mary temporarily suspended Penn's charter to Pennsylvania and put the colony under Fletcher's supervision. The New York governor met with the Upper Delaware River Indians between meetings, interviews, and interrogations with various colonial officeholders and aspirants to office. Their speaker complained that Senecas angered by the Delawares' failure to help them against the French had attacked some of their people who were out hunting the previous summer. Fletcher promised that he would order the Senecas and other Covenant Chain Iroquois allies to halt further attacks and suggested that the Senecas and the Upper Delaware River Indians send some men to Albany.

Meanwhile Indians throughout the rest of Munsee country were trying to keep as low a profile as possible in the foreign wars and colonial infighting that threatened the fortunate few survivors of the late epidemics. On the Hudson, inexperienced sachems, unsure of what to make of recent political developments in New York, kept their warriors at home and put off welcoming Fletcher, waiting for the dust to settle. A miffed Fletcher would have none of it. In July, he addressed the River Indian sachems as children when they finally met with him in Albany on the last day of Covenant Chain renewal meetings with the Five Nations and Schaghticokes. Taking his time to make his points, Fletcher reprimanded them for not coming sooner and rebuked them for leaving their families defenseless while they went off hunting and drinking. He ordered them to send warriors to scout the frontier, offering a substantial reward for the head of any enemy killed within three miles of Albany or Schenectady.

Rumors that Long Island Indians were plotting against English neighbors thought to be planning their extermination kept Tackapousha and the other sachems away from Manhattan for a time. Sachems representing the reportedly ailing elder Long Island statesman finally officially paid their respects to Fletcher in early May, 1694. Tales allegedly spread by a River Indian three months later evidently panicked younger sachems on Long Island. It took Fletcher another round of good words and gifts presented at another meeting held the following October to finally assure the chiefs of his friendship.

Earlier that year, a distressingly more plausible rumor reached New York from New Jersey that 150 snowshoe-shod French and Indians were said to be on their way to detach the Minisinks from the Covenant Chain. Knowing the French predilection for launching raids during snowy weather, Fletcher dispatched Arent Schuyler to

Minisink country that very day to look into things. Schuyler crossed onto Minisink Island on February 7 to find that the alleged French and Indians were in fact three New Yorkers and two Shawnees who had stopped by the town six days earlier. They were sent by Viele to bring news of his progress with the Shawnees and to fetch gunpowder and supplies from Albany. These provisions, they said, would be needed by the seven hundred Shawnees who planned to come loaded down with beaver pelts in the spring. The Minisink sachems also told Schuyler that one of their hunting parties was overdue. They feared Senecas may have waylaid it in reprisal for their not having paid their tribute that year. Schuyler promised to let the governor know about these developments and immediately left, arriving three days later in New York with the news.

It is not known exactly when the Shawnees arrived, how many came east, or where they first settled. The first Shawnee contingent probably made its way to Minisink country by the summer of 1694. Others soon settled along the Susquehanna and Potomac rivers. Like the Susquehannocks, who ultimately moved from the Delaware to the new town of Conestoga built under Anglo-Iroquois auspices in the heart of their old homeland by 1690, Shawnees tried to live inconspicuously in their new settlements on the west side of the river just above the Delaware Water Gap.

They had good reason to do so. The Shawnees evidently relocated among the Minisinks before making peace with the Five Nations. Two years after their arrival, Fletcher heard their complaints that Senecas had killed thirty of their people during the journey east. The governor sent Arent Schuyler to Albany to confirm the disturbing report and to ask the Five Nations if they would receive the Shawnees as friends. King William's War would end before the Iroquois finally agreed to peace with the Shawnees and issued the requested invitation.

In the meantime, Senecas ignored Fletcher's appeals to stop attacking what he called the "few miserable Indians upon the Delaware River . . . who hurt nobody and belong to Pennsylvania which is in the Covenant Chain and under my government." Such intransigence did not aid formation of an effective united front against the French. Infighting and defections further threatened to tear the Covenant Chain alliance apart from within. River Indians, for example, were so frequently assaulted when traveling in New England that Fletcher ordered them not to cross into Massachusetts until the war was over. And in the crucial center, Iroquois who had suffered most from the fighting listened with increasing interest to French invitations to join expatriate relatives now living near Montreal in the Catholic mission town of Caughnawaga.

Europeans armed and supplied Indian warriors, and fed and sheltered their displaced families. The Indians, however, grew tired of the endlessly inconclusive war of raids and counterstrikes. No decisive blow had been struck, even though many had died and entire villages, like Schenectady and Lachine, and nearly every Seneca and Mohawk town, had been destroyed. And nothing could hide the fact that the Five Nations and their Indian allies were bearing the brunt of the war. The French governor emphatically drove the point home during the summer of 1696. Marching from a newly reconstructed fort at the head of the St. Lawrence, named Frontenac in his honor, the governor led two thousand men through Onondaga and Oneida towns thus far untouched by the fighting. As they had done with almost every other Iroquois town, they burned the hastily abandoned settlements and destroyed everything they could not carry away. Moving quickly during the height of the campaigning season, Frontenac's force was able to return to Montreal unmolested.

Fletcher knew that the gifts, promises, and supplies he distributed to Five Nations sachems at a meeting with them a month later could not condole them for their losses. In his report to the home government, Fletcher wrote, "we cannot expect the assistance from the Five Nations as formerly." Although some River Indian warriors continued to guard the frontier, the governor also knew he could no longer depend on their support. They ignored his request that they concentrate their settlements at a few designated locales. Many had already left for Canada or moved east among Abenaki friends still fighting against the New Englanders. Several of the latter were probably among the River Indians arrested in Massachusetts for killing some settlers while out hunting during the spring of 1697. Two women

from the party escaped from jail and made their way back to Schaghticoke after the settlers put two of their companions to death for the
killings. On hearing the news, the Schaghticoke sachem quickly traveled to Albany, where he reported the arrests and demanded release
of the surviving prisoners.

In Europe, exhausted combatants signed the Treaty of Ryswick,
ending King William's War on September 30, 1697. Like most earlier
treaties, the peace of Ryswick left things pretty much as they were at
the start of the fighting. Prisoners were exchanged, and captured territory was mostly returned.

River Indians and their Five Nations Covenant Chain allies were
still formally at war with France when Fletcher received word that
orders for his replacement had been prepared in London during the
spring of 1696. Determined to do everything possible to secure Indian
support for the war, Fletcher had held a tight rein over purchases of
Indian lands up to that time. This did not mean that he halted all sales.
Fletcher and his predecessor Leisler sanctioned at least fifty sales of
lands in Munsee country and granted purchase licenses for others between 1689 and 1696. The frequency of these sales increased in direct
proportion to their distance from the frontier. Few colonists wanted
to buy, and even fewer Indians wanted to sell, land liberally watered
by the blood of its defenders. More than half of lands sold at this time
were on western Long Island, far from the fighting.

Identifying themselves as Massapequa Indians, Tackapousha, Suscaneman, and their kinsmen signed deeds conveying fourteen tracts
at the south end of the town of Oyster Bay. The same people, mostly
identified as Secatogue Indians, sold several necks and tracts of sandy
pinelands in ten deeds to lands farther east in the town of Huntington.
At this time, a man named Wamehas rose to prominence as one of
the more influential Secatogue sachems, signing twenty-six alienation
and confirmation deeds to Indian lands mostly within Huntington
town bounds.

In two deeds signed on one day in March 1693, Suscaneman gave
three town residents gifts of land around and overlapping part of the

unsurveyed two-hundred-acre reservation Dongan had set aside for his people at the head of Hempstead Harbor. Unsanctioned by provincial authorities, the deeds failed to end disputes over the reservation, which still straddled the long-contested border between Oyster Bay and Hempstead. A little more than a year later, Suscaneman complained to Fletcher that Hempstead men were cutting timber on reservation lands. Fletcher ordered new surveys for both the town border and the reservation.

Other sachems primarily sold gores (wedges of unsold land between purchased properties revealed during surveys) elsewhere in Munsee country. Katonah and several of his compatriots sold five small tracts on both sides of the lower Hudson. Farther southwest, Taphow, Claes, and a number of other sachems conveyed parcels along the Pequannock River above present-day Pompton Lakes, New Jersey.

Fletcher gave his blessing to much larger grants, and collected much higher commissions, once it was clear that the war was ending and he would be returning to England. In the space of less than a year, the lame-duck governor sanctioned twenty purchases of considerable tracts from Indians in every corner of Munsee country. In late June 1696, Taphow and several of his people signed over the Kakiate Patent, a territory embracing more than 100,000 acres west of Dongan's former 300,000-acre estate. Fletcher subsequently sold most of the land at Kakiate to a crony named John Evans, who christened the vast manor Fletcherdon in his benefactor's honor.

On Long Island, Tackapousha made his last appearance in colonial records as the primary signatory to an October 1696 deed turning his people's share of land at Fort Neck over to Oyster Bay townsfolk. His children sold their rights to other parts of Fort Neck and to small tracts in the interior of Huntington around the same time. On the other side of the still-disputed Keith Line, the West Jersey Society, a syndicate of forty-eight London merchants and gentlemen, purchased the controlling interest in the province in 1692. Not content to stop there, they also bought up a good-sized chunk of East Jersey proprietary shares. Along those stretches of the Delaware in West

Jersey where Indians still held title to their land, however, Munsees remained largely unmolested while new proprietors fought old for control of proprietary interests in the province.

The arrival in New York of Richard Coote, Earl of Bellomont, on April 12, 1698, brought a temporary halt to the reckless deed spree. Like everyone else in English America, Lord Bellomont knew that the new peace with France was little more than an uneasy truce that could easily be broken and in any event would not last very long. He was also aware that feelings over the Leisler affair still ran high. Making matters worse, Fletcher's extravagant land grants had angered the overwhelming majority of settlers, who did not benefit from them, and had alienated the Indians who lost their lands. Bellomont carefully felt things out before granting privileges and handing out positions. He knew his placemen would waste little time pressuring already sorely pressed Indians for ever larger portions of their shrinking ancestral estate.

The question of how much was too much assumed new dimensions as the Indians of Munsee country, for the first time since the coming of Europeans, faced the real possibility of losing virtually all of their remaining ancestral territory. Bellomont was determined to retain the loyalty of remnants of Indian communities that clung to remaining lands in Westchester and Long Island. Most, he knew, would surely go to Canada if displaced from their homeland. Once there, their knowledge of the English colonists and of local geography would provide assistance to the French out of all proportion to their small numbers. Such help would put the English at a severe disadvantage when hostilities inevitably broke out again. Bellomont would have to move cautiously to prevent the defection of River Indians along with friends and relatives elsewhere who might follow their example.

The Indians of Munsee country were by no means the only constituency Bellomont had to worry about where land was concerned. The new governor arrived as opportunities to acquire cheap territory, long a major drawing point for immigrants, were shrinking to insignificance. In the Jerseys and in Pennsylvania, which regained its charter in 1696, proprietors monopolized access to all but the contested unsurveyed borderlands of their provinces. Along the Hudson River in New York, a few powerful families held more than 75 percent of all unfenced open land not still in Indian hands. Bellomont had to deal with an angry, apprehensive, and war-weary citizenry still polarized by Leislerian rifts, who felt they owed little to Indians and cared even less about Indian rights to land or life.

Bellomont attempted to mollify settlers outraged by some of Fletcher's more flagrantly excessive grants by starting annulment proceedings that finally threw the three hundred thousand acres of Evans's Fletcherdon Manor open to new buyers in 1699. Determined to keep restive River Indians in the English fold, he had officials all but halt new acquisitions of Indian land for two years. Settlers were able to make only three purchases from Indians in Munsee country during the year following receipt of the news that King William's War had ended. These small plots were located in Oyster Bay, Huntington, and the Westchester County town of Bedford. Sachems in these locales, no longer able to easily play off rivals, increasingly concentrated on reducing sources of friction with their neighbors in order to maintain access to vacant sections of sold lands. In pursuit of this goal, several sachems confirmed earlier sales while others helped local townsfolk mark out more precise borders of earlier purchases.

This temporary respite in the transformation of Munsee home-land into colonial private property did not last long. In 1699 colo-nial officials started reissuing purchase licenses. Indians subsequently signed no fewer than fifty-one deeds to lands in every part of Munsee country before a new governor arrived from England in late 1702 to replace Bellomont, who had died suddenly on March 5, 1701. While numerous, most of these deeds conveyed only small tracts, mostly around the edges of existing settlement.

The fact that the names of Taphow and others first appear above and before those of older leaders like Claes on the twelve deeds to land in northern East Jersey negotiated at this time suggest that a transfer of power was underway. Taphow's rise to prominence was made explicit in the July 29, 1702, deed to land along the Rockaway River, which rather grandly identified him as the "sagamore and commander in chief of all the Indians inhabiting what the English call the northern part of the Jerseys."

Farther south, the primary position of Weequehela's mark on six deeds to lands near the provincial capital at Perth Amboy signaled his own rise to prominence as the Indian King of New Jersey. In Esopus country, Dostou, a daughter of Mamanuchqua and wife of the sachem Harman Hekan, sold some land around present-day High Falls about the same time as their son Hendrick Hekan and some of his associates conveyed two tracts closer to Port Jervis. On Long Island, sachems continuing to identify themselves as Secatogue Indians sold six more tracts to Huntington townsfolk between 1699 and 1702.

Wishing perhaps to avoid being troubled by landless Indians and certainly interested in attracting Indian laborers, New York's then–chief justice William "Tangier" Smith set aside four small tracts in his vast Manor of St. George as Indian planting and fishing reserves on July 2, 1700. Terms of the deed allowed Indians to plant, sow, but not sell reservation lands. The tracts were guaranteed to them in perpetuity on condition that they annually pay Smith or his assigns two ears of yellow Indian corn. The reserves comprised a total of 175 acres of the 64,000-acre estate Smith had put together in the Suffolk County town of Brookhaven just east of Huntington.

In Westchester County, Katonah and his colleagues still held title to much territory in the more remote northeasternmost hills bordering Connecticut. A small number of their relatives retained some lands closer to Long Island Sound. Surveys of hazily bounded earlier Indian deeds, moreover, revealed other gores and gaps of unsold land that Indians could still claim. Katonah and several other local sachems accepted gifts and took payments in return for signing deeds to gore lands and for confirming or clarifying boundaries of several earlier conveyances.

Settlers purchasing land from new colonial landowners felt no particular obligations to the former Indian owners, who had given up the land in hopes of protection and justice. Alarmingly for the River Indians, settlers were not the only people who forgot them. Neither French nor English diplomats signing the Treaty of Ryswick made any provisions for them or any other Indians fighting alongside them. Although formally at peace, the former adversaries continued to try to use Indians as cat's-paws for imperial ambitions. Louis-Hector de Callières, the governor of Montreal who became governor-general of New France after Frontenac died in 1698, urged his Indian allies to continue fighting until the Five Nations repudiated their Covenant Chain alliance. In New York, Bellomont continued to provide arms and supplies to Covenant Chain Indian allies resisting French blandishments and French Indian threats until his own death in 1701.

The Europeans' machinations made little difference. The Five Nations had had enough. They dispatched an embassy to Montreal, where they agreed to an armistice with the French and their Indian allies on July 18, 1700. Two delegations of Five Nations diplomats traveled from Iroquoia the following summer. At a meeting in Albany held the following summer, the first delegation, largely consisting of Mohawks, Oneidas, and Onondagas, assured the New Yorkers that although they might stop fighting the French, they would not abandon the Covenant Chain alliance. Pledging enduring friendship, they deeded over what they claimed were their western hunting lands around the Great Lakes.

Farther north, the other and much larger Iroquois delegation, made up of sachems from the four western nations, assembled in Montreal in late July 1701. Over the course of the next two weeks they made peace with representatives from thirty Indian nations allied with the French and proclaimed their neutrality in all future wars between the European powers. A small Mohawk delegation belatedly signed on to the agreement a few days after the meeting ended. In two close-cut strokes, Five Nations diplomats formally ended nearly a century of warfare and extricated themselves from involvements in European political differences. These agreements helped set the pattern for separate peaces that Indians would make in pursuit of their own interests to the end of the colonial era and beyond.

9

GREAT PEACE, 1702–1713

No one at the 1701 Montreal meeting mentioned anyone from Munsee country. This was not an oversight. It was instead a statement made by the Five Nations, and tacitly accepted by the French and their Indian allies, that the Munsees had been subordinated. Through this simple act of omission, this nonevent, the Five Nations signaled that they regarded Munsees and other less powerful Covenant Chain affiliates as "women" whom they would represent at diplomatic conclaves.

Iroquois used the metaphor, and Indians living within their sphere of influence evidently accepted it, in the peculiarly Iroquois sense of the term. Five Nations clan mothers quietly met among themselves when exercising their exclusive right to appoint and remove kinsmen as sachems. The Esopus squaw sachem Mamanuchqua and women from other Northeastern societies, including the Iroquoian-speaking Susquehannocks, strode seventeenth-century diplomatic floorboards as full-fledged leaders, signing treaties and selling land. In Mamanuchqua's case, her sex was of so little relevance to her role as sachem that it was often not even mentioned in meeting minutes.

Iroquois use of the term "woman" to address River Indians, Shawnees, and others they considered lesser links in the Covenant Chain did not do much to change existing relationships. Five Nations and other tribute-takers had compelled less powerful nations to pay for protection for many decades. Metaphorical violence threatened against those failing to pay was made real in many chronicled assaults. Far from ending tribute-taking or mitigating the consequences of nonpayment, symbolic references to people like River Indians as women reflected the view that tribute payment was the proper province of women.

It is hard to imagine that Indians in Munsee country would have regretted their lack of formal involvement in political problems embroiling the Five Nations with more distant adversaries like the French. They had always acted as their own agents in affairs closer to home that really mattered to them. Munsee people would continue to represent themselves at meetings with English authorities at all political levels as long as they retained unchallenged control over some portion of ancestral homeland. They would do so as Loups, Delawares, or Mahicanders when living with foreigners beyond their borders, as River Indians when acting in concert with Schaghticokes and Mahicans, as Lower River Indians when conducting affairs more independently, and as residents of particular places or members of particular kin groups when dealing locally. English and Iroquois Confederacy Covenant Chain partners might use varying degrees of emphasis when suggesting particular courses of action to them, but Munsees remaining on ancestral land remained free to make their own choices.

This freedom to choose was reflected in their settlement patterns. Unlike most Iroquoians, River Indians and many other Eastern Algonquians traditionally tended to avoid living close to one another for any extended period of time. Neighborliness, of course, can be a virtue. Concentrations of people in one place at one time can help communities focus attention on problems and take advantage of opportunities. Closeness also has drawbacks that transcend cultural boundaries. Familiarity breeds contempt; resulting contentions often lead to conflict. Proximity can also lose its charm in tightly clustered towns filled with cramped houses lacking sanitation and running water. Large numbers of people stuck within the confines of smoky, combustible longhouses can quickly burn through accessible nearby timber fuel supplies, exhaust fertility of nearby soils, and foul springs and other water sources.

Firsthand observations of colonial surveyors and travelers confirm archaeological findings that people throughout the Northeast spread out across their territories following restoration of lasting peace. Even the Five Nations adopted a more expansive settlement pattern once the Great Peace removed the need to concentrate in fortified towns. River Indians already moving along networks long held together by ties of family and friendship continued to go to and from places whose limited resources could only briefly support large populations. They could, however, no longer gather in the more salubrious places along the coast and lower river courses now densely settled by colonists. Just as Indians never again uttered dead ancestors' names, they avoided mention of lost places, whose names fell into disuse.

How, then, to account for the survival of so many names never again uttered by Indians observing postmortem ritual prohibitions? Europeans documented virtually all Munsee-language names that have come down to us. They were not, however, the only people who kept dead Munsee names alive. Some Indian families began getting around postmortem prohibitions by turning the names of prominent ancestors into European-style surnames representing living families and lineages. And all Munsees continued to use names of socially functioning places like Manhattan, Raritan, and Hackensack no longer owned by them but adopted by colonists, and thus kept alive.

Large numbers of River Indians continued to congregate at Manhattan and other colonial cities for treaty meetings. Focal points for their social networks, however, shifted farther inland to opposite ends of the Great Valley of southeastern New York and northern New Jersey after 1701. To the north, Mahican was the dominant tongue where River Indian towns nestled within remote mountain hollows at Catskill and Taghkanick. Munsee, by contrast, was probably the language most often heard at neighboring Esopus and Wappinger settlements along streams flowing into the Hudson above the Highlands. Off the beaten path of colonial expansion, these and other places in and around the Catskill and Berkshire mountains ultimately served as gathering points of departure for destinations beyond the borders of Munsee country.

At the other end of the Great Valley, mostly Munsee-speaking families found refuge at Pompton and along the flats lining both banks of the Delaware at and around Minisink. Sheltered behind the mountain wall of the Kittatiny Ridge and centered around a defensible island far but not too far from big colonial settlements, Minisink contained the largest expanse of level, well-watered land left under Indian ownership in the Munsee homeland. Steep ridges and an often fast-running river that pierced the Kittatinys only at the Delaware Water Gap many miles downriver screened Minisink from three sides. Trails winding through passes in the surrounding hills joined at Minisink to link the place with other locales beyond its mountain fastness. Years after the Great Peace was signed in faraway Montreal, Minisink remained the last best gathering place for Indians traveling to and from the more westerly lands in the Susquehanna, Allegheny, and Ohio river valleys that the 1701 treaty opened to safe settlement by River Indians and others.

Growing numbers of Munsee- and other Eastern Algonquian–speaking people congregated at places like Minisink, Catskill, and Taghkanick on their ways from coastal lowlands to more distant inland locales. These trips grew in distance, duration, and frequency as successive waves of European immigrants took up the last open lands around colonial centers and pressed outward into remaining Indian lands in the Munsee homeland. Pressures brought to bear by land-hungry settlers were most keenly felt along the tidal reaches of Munsee country. Shore lands were places where colonial populations were now thickest and Indian numbers fewest.

In western Long Island, descendants of Tackapousha and Suscaneman still held title to the two small reservations on Hempstead Harbor established for their use by Dongan in 1687. Indian people also continued to hold on to the four tiny tracts Smith had granted them in Suffolk County. Aside from these reserves, Indians also still held title to substantial expanses of sandy pinelands in the interior of the island and a few necks along Long Island Sound and the Great South Bay in the more easterly parts of Queens County that are now within

Nassau County. Elsewhere on western Long Island, Indians had given up title to nearly all of their remaining shore lands by 1701.

Indian journeys to and from tidewater camps decreased in frequency as colonial population growth along the coastlands increasingly limited shore access and colonial demand diminished for shore products provided by Indians. Fish and shellfish formerly harvested by Indians were now often caught or gathered by slaves and brought to markets by their owners. Colonists increasingly eschewed wampum as currency, preferring to use locally printed paper money along with the growing stocks of hard cash flowing into the provinces. Soon, only inmates confined to poorhouses in New York and Albany (often Indian women, children, and the incapacitated) were making wampum, used almost entirely for trading with Native nations.

Although they would never entirely abandon the shore until finally forced from their homeland, most River Indians gradually turned inland. Those not leaving Munsee country altogether spread themselves out across the considerable expanses of their remaining interior territories. Among other benefits of spreading out best appreciated by those who prefer wide-open spaces was that doing so enabled Indians to maintain a presence on lands that colonists might otherwise claim for themselves as vacant wastes apparently unwanted by their owners. Those spending time outside Munsee country built on existing relations with foreign Indians. Contacts in these communities allowed them to move across an increasingly far-flung network extending from New England and the Mid-Atlantic provinces beyond Iroquoia to Acadia, the St. Lawrence Valley, the Great Lakes, and Ohio country.

The physical as well as cultural survival of Indians in Munsee country increasingly depended on their maintenance and extension of networks with people from other Indian nations as sachems surrendered remaining ancestral lands and homeland populations plummeted. By 1701, the Indian population of the Munsee homeland was nearly 95 percent less than what it was when colonists purchased their first tracts of land from River Indians some seventy years before. The hypothetical Indian population in the Munsee homeland was around 2,400 in 1686, significantly below pre-contact numbers.

In 1697 Albany magistrates noted that the number of warriors living in River Indian towns had dropped by more than 50 percent between the beginning of King William's War and its end. Based on this figure, the Munsee population may have sunk to little more than 1,000 by the time the fighting stopped.

Whatever the actual numbers, this population was neither uniformly nor evenly distributed within Munsee country. Documents recording activities of nine sachems in the central Long Island pinelands and lower Berkshire Mountain borderlands between New York and New England suggest that sachems in both places may have led a combined total of between 150 and 200 people. At Esopus, sachems represented four extended family clans that together numbered something in the vicinity of 100 people. The eight sachems active in Indian communities astride the border between East and West Jersey would also have represented from 150 to 200 people. Twenty sachems at Minisink and its surrounding hinterland, may have represented around 400 people in their refuge at the southern end of the Great Valley. In addition, between 100 and 300 Shawnees probably were then living above the Delaware Water Gap.

Small numbers of Munsee people also continued to live beyond the borders of their ancestral homeland in 1701. Most were probably associated with Mahican and Northern Indian people moving to and from Schaghticoke, the long-established Catholic missions at Sillery and Three Rivers near Quebec, the newly erected St. Francis Odanak mission just above Montreal, and the Jesuit mission stations built in present-day Maine between 1693 and 1695 at Ameseconti on the Sandy River (where the college town of Farmington stands today) and Norridgewock (twenty miles downstream, where the Sandy River flows into the Penobscot River at Madison). Although the population and composition of the Loup community still in Michigan at this time is unknown, the percentage of people from Munsee country among them probably continued to be small. Together, as many as 300 River Indian expatriates may have been living at various locales from Maine to Michigan. Adding this number to the 1,000 to 1,300 or so Indian people in the Munsee homeland (a number that includes the Shawnees on the Delaware), an estimated total of around 1,600 Indians probably maintained connections of some sort to the ancestral Munsee homeland in 1701.

Much of the Indian leadership in Munsee country at this time was fairly new to European records. Although only thirteen out of the fifty-one sachems active at the turn of the century first appeared after 1686, the majority of the remainder had been junior or local leaders who were first mentioned in colonial documents just a few years before. Communities centered around Navesink, Raritan, and Crosswicks territory were mostly led by young or newly chosen descendants of Ockanickon and his brothers. Most of these people rose to prominence during the late 1680s and early 1690s.

The largest concentrations of experienced sachems lived in central Long Island and Minisink. Elders like Suscaneman on Long Island and Taphow in the North Jersey uplands would continue to be mentioned in colonial records for only a few years after 1701. During that time, they and other experienced sachems concerned for the future of communities facing colonial expansion would have worked closely with younger people to preserve a measure of continuity.

This sense of continuity would spill over into the colonial community, allowing both peoples to explicitly recognize or tacitly accept the legitimacy of each others' rights and claims. Sachems' abilities to maintain provincial acknowledgments of their people's rights became an increasingly crucial survival skill as a colonial population hemmed in by decades of war was set to explode outward in 1701. Immigrants, primarily from the Celtic fringe of the British Isles and the German-speaking areas of Europe, would join native-born colonists moving from large regional centers in Boston, New York, and Philadelphia. Many would stop at smaller staging areas along the edges of remaining Indian territory, such as Albany and Kingston in New York; Newark and Trenton in soon-to-be-reunified New Jersey; and Newtown and Wrightstown above Philadelphia in Pennsylvania.

Of the total colonial population of some 53,000 in New York, the Jerseys, and Pennsylvania, the vast majority were Europeans of mostly English, Scottish, or Dutch descent. Nearly 4,000 were enslaved Africans and their descendants, mostly confined to farms and households in New York and the Jerseys. Within twenty years, the number of African slaves nearly tripled and the European population almost doubled in size. The European population doubled again to more than 200,000 by 1740. Although the rate of increase in the Afro-colonial population slowed somewhat during this time, slightly less than 17,000 mostly enslaved Africans were living in the Mid-Atlantic colonies in 1740. And both European and African populations roughly doubled again by 1760, to a combined total of almost 428,000.

Nearby, even larger colonial populations burgeoned in New England and Chesapeake Bay. Population numbers in the French colonies, by contrast, remained transient and small. Unlike the densely settled English provinces, whose ever-growing immigrant population farmed fields and built up new markets, French possessions in Canada and Acadia were primarily regarded by their mother country as trading outposts and strategic assets. Most habitants were expected to return home to France after fulfilling their contract obligations. Of the twenty-seven thousand people contracted to trade, trap, or work as farmers, fishermen, or soldiers in New France during the eighteenth century, only a third of that number were living in New France at the time of the French surrender in 1762.

Indians in the Munsee homeland in 1701 found themselves in the way of more than fifty times their number from New York, the Jerseys, and Pennsylvania intent on taking their lands. Several times that number in New England, Maryland, and Virginia also hungrily eyed Indian territory. Royal officials in all colonies faced a common dilemma when weighing matters of equity and expedience. First and foremost, all were charged with implementing policies intended to manage colonial growth rather than help Indians. Even the most venal official knew, however, that growth and profits depended on peace with all Indian nations, not just the powerful ones. Unjust treatment of small nations could alienate more powerful Indian allies and displease royal authorities at home. Governors recognizing this fact extended a considerable measure of legal protection to Indians living under Crown rule. They investigated thefts, assaults, and killings of Indians and settlers alike. Malefactors from both communities often escaped justice by fleeing to other jurisdictions. Apprehended felons were tried, and those found guilty punished.

Although ordinances prohibiting sales of guns and alcohol to Indians were openly flouted, laws regulating purchases of Indian lands were strictly enforced. Anything disrupting title integrity threatened everyone's well-being. Officials who did little to stop Indians from pawning guns and furs tended to draw the line at land seizures. There are few documented takings of Indian lands in Munsee country for debt. Only four examples of Indians mortgaging land in Munsee territory are known. Dostou's husband and Mamanuchqua's son-in-law Harman Hekan took out the first two of these, payable in wheat and corn, when he agreed to purchase two tracts where he lived in Marbletown in 1674. Hekan was fluent in Dutch and was a well-known figure among colonists at Esopus. The nickname they gave him, Ankerop (literally "bottom's up," one who raised up his *anker,* a Dutch unit of liquid measurement), indicates that mortgages and surnames were not the only aspects of Dutch culture he adopted.

Drink had lubricated land deals and a host of other creative misunderstandings woven into the fabric of intercultural exchanges in Munsee country from the very beginning. These were not limited to local relations between Indians and colonists. Colonists living in Munsee country also maintained working disagreements with covert competitors in other English colonies, with open enemies in New France, and with government officials and businessmen in their home countries. Like those formed with Indians, such arrangements provided profits and other benefits that could not be gained through official channels. Quiet accommodations helped colonists circumvent highly restrictive mercantile trade regulations in times of peace. Others maintained informal truces in places where royal forces failed to safeguard settlers or commerce during wartime.

The great distances of space and time separating colonies from imperial centers further fostered working disagreements and creative misunderstandings. Frontier improvisations necessary for survival at the edges of empire created opportunities for profit and freedom of action unavailable in Europe. These often expressed themselves in what might best be described as waves of enthusiasms. Enthusiasm for landownership sparked deed frenzies. Enthusiasm for greater degrees of self-government and personal freedom triggered everything from rent strikes to revolutions. Enthusiasm for extralegal profits made Albany a center of the clandestine smuggling trade with New France and turned New York Harbor into an actual pirates' nest. And spiritual enthusiasms would soon set off religious revivals and sustain great awakenings in many parts of the English colonies.

A new governor singularly enthused by the prospects for profit landed at Manhattan on May 13, 1702. He was Edward Hyde, Third Earl of Clarendon, Viscount Cornbury, most widely known as Lord Cornbury. He had been sent by his cousin, the newly crowned Queen Anne, who succeeded to the English throne following the death of King William earlier in the year. Cornbury arrived just as another smallpox epidemic was raging through the region. Around the heads of the sick and scared, the North Atlantic world was again tumbling toward war.

Lord Cornbury could not know that England had declared war on France just one day after his ship hove into New York Harbor. The new governor was not, however, totally surprised when the news finally arrived. He had left England expecting a fight. Cornbury started putting his province on a war footing shortly after informing East and West Jersey officials that the queen had united the governments of their fractious proprietaries into a single royal colony. Allowing the proprietors to maintain control over lands within their respective charter bounds, the queen grafted the new royal government of New Jersey onto New York and placed the consolidated provinces under her cousin's control. These decisions went far in easing political differences that were bringing the Jerseys to the edge of anarchy. They did not, however, put an end to contentions between resident and nonresident proprietors, nor between the proprietary and antiproprietary factions. Neither did they do anything to ease tensions between Anglicans, Calvinists, Quakers, Lutherans, and other contending denominations.

In New York, old political hatreds continued to crystallize around Leislerian and anti-Leislerian factions. Power, however, was still in the hands of the anti-Leislerians. Lord Cornbury had no trouble finding properly placed, politically powerful partisans from both factions willing to take positions and fill contracts to help themselves as they furthered the war effort. Preparations for the war, however, progressed slowly in smallpox-ravaged New York. Although privateers and war contracts promised spectacular short-term profits, few merchants in the province had much stomach for a struggle that would only throttle the fur trade. Indians trapping or trading furs from as far away as the Great Lakes and Hudson Bay had been carrying beaver and other pelts to merchants in Albany and Montreal for more than ninety years. Indian trade made up as much as 25 percent of the exports shipped out of the port of New York in 1701.

Merchants extended loans and offered other inducements to more closely bind Indian clients to their interests. Such efforts were only partially successful. Indians could and would take their furs where they pleased. They worked along what strategists call interior lines. Their relative proximity to market rivals allowed them to carry pelts to whichever merchants offered products they wanted at the lowest possible prices. News and rumors traveling as swiftly as those carrying the trade along these interior lines could quickly stanch the flow of furs or shift it to competitors. The fluid nature of this commerce, and the practical needs and desires of those serving it, made trade possible even between enemies whose home nations were officially at war with one another.

Despite losses suffered during the last war and the diseases that even then were ravaging their towns, Indians still held the balance of power on the frontier. A political realist, Cornbury really cared only about the more powerful of these nations: the Iroquois Confederacy, the Schaghticokes, and the Shawnees. Although they carefully cultivated their image as the region's most powerful Indian nation, the sachems of the Iroquois Confederacy no longer totally dominated military equations in Covenant Chain councils. Having attracted hundreds of displaced Northern Indian expatriates to their town, Upper River Indians at

Schaghticoke could call on more than two hundred warriors when renewed fighting with France, known today as Queen Anne's War, broke out in 1702. Shawnees living in Minisink country could field nearly as many men. Only the Senecas could raise a larger body of troops. The new governor would have to move carefully if he was to keep powerful allies on the frontier happy while giving in to pent-up colonial enthusiasms for remaining Munsee lands near settlement centers.

As Indian numbers tumbled toward their nadir and Indian people in Munsee country ran out of lands to sell, many colonists, especially newcomers, increasingly came to feel that they no longer needed to fear or depend on Indians. Many were prepared to abandon discreet fictions in favor of naked lies and outright fraud. Cornbury, however, was realistic enough to know that the time was not yet right to give up pretenses and run roughshod over Indians who still had powerful friends and influential connections. This does not mean that he or any other officials maintained matters as they were. Deals struck with Indians in Munsee country after the governor reopened the floodgates to Indian lands around New York City reflected new demographic and political realities. Settlers began to petition Cornbury for permission to purchase tracts of Munsee territory almost as soon as he settled into his office at the now renamed Fort Anne. Those who succeeded in gaining his favor and favors came to be known collectively as the Cornbury Ring.

Unlike Livingston and his prestige-hungry rural brethren along the upper river, most colonists admitted into Cornbury's circle were city folk uninterested in taking on the burdens and responsibilities of a manorial estate. At home on Manhattan, and on the lookout for no more than a country seat or two for themselves, they were speculators who intended to resell newly acquired Indian lands at a profit as soon as possible. They and their mostly anti-Leislerian rivals quickly formed syndicates of investors. Each investor received title to particular portions of syndicate lands in proportion to his connections, size of investment, and other factors.

Rival partnerships vied with one another to snap up licenses to purchase Indian lands. Most turned their attention north and west of

Manhattan, where the largest expanses of still unsold Munsee territory remained. Colonists considered the farther reaches of these territories howling wastelands inhabited by wild animals and open to depredations of French raiders and itinerant Indian war parties. Visions of mineral riches mined from stony uplands and bumper crops harvested from fertile bottomlands at places like Minisink, however, beckoned investors. They soon started setting up meetings with sachems from those places to arrange purchases.

Syndicate partners worked with the speed of driven men in wartime to purchase and patent as much Indian land as they could in Orange County. Within the space of two years, they managed to get Taphow and other sachems to sign deeds conveying considerable tracts within what became known as the Wawayanda and Cheesecocks patents. Just west across the Kittatiny Ridge, rival anti-Leislerian syndicates from New York City contended with pro-Leislerian country gentry for the glittering prize of Minisink.

Minisink was indeed a desirable prize. Both New Jersey proprietors and New York merchants had lusted after land there long before Arent Schuyler obtained the first Indian deed in the region in 1695. The real struggle for Minisink began in September 1702, when rival syndicates petitioned Cornbury for permission to purchase Minisink Island from the Indians. This touched off a competition that resulted in some of the more controversial Indian land deals made by Cornbury Ring men. One syndicate purchased the westernmost of the two tracts of land sold by their Indian owners between Minisink Island and the Drowned Lands (referring to the former bed of a large Ice Age lake) during the first week of March 1703. A second group led by Philip French, New York City mayor and Cornbury Ring member, secured a deed to a large tract at Minisink three months later.

Spellings of Indian names on these and many other deeds written at the time were peculiarly garbled. There is, however, no clear evidence supporting French's assertion that his rivals' deeds were invalid because they had purchased their tracts from "strange Indians not inhabiting on or claiming any right to the same." In addition to familiar figures like Taphow and Claes, the names of less-prominent local sachems can be picked out of the orthographic haze of the 1703 conveyances.

Meanwhile, the first syndicate spun fictions to wring every possible acre from their land purchase. Later told of the claims, two of the Indians who had put their marks on the Drowned Lands deed said that they had parted with only two small tracts at the locale. They emphatically denied that they had sold Minisink Island in this or any other deed. Both further affirmed that Tatapagh, the principal sachem at Minisink, whom they insisted was the only person with the authority to sell the island, had not signed the deed.

This did not stop the go-ahead men from the city from applying for a patent that included Minisink. The overreaching grasps of the rival syndicates went beyond Minisink Island itself. Together, they claimed patent rights to twice the amount of the sixty thousand acres thought to have been originally purchased. Unwilling to spend too much time haggling over land claims while a war was going on, Cornbury ordered the syndicates to come to some understanding. Both groups put aside their differences and came together long enough to establish a new partnership whose combined membership included twenty-three of the governor's most loyal and generous supporters. In August of 1704, an appreciative Cornbury granted the partners a patent to more than 175 square miles of land. Predictably, the grant included Minisink Island.

Even greater chicanery was afoot just to the north. In April 1708 Cornbury granted what became known as the Hardenbergh Patent to another syndicate. This deal was the brainchild of Johannis Hardenbergh, an Albany-born settler determined to make his fortune in real estate. Two years earlier he had petitioned Cornbury for a license to purchase a small tract of land just beyond Marbletown. Using this deed as his base, he threw in with his brother-in-law Jacob Rutsen and six other men who had also purchased interests in Indian lands west of the Shawangunks to form a partnership. This allowed them to extend their claims beyond the recently enacted two-thousand-acre legal limit placed on individual Indian land purchases. The partners petitioned the governor for a patent to secure title to their purchases in early February 1708. Despite their failure to provide a good survey, Cornbury granted the letters patent to Hardenbergh's syndicate the following April. The amount of land granted under this patent ballooned individual deeds to six thousand or so acres of land into a syndicate estate totaling one and a half million acres that took in most of the present-day Catskill Mountains in Sullivan, Delaware, and Otsego counties (see map 7). In one stroke of a pen, the New York governor signed over the largest single taking of Munsee territory made during the colonial era.

Neither the Minisink Patent syndicate associates nor Hardenbergh and his partners had much luck finding settlers interested in purchasing property in their unsurveyed and forbiddingly stony mountain estates. Like Minisink, most of the Hardenbergh lands would largely remain Indian territory penetrated only by a few hardy settlers, mostly squatters unable or unwilling to buy land or pay taxes, up to the end of the Revolution.

East and West Jersey proprietors also did what they could to obtain title to as much Indian land as possible within the boundaries of their proprietaries while the exigencies of Queen Anne's War presumably distracted the attention of royal administrators. Several investors in the rival combines haggling over claims at Minisink also pressed Indians for other lands in the northern reaches of New Jersey. Initially, the Indians there, who acknowledged Taphow as their sachem and commander in chief, were able to put off most demands. They were inadvertently helped by opponents of the Cornbury Ring like Lewis Morris, lord of Morrisania manor in the Bronx and an avid investor in Jersey lands. Morris was among the many colonists determined to prevent Cornbury from taking over New Jersey's land along with its government. The opposition of Morris and men like him limited Cornbury's cronies to a few small purchases of Indian lands at Saddle River and some other mostly swampy portions of the lowlands between the Rockaway and Whippany rivers.

Farther south, Weequehela and his people sold some, but again not all, of their remaining ancestral lands in Monmouth and Middlesex counties. West Jersey Society proprietors had greater success getting

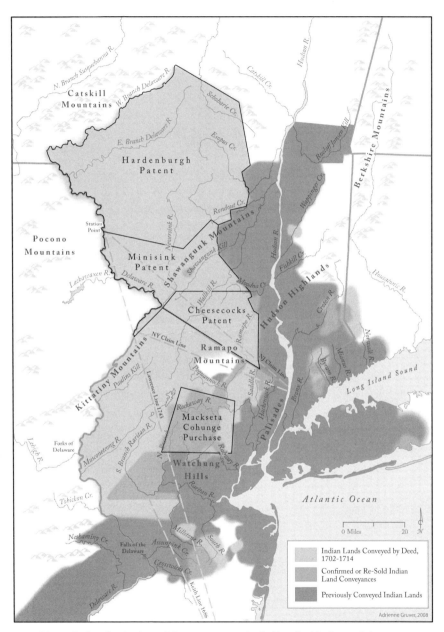

Map 7. Indian land sales in Munsee country, including the Mackseta Cohunge, Cheesecocks, Minisink, and Hardenbergh patents, 1702–1714.

a very young man who later became well known to colonists as Nutimus to join some of his relatives in selling lands around and above the Falls of the Delaware. Although colonists gained considerable ground in what is today Hunterdon County, the longed-for goal of the Delaware Water Gap still remained tantalizingly out of reach.

In Dutchess and northern Westchester counties, Katonah's name headed lists of Highland Indians selling much of the area's remaining Indian land. Other Indians sold their last parcels around Rye and Byram Pond. Across Long Island Sound, Wamehas and his people conveyed nearly all of their remaining title to lands in Huntington to town fathers between 1703 and 1707. Farther north in Esopus country, Harman Hekan and his son Hendrick placed their marks alongside those of Tatapagh and several other sachems on deeds in Ulster County.

No one, by contrast, seems to have made any demands on Shawnees for lands at the Delaware Water Gap during these years. Although the Shawnees kept a low profile, they did occasionally put in appearances at New York and Philadelphia. A substantial number of Shawnees, for example, showed up at Philadelphia in April 1702 in company with "Sasquehannah Minquays or Conestogo Indians" and Conoys from Maryland. Meeting with proprietary representatives and the governor, they signed a treaty guaranteeing trade and security so long as they conducted themselves peaceably.

Another delegation of Shawnees met with Cornbury at New York during the second week of July 1703. Nothing of the propositions discussed at the meeting can be made out from the badly scorched pages recording the get-together. Some idea of Shawnee concerns can be formed from other records kept at the time. One of these noted that French traders who had accompanied the Shawnees on their eastward migration carried a message to Philadelphia in May 1704, reporting threats made by the Five Nations to carry off "those Shawanah Indians, both those settled near Conestogoe and those near Lechay" (Lehigh, near the Water Gap). Trade, it seems, was also on the Shawnees' minds. Nearly a year later, "two Indians from the Shawannais upon Delaware" came to Philadelphia to inquire after trade opportunities.

The Pennsylvanians told them that they had little more than powder and lead in stock. They said that they were expecting another shipment in the fall and invited the Indians to come down then with their furs.

Philadelphia was not the only place where trade goods were scarce, as inventories in every colony continued to dwindle while Queen Anne's War dragged on. Cornbury was recalled in 1708, due as much to anger over a collapsing economy as to attacks on his character made by his political enemies. He was replaced when John Lord Lovelace, Fourth Baron Hurley, landed in New York in late December 1708. As far as Indian affairs were concerned, Lovelace was able to do little more than ship Cornbury back to England and suspend issuance of further new land-purchase licenses before dying suddenly the following May.

Richard Ingoldsby once again stepped in as interim governor until another replacement arrived from England. In the meantime, the interim governor, who had been a member of the Cornbury Ring, kept access open for those wanting land in Munsee country. A career soldier by trade, Ingoldsby also showed a passion for combat with the French. He quickly committed New York to an ambitious scheme to seize both Acadia and Canada simultaneously in a coordinated, two-pronged assault. Ingoldsby had difficulty persuading Indians in Munsee country to join the expedition. In New Jersey, Weequehela politely told authorities in Perth Amboy that he would look into the matter and get back to them. Shawnees on the Delaware refused several invitations. And the sachem at Minisink rebuffed recruiters, saying his people "were only squas, and not fighting men." Orders requiring sheriffs in Queens and Suffolk counties to bring in Indians produced few warriors.

Not all Indians, however, were uninterested in joining the expedition. At least sixty River Indians, mostly from Schaghticoke, joined Mohawk and other Iroquois warriors in the army that marched up to the south end of Lake Champlain. There they built Fort Anne, where they wound up cooling their heels as the expected British support never arrived. When September frosts put an end to the fighting season, the little army was disbanded and its men sent home.

Indians and Albany traders were probably secretly glad that the expedition had failed to materialize. Neither really wanted to break the informal truce with New France or give up their smuggling operations. War hawks, however, were determined to strike a blow against the French. They packed three prominent Mohawk men and a Schaghticoke sachem off to England during the spring of 1710 to drum up support for another attempt. Chaperoned by Pieter Schuyler, the Four Indian Kings of America, as they were called, created a sensation wherever they went. The trip was a public relations success. The Indian Kings got their portraits painted and made a favorable impression in a royal audience with the queen. The entourage left London with a firm promise that more than adequate support for a major effort against New France would be forthcoming by the time the next campaign season opened in the spring.

This time the British were better than their word. It helped that the Board of Trade had already authorized a more limited strike against Acadia before the Four Kings arrived. The fleet of warships left Portsmouth a short time after the Indian delegation and their escorts embarked for New York. Capturing Acadia during the first week of October 1710, the newly established United Kingdom of Great Britain renamed it Nova Scotia in honor of England's 1707 union with Scotland.

A subsequent expedition sent against Quebec failed disastrously. News of the debacle reached Fort Anne, where Shawnee, Upper River, and Long Island Indians were camped with a colonial army assembled to attack Montreal. Again left in the lurch, the disappointed troops burned Fort Anne to the ground before returning home. Two years later, on April 11, 1713, diplomats in Europe signed the Treaty of Utrecht, which turned Nova Scotia, Newfoundland, and all of Hudson Bay into sovereign British territory.

Although formal protestations of peace and amity like the Utrecht Treaty cooled the mostly tepid ardor of most northern colonists, they did little to end animosities that had long kept conflict on the boil in the southern provinces. The first intimations that old problems were causing new troubles filtered north when a delegation of Tuscarora sachems appeared at the Conestoga town in early June 1710. Tired of being defrauded by North Carolina traders and abused by squatters trespassing on their lands, Tuscaroras carried wampum belts and messages to the Senecas, asking permission to move north to join Shawnees and others living under Five Nations' protection. A delegation of Conoys from Maryland soon followed, making a similar request for asylum.

Resentment exploded into violence when open war broke out between the Tuscaroras and North Carolinians a year later. The war was a calamity. Cherokee, Yamasee, and other warriors helped provincial militiamen kill Tuscaroras and burn their towns. Hundreds of Indians died in the fighting. Tuscaroras taken captive by Indian English allies were put to death or adopted. Most taken by colonists were enslaved. Tuscarora refugees seeking asylum started showing up at various spots in Pennsylvania and New York by the spring of 1712. They arrived at a bad time. Nearly bankrupted by the collapse of trade caused by the still-raging war with France and panicked by rumors of French, Shawnee, Seneca, and River Indian attacks, colonists in New York City were also in the process of savagely suppressing a slave revolt.

In the middle of all this, Esopus sachem Harman Hekan told magistrates at a Nicolls Treaty renewal meeting at Kingston in June 1712 that about six hundred "Shawannos who cannot live at peace in their own native country" had asked to settle as his subjects "to the west and northwest of the blew hills in Ulster County where said Esopus Indians now reside." Ordered to return to Kingston just three weeks later to clear up a rumor that three strange Indians had been circulating wampum and calling on the Esopus to rise up and massacre their neighbors, a chastened Harman Hekan denied the report. He further denied reports that warriors from his nation were heading south to help Indians "going against North Carolina." He then tried to ease the fears of the nervous officials by admitting that the six hundred Indians mentioned at the last meeting were actually "but one sachimo and about thirty or forty souls." Remembering that New York authorities had dispatched a River Indian envoy to the Susquehanna River several years earlier to invite Shawnee Indians living there to come to New York, he tried to convince the magistrates that his Shawannos "had lived about menesinck above twelve years."

The magistrates were not fooled. They soon found out who Harman Hekan's "Shawannos" really were. On July 3, 1712, Governor Robert Hunter, who had arrived in 1710 to take over the government of New York and New Jersey, formally gave a Tuscarora delegation permission to remain at a fort they had built "beyond the blue hills." This was not, however, on the Delaware headwaters, nor did the Tuscaroras become subjects of the Esopus. More than five hundred families of Tuscaroras instead gradually settled at various spots in the Upper Susquehanna Valley during the next few years. By September 1714 Five Nations sachems were telling Hunter that the Tuscarora Indians "are come to shelter themselves among" them. They were more specific in a speech made at Albany two years later. At this meeting, their speaker informed Albany magistrates that Tuscaroras were living under their sponsorship and protection "about the branches of the Susquahanna River." He went on to say that presents to the Five Nations should thenceforth be divided into six portions. Colonists themselves began referring to Tuscaroras as the sixth Iroquois nation, and to the confederacy as a whole as the Six Nations, by 1722.

Iroquois warriors and their Covenant Chain affiliates joined Tuscaroras sending warriors out against the Indian nations in league with the North Carolinians. The narrow Appalachian ridge valleys traversed by the ever-shifting route of the Warrior's Path became desolated no-man's-lands as the conflict Indians called the Great Southern War intensified. Those at the southern end of the Great Valley—like the Yamasees, who had taken an active part in the war against the Tuscaroras—were soon destroyed in their own war with North Carolina in 1715. Indians from Munsee country joined Iroquois warriors helping Tuscaroras take their revenge on the Yamasees. Among "the sachims of Susquahanna" reporting receipt of several presumably Yamasee scalps and captives from Carolina in the fall of 1715 were Minisink sachem Tatapagh and Manawkyhickon, a young cousin of Weequehela.

Except for war parties, most Indians in Munsee country avoided traveling south. Although vengeance, glory, captives, and peltry worked their enduring charms on those willing to be seduced by them, few from the Munsee homeland were interested in journeying to places where Virginian and Carolinian slavers lurked, waiting to drag unwary Indians off to markets in Williamsburg and Charleston. Even fewer were willing to journey on paths where mourning warriors might kill or capture the first people they encountered. More westerly destinations held greater allure. Indians in Munsee country still had friends and relatives farther west, where furs, game, and fertile soils could be found in abundance. Beyond the Appalachians and distant from Iroquoia, Far nations like the Ottawas and Miamis respectfully addressed River Indians and other easterners as grandfathers whose long experience with colonists had made them seem wiser than any may have wanted to be. During the decades that followed, help from metaphorical grandchildren would help grandparents forced from Munsee country endure the worst strains and stresses of dispossession and dislocation.

10

UNMOORED, 1708–1742

Trips farther north and west became more frequent as Indians in Munsee country finally were forced to give up title to nearly all of their remaining ancestral lands east of the Delaware River. Syndicate partners in New York and New Jersey had cut out vast hunks of Munsee territory for themselves at Minisink and other places during Cornbury's administration. Buoyed by these successes, colonists finally felt the time was right to press Indians for their remaining lands in the combined provinces. Although the settlers were as divided as ever, they finally were of one mind in their determination to own the whole of the Munsee homeland and would no longer allow themselves to be put off or manipulated by the few Indians still living there.

There was little the Indians could do about the situation. Their political position was weak, and the colonists knew it. The Indians also knew that they now had few friends among the Europeans. The generations that had put up with working disagreements and creative misunderstandings were passing away. The reluctance of Indians in Minisink, central New Jersey, and western Long Island to step forward during Queen Anne's War, moreover, added substance to rumors that they were conspiring with slaves, Senecas, and Shawnees to drive settlers away and regain lost lands. Distrusted and alone, they had to face hard-nosed businessmen intent on extinguishing remaining Indian title to land in the provinces.

In late September 1708, Norwalk town fathers from Connecticut persuaded Katonah to sign over title to his people's last twenty thousand acres along the border with New York. Four years later, Nimham (a relative of Ockanickon known in the Jerseys as Sehoppy) headed the list of sachems selling a small tract just above the Hudson Highlands in Dutchess County. A bit farther north, Robert Livingston purchased yet another piece of Indian land within his manor boundaries from its Munsee- and Mahican-speaking residents in May 1713.

One by one and in small groups, Taphow, Weequehela, and their compatriots had to give ground in northeastern and central New Jersey. Between 1708 and 1710, East Jersey proprietors and their agents used licenses granted during Cornbury's and Ingoldsby's administrations to acquire vast tracts of land in the upland reaches of the Passaic and Raritan valleys. The largest of these East Jersey purchases, the Mackseta Cohunge deed, signed on August 13, 1708, conveyed an enormous expanse of territory west of the Watchung Mountains that included most of present-day Morris County (see map 7).

On the other side of the province line, agents working for West Jersey Society shareholders finally acquired the long-desired lands at the Delaware Water Gap. They got Taphow, Weequehela's cousin Manawkyhickon, and several other leaders to sign a series of deeds to large tracts of land there between 1709 and 1714. A group of four deeds signed in one day in August 1713 conveyed lands at and around the Delaware Water Gap to Daniel Coxe and his partners; those sales together with another in the area finalized a year later represented the single largest block of Indian land surrendered in West Jersey.

Together, these deeds transferred title to more than one and a quarter million acres of Munsee country to West Jersey Society buyers. The land lost through these deeds represented virtually all remaining ancestral Indian territory east of the Delaware. Taphow and the other sachems who had held settlers back from the Kittatinys for so long could take small comfort in knowing that the Water Gap gateway that had so dazzled Daniel Coxe and his proprietary partners was actually a blind door. Munsee- and Northern Unami–speaking Indians still held title to all lands west of the gap. With a little help from Pennsylvanians eager to draw trade to their own province, they could block West Jersey efforts to press farther into the interior. Even if the Jersey men could somehow get through the Gap, it would be many years before settlers would obtain Indian title to the passes through what some called the Kittatinys and other knew as the Blue Mountains.

It took less than five years to extinguish most of the remaining ancestral Indian titles to lands east of the Delaware River. Yet it had taken more than a century to turn the Indians of Munsee country into the nomads colonists originally thought they were. True, they had not been entirely sedentary, settled agrarian farmers in the Old World model when Europeans first sailed to their country. But their movements were mostly limited to relatively modest moves among network affiliates made on lands that were clearly their own. Unlike Europeans, who drew on winds and wheels to carry their bodies and bundles from place to place, Indians relied on mind and muscle power. People with limited mobility—elders, the infirm, mothers with very young children—tended to stay with family and friends on ancestral lands. Hunters, warriors, traders, and sachems, especially men with several wives in different towns, traveled farther from home. Even with firearms, fruit trees, fine fabrics, and other labor-saving innovations that made it easier to make a living close to home, most Indian people, and especially the young and fit among them, preferred the excitement of travel to strange lands beyond their hearths and homes.

With near total displacement, however, most Indians could no longer count on stable home bases. Some Indians from the region held on in Lehigh Valley towns at the Forks of Delaware, in small towns in and around the Great Valley, in others in the central New Jersey pinelands, and on small reservations and pieces of vacant land on western Long Island. Most, however, soon moved to Indian towns and Christian missions located beyond their homeland's borders along the upper reaches of the Susquehanna and Housatonic rivers. Those who still wanted to live for at least part of each year on vacant stretches of ancestral lands now owned by colonists, and their numbers were not small, became wanderers.

They spent the year as travelers, camping in out-of-the-way spots as they shuttled between towns, missions, and reservations. Small knots of friends and families began moving along increasingly far-flung networks that could carry them from trapping grounds in Ottawa country or even farther to the Wabash Valley (in present-day Indiana) during winter to spring trade fairs at Montreal or Albany. Joining up with new partners and saying goodbye to old companions, some might journey during warmer months to relatives living on Long Island reservations or to ocean-side back lots at Rockaway, Merrick, and Massapequa.

Others might visit families and friends still hanging on to tiny tracts surrounded by settlers in Monmouth, Somerset, or Westchester counties. Some could also settle for the summer around still-unfenced old planting fields and orchards in the Great Valley. Together, people from these and nearby places, who increasingly were collectively called Munsees by colonists, might gather again for treaty meetings in Albany, Kingston, or New York City. They could then journey to Lehigh, Susquehanna, or Housatonic valley towns for fall religious festivals. After mending political fences and giving thanks for their blessings, families would leave to hunt deer and tend winter trap lines in nearby Pocono and Catskill mountain valleys or journey back to Far country forests beyond the Appalachians.

Just as no document records Indians' views on the patterns of land sales chronicled in this book, no single set of sources chronicles the movement of a particular person or group through a network of the kind reconstructed here. The existing record, however, contains scores of references noting the presence of Munsee people identified by name and affiliation in the above-mentioned places (and others) at various times during the decades after they lost most of their last ancestral lands. A more concrete idea of what this network looked like can be gained by examining references documenting the changing residences of Weequehela's cousin Manawkyhickon. Manawkyhickon first appeared in colonial documents as one of the more important sachems selling land between the Musconetcong River and the Delaware Water Gap between 1711 and 1713. He was next mentioned in

1715 as one of the sachems on the Susquehanna whose warriors were going to war against Indians to the south. In 1728, he was noted as living at a place called Chenastry, on the upper reaches of the West Branch of the Susquehanna River. By 1737, Manawkyhickon had returned to the Delaware River, where he was repeatedly mentioned in colonial documents as a senior sachem at Minisink until his last appearance in colonial records made at a major Easton Treaty meeting in the fall of 1758.

Survey notes and other records indicate that Munsees maintained their preference for living whenever possible in settlements consisting of single longhouses sheltering extended families well into the eighteenth century. Initially depicted symbolically on early maps, this settlement pattern was first directly documented in deeds to Raritan Valley lands signed during the last quarter of the 1600s. Places were often known by the names of their most prominent residents, like "Metapas [Metapis's] Wigwam" and "Amirents [Emerus's] Plantation." These and other communities tended to come to colonial attention following conclusion of some kind of land agreement, and most disappeared from settlers' records shortly thereafter. This does not mean such settlements appeared and disappeared in accordance with their notice in colonial records. Instead, deeds and surveys revealed specifics of Indian settlement geography in Munsee country that had earlier been overlooked, ignored, or kept from colonial notice.

Between 1715 and 1719 surveyor John Reading chronicled an Indian world in northern New Jersey that previously had been largely hidden. Among observations assessing land quality; reporting weather conditions; and chronicling finds of potentially exploitable lead, iron, and copper deposits, Reading recorded Indian fields and houses he saw and, on occasion, slept in. Some of the place-names recorded in his journals were familiar to but rarely visited by colonists up to that time—places like the Upper Delaware Valley town of Cochecton, Pomptown on the Ramapo River, Whippany and Peapack in present-day Morris County, and the Shawnee towns at the Water Gap that Reading was able to glimpse only from a distance. Others are documented only in his journals, like the formidable mouthful Essakauqueamenshehikkon;

towns called Allamuch Ahokkin, Chanongong, and Mensalockauke; a settlement in the upper Wallkill Valley named Chechong (noted as "an Indian plantation in good fence and well improved [whose people] raise wheat and horses"); and several unnamed houses and campsites unoccupied when Reading rode by.

Except for the knot of settlers around Maghkaghkemeck (present-day Port Jervis, New York) and some isolated families along the fringes of frontier settlement, he encountered no other colonists in the Minisink region. Ironically, Reading never got the chance to see the Minisink town itself. Indians living where the Minisink Path crossed today's Paulins Kill refused to let his party pass farther west in 1715. Maringoman, who was Reading's Indian guide, refused to help with a second attempt to cross at a different spot, saying "that Tohokkonet-kong [Paulins Kill] Indians would be angry with him for showing their land." When the party decided to press on regardless, the guide went home. Without Maringoman, Reading finally thought better of the idea and quietly redirected the party east of the Paulins Kill.

Reading also avoided Minisink when he returned to the region in 1719 to help survey the New York–New Jersey border. After passing by the Shawnee towns on the Pennsylvania side of the Delaware, he left the river three miles below Minisink and took a more inland route to Maghkaghkemeck before traveling on to Cochecton. Even with this detour, armed Munsees again stopped his party short of its goal. Like the Tohokkonetkong Indians four years earlier and Manawkyhickon some twenty years later, Munsees at Minisink refused to acknowl-edge that they had sold their land to anyone. They let the surveyors pass only after being assured that the party was merely establishing a station point marking the provincial border and not taking Indian lands. It would take a war and a final comprehensive settlement to finally shake the Indians' grip from their beloved upper valley island fastness. Even then, Munsees would take care to retain their rights to hunt and fish on the land.

Many Indians from more northerly reaches of Munsee coun-try seeking new places to live intensified historically close connec-tions with Pocumtucks, Pennacooks, Sokokis, and other Northern

Indians. Indians and colonists living farther north and west gradually extended the name Abenaki, "Easterner," to refer collectively to Northern Indian communities that often included Munsee people. Schaghticoke residents began making longer and more frequent visits to Abenaki towns as Albany commissioners, led by Pieter Schuyler, started buying up the lands of those Indians they were supposed to protect. Although authorities in New York regarded the Upper River nation as their first line of defense against Canada, Schuyler himself never trusted the Indians living at Schaghticoke. He knew that nearly all were at least nominal Catholics with strong ties to French missions. He was also aware that many Schaghticokes still cherished ancient hatreds for New Englanders, and that most, including the people from Munsee country living among them, were considered spies and smugglers.

These beliefs led Schuyler and his board of commissioners to be less than careful in protecting Schaghticoke interests. The board men started small, using the highly irregular tactic of calling in a mortgage for sixty beaver pelts and other skins from one "Taspelalet alias Murhank" to claim land at Schaghticoke in January 1702. Five years later, they obtained a deed to all but twelve acres of Schaghticoke land between the mouths of the Mohawk and Hoosic rivers from a group of sachems.

By 1714, the Indians at Schaghticoke were desperate. Meeting with the board at Albany that September, their speaker demanded to be "confirmed in some particular place under certain metes and bounds, that they might live no more like dogs." Many did not wait for the Albany men to break the promises made at that meeting. Schaghticokes suddenly released from wartime duties following the restoration of peace that year began to drift away from the Hoosic Valley. After a long string of violent incidents, most finally left for Canada to join their Abenaki brethren against the New Englanders when open war again broke out between the old adversaries in 1722.

At about the same time, other people born in and around Munsee country were spending increasing amounts of time in fast-growing settlements above Shamokin along the upper reaches of the West and

North branches of the Susquehanna River. Although records from this time are sketchy, it appears that Munsees were already building houses and planting crops near Tuscarora and other expatriate communities on the North Branch at sites of later multicultural Indian towns like Wyalusing, Tioga, and Ochquaga. On the West Branch, Manawkyhickon and his people lived near Shawnee and Six Nations people in towns built on the flats between present-day Muncy, Williamsport, and Lock Haven, Pennsylvania. Farther south, Munsees visited Delaware-speaking friends and relatives living among Shawnees, Conoys, and other Indian expatriates on the main stem of the river between Conestoga and Shamokin.

It is not known what happened to the people from Munsee country living among the Loups along the St. Joseph River after 1687. Governor Dongan asked the Five Nations to invite "Mahikanders that are at Ottowawa and further nations" to return east that year. It is unclear whether the invitation was proffered or, if it was, whether it was accepted. It may be that violence brought on by King William's War forced Loups remaining in Miami country finally to come back east with Viele, Mattaseet, and the Shawnees in 1694. A very detailed account of an Indian siege of Fort Pontchartrain at the newly established French outpost of Detroit during the spring of 1712 contains no references to anyone representing themselves as Loups or easterners during this pivotal event in that region's history. That silence does not prove anything, but is suggestive that the Loups had moved elsewhere.

Wherever they traveled, the original inhabitants of Munsee country trod softly. Whether they journeyed through or beyond the borders of their home territories, they fell into routines that helped them lead unobtrusive lives on lands now dominated by strangers. This approach was a sensible if not particularly ennobling way of dealing with the loss of a homeland. Although defiant voices like Manawkyhickon's occasionally threatened retaliation, most Munsee people resigned themselves to living obscure lives, leaving the risks and worries of power politics behind for the time being. Ceding center stage to others, they focused on rebuilding their families as they struggled to come to grips with hard new realities.

Sachems determined to remind colonists and Indian allies of past promises and pledges paid special attention to the diplomatic niceties. They took care to periodically sign new agreements and renew old ones like the Nicolls Treaty. Munsee delegations also continued to welcome arrivals and condole deaths of Crown officials. At these meetings, Munsees mostly conducted themselves unobtrusively. Although they would always have a day or two of their own to have their say, they tended to remain in the background as Six Nations diplomats and colonial officials made the big decisions.

Authorities who tended to forget about Munsees most of the time always seemed to remember them when there was a need for their services. Munsee sachems responded by making a show of answering summons and responding to requests. They were careful, however, to minimize expectations. Assured of the Munsees' fidelity and constantly reminded of the constraints they operated under, officials tended to forgive and forget when those Indians failed to obey orders or fulfill promises. Sachems pledging enduring friendship did not neglect to remind the authorities of laws and treaties when their people were cheated, assaulted, or arrested. Although feelings might run high, Indians as well as colonists had to forget about offenders who fled out of the reach of justice.

The desire for land that had kept Munsees firmly in the minds of colonists did not pass with acquisition of most of the last Indian territory east of the Delaware in 1714. Now, however, deeds mostly preserved fading memories of past deals and arrangements. This did not mean that Munsees stopped doing land deals or that colonists stopped producing records to remind them of who owned what. Land records, however, increasingly took the forms of terse affidavits confirming earlier sales or of depositions identifying buyers, sellers, place-names, and boundary markers. A substantial body of this documentation chronicled proceedings dealing with unfulfilled promises, blocked boundary-marking parties, and survey plats and property patents that always managed to take in far more land than anyone intended to sell.

Weequehela and other sachems regarded as Indian spokesmen worked hard with Governor Hunter and William Burnet, the man who replaced him in 1720, to keep the peace that Indians and colonists had dreamed about during the long decades of struggle and uncertainty. They kept contacts open with one another and relied on laws and customs short of war—such as circulating wampum belts or setting pens to paper—to deal with serious problems. This tranquil state of affairs was threatened only once during the era of the Great Peace. Like the incidents that led to so much trouble in 1675, trouble began with a string of unpleasant but not particularly uncommon incidents occurring in several places at about the same time. The first of these took place in New Jersey. One day in the spring of 1727, Weequehela shot and killed a local tavern keeper and sometime ship captain and pilot named John Leonard during what most seem to agree was a drunken argument.

By any measure, Weequehela was the best-known and most influential sachem in New Jersey. Depending on who was talking about him, he was either respected or feared as head of a powerful family with close connections in Munsee- and Northern Unami–speaking communities. He was also a highly cultivated man with refined and expensive tastes, rare among all but the most cultivated colonists at the time. He is said to have lived in a well-furnished frame house, with barns housing cattle and horses, surrounded by fields of wheat tended by enslaved Africans. It is also thought that he operated at least one mill on the banks of the Manalapan River.

The circumstances of the shooting and the subsequent trial are murky. The result is not. At Perth Amboy on June 30, 1727, New Jersey authorities hanged Weequehela for murder. Two months later, newspapers reported that three "Indian Kings" gathered with fifty of their principal men at the late sachem's plantation to "crown a new king." Nearly all of Weequehela's people packed up and moved to the Forks of Delaware shortly thereafter.

Trouble broke out in Pennsylvania almost as soon as the New Jersey Indians arrived at the Forks. A message reaching Philadelphia on September 27, 1727, contained the earliest known colonial reference mentioning Munsees by name. The report stated that "Munscoes Indians, who live on an eastern branch of the Sasquehannah" had killed a trader at a place called Snake Town. Just two months later, New Jersey émigrés at the Forks of Delaware drove off surveyors trying to lay out lands at Durham where the Penn family proprietary secretary James Logan was setting up an iron furnace. Durham was located just below where South Mountain formed the natural border between the piedmont lands to the south and the part of the Great Valley drained by the Lehigh River immediately to the north. The Indians claimed that they had not been paid for the land. A meeting was convened at Philadelphia in early June 1728, to deal with tensions caused by this and other, more serious incidents. At that meeting, Logan responded to the Indian complaints by dramatically producing what he claimed was a ten-year-old deed bearing the standard indorsement affirming that the Indian signatories had received what they had been promised.

A flurry of panicky reports reached Philadelphia around this time. Several stated that Manawkyhickon was circulating war belts among the Six Nations and the Miamis, calling on them to help him avenge his cousin Weequehela's execution. Even more worried messengers brought word that a brawl had broken out at another ironworks at Maxantawny (near present-day Kutztown) between some "Shawanese from about Pechoquealin [their name for the Water Gap]" and local colonists. Settlers were said to be banding together to defend their families from further attacks. Shortly thereafter, Philadelphia authorities learned that three men belonging to one of these bands had murdered two Delaware women and an elderly Delaware man passing through the colonists' village at Cacoosing in the nearby Tulpehocken Valley.

Determined to stop these outrages from spiraling into war, Pennsylvania's resident lieutenant governor, Sir Patrick Gordon, who had taken office only a year earlier, acted quickly. On May 16, 1728, he issued a proclamation that called for calm and ordered vigilante bands to disperse. He also saw to it that the murderers of the Indians at Cacoosing were swiftly captured and brought to trial. Gordon then met with Susquehanna Valley sachems at Conestoga two weeks later, and with the leaders of the Schuylkill and Delaware Valley nations ten days after that at the aforementioned Philadelphia meeting.

Gordon condoled the Indians for their losses at these meetings. Announcing that two of the three Cacoosing murderers had been executed, he assured the sachems that his feelings of friendship toward them remained unchanged and urged them forget about the late unpleasantness. He also promised to hold a more general convocation in the fall to formally reaffirm friendship with all Indians in Pennsylvania.

Several important developments came out of these meetings. At Conestoga, everyone agreed to recognize the Oneida leader Shikellamy as the Six Nations regent over all Indians living in and around the Susquehanna Valley. Shortly thereafter in Philadelphia, James Logan browbeat the Delaware sachem Sassoonan and his people, then living mostly in the upper Schuylkill Valley, into acknowledging the validity of the irregular, unrecorded 1718 deed to their lands below "the mountains on this side Lechay" between the Delaware and Susquehanna that he had produced at the June meeting. Ominously, the most aggrieved parties did not appear at these or other meetings convened at the time.

It is not that invitations were not issued. Gordon had sent substantial gifts along with his invitation to Manawkyhickon, whom he addressed as a man of worth and note among his people. Neither these sentiments nor the proffered gifts evidently mollified the sachem, who fervently wanted war. Subsequent Six Nations and Miami rejections of his war belts, however, forced Manawkyhickon to reconsider his options. Hoping to ease tensions with the Shawnees on the Delaware as well, Logan dispatched a message to their sachem in late May, reaffirming the Pennsylvania government's wish for peace and inviting him to meet at Durham in the fall. Logan then sat back and waited for the Shawnees to come to him.

The Shawnees had no intention of answering a call to a meeting where Logan would have a chance to spring another surprise deed on them. As summer began, the Shawnees seemed to be avoiding any contact with settlers. Then news reached Philadelphia in late August that Shawnees had hanged a trader from one of the rafters of a cabin at Shamokin in what could be seen as a grim simulacrum of Weequehela's execution. Another report soon revealed that the trader had survived the ordeal. Just days thereafter, word reached the provincial capital that the Shawnees had completely abandoned their towns at the Water Gap. They had moved with such haste, the report ran, that they left their corn standing. The circumstances of this Shawnee move remain as unclear as those surrounding the relocation of Weequehela's people. Six Nations sachems claimed they ordered the Shawnees west to place them under Shikellamy's closer supervision. A few years afterwards, Shawnees themselves said that their Munsee neighbors at Minisink had asked them to leave, adding that they had been happy to go since the Minisinks and Iroquois had then been plotting to attack the Pennsylvanians.

Whatever their immediate reasons for going, Shawnees on the Delaware probably had patiently put up with as much Pennsylvanian protection, Iroquois supervision, and colonial neighborliness as they were going to take. There is some evidence suggesting that the Shawnees may have been thinking about moving for some time. As recently as 1726, Logan had directed that a notice be posted at Kingston, New York, complaining that people from that place were purchasing some land from Indians "on the west side of the Delaware River above Pechaquealin Hills." Stating that unauthorized purchases were against Pennsylvania law, he warned Kingston residents that his province would only allow purchases from Indians made with proprietary approval.

It appears that Logan was working from good intelligence. A grandson and namesake of the old Hudson Valley land shark Nicholas Depui secured a private deed for three thousand acres of Indian land at and around Shawnee Island in September 1727. Signed by two otherwise unknown individuals identified in the deed as "Waugoanlenneggea and Pemnogque," the younger Nicholas's deed anticipated the Shawnee departure by a year. He subsequently parleyed his deed first into a lease and later into a more regular title issued by proprietary owner William Allen for 426 acres that included what are today known as Depue and Shawnee islands. A couple of years later, another enterprising settler named Johannes Westbrook made a private deal with a man he identified as Syacop (perhaps a garbled rendition of

Ankerop, a nickname that settlers sometimes used when referring to Harman Hekan's son Hendrick) for some acres of land several miles upriver on the New Jersey side, just across from Minisink Island.

Whoever sold the land at Shawnee Island, Canadian documents suggest that French authorities had been trying to draw off Shawnees living there since 1724. It is also clear that a substantial number of the Shawnees who left both the Delaware and Susquehanna valleys in 1727 settled far to the west on lands beyond the reach of Shikel- lamy and the Six Nations. Many evidently moved near the sheltering walls of French forts at Detroit housing traders, trade goods, and gun- smiths. Others set up new towns in the still-remote heart of the Ohio Valley, where only the most enterprising Iroquois, British, or French intruders might disturb them.

The Shawnees were not the only people getting fed up with living near British colonists in 1728. The patience of the long-suffering In- dians at Schaghticoke finally wore thin late that summer when they returned from their hunting and fishing camps to find their fences broken down, their crops trampled by cattle, and hostile colonists planting their land. Formally greeting Burnet's newly appointed replacement, Colonel John Montgomerie, at Albany on October 5, 1728, they must have quietly boiled as they listened to the clueless governor blandly assure them of his continuing protection. Their at- tention may have perked up when Montgomerie urged them to go to Canada to fetch back those of their people who had deserted the province. They politely thanked the governor for his kind words and promised they would leave at the earliest opportunity. The Indians were as good as their word. Many soon joined friends and family at the north end of Lake Champlain at Mississiquoi. Others went farther east to Cowas country along the uppermost reaches of the Connecti- cut River between Vermont and New Hampshire. Although Indians did not entirely abandon the place, few ever returned to Schaghticoke for more than a brief visit.

Lower River Indians east of the Hudson River started selling off their last remaining tracts of territory in the Highlands at this time. Robert Livingston made his final three purchases of Indian lands

around Taghkanick in the remote, hilly back lots of his manor between 1718 and 1724. Nimham and several other sachems put their
marks on another three deeds between 1723 and 1730, thereby conveying much of what remained of their lands in the Berkshire foothills. A few years later, most of the sachems signing these and other
deeds moved with their people east to the still uncolonized uppermost
reaches of the Housatonic Valley, where missionaries inspired by the
Great Awakening were starting new Indian missions at places like
Stockbridge, Massachusetts, and Scaticook, Connecticut.

Across the Hudson, Esopus people continued to lodge complaints
during Nicolls Treaty renewal meetings, claiming that Johannis Hardenbergh and others failed to pay for or took too much of their lands.
Farther south, Nutimus and a younger kinsman named Teedyuscung
began selling off some of their people's last remaining enclaves in
New Jersey (see map 8).

Together, conveyances made at this time in New York and New
Jersey were little more than nips and tucks smoothing out gores and
gaps left from earlier sales. Experienced sachems like Manawkyhickon
and newcomers like Teedyuscung and a young man named Daniel
who took Nimham as his surname, would soon have to face a new
generation of ever more numerous colonists. These would be a mix
of ambitious younger sons of old colonial families and mostly impoverished Scotch-Irish and German immigrants. Few would have had
prior dealings with Indians, and most would share a distaste for them,
a sentiment the Indians heartily reciprocated. Unfettered by any sense
of obligation or regard for the tiny Native communities clinging to
remnants of ancient lands, they would instead concentrate on driving
all Indians beyond the pale of settlement.

Sachems who chose to remain upon ancestral lands would spend
the remaining years of their lives defending their peoples' last pieces
of native soil from these newcomers. This critical stage in the struggle
between colonists and Indians would furnish some of the more iconic
moments in American history. Memories of battles, treaties, and land
purchases bound up in this climactic conflict still make up much of
the present-day American sense of the colonial past. Already fading as

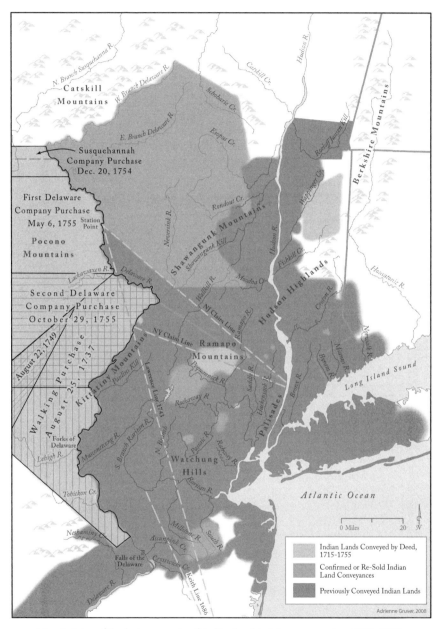

Map 8. Sales of the last remnants of Indian land in Munsee country, 1715–1755.

colonists rushed onto the Indians' last lands, memories of earlier Indian efforts to hold onto their territory in the Munsee homeland disappeared as succeeding waves of settlers ran roughshod over Indians and British officials alike, flooding across the Indians' lost territories in search of new homes of their own farther west.

Few land sales in American history weigh more heavily on modern consciences than the Walking Purchase. The story itself has been told often, and the best accounts leave little out. Although writers consistently identify the Indians involved in the sale as Delawares, very few acknowledge that very nearly all of the Delawares involved in the Walking Purchase were either Munsees or people closely connected to them. This omission has had the same effect on collective memory as the failure to identify the Indians who sold Manhattan in the most memorable of all American land deals. Although use of general terms like "Delaware" allows scholars to sidestep nitpicking arguments over exactly who had rights to what, their use has also blotted out memories of the significant roles that Munsee-speaking Delawares played in the nation's early history.

Munsees were not the only Indians involved in this pivotal purchase. For the first time, Iroquois Confederacy sachems played a deciding role in a sale of land within the ancestral Munsee homeland. Their involvement began just as the newly arrived proprietary governor Thomas Penn was settling in at Philadelphia. Penn had come to Pennsylvania to drag his family out of debts that had plagued them since the time of his late father. Before Thomas even sailed to America, the Penn family had already countenanced purchases of large tracts of Indian territory in the Lehigh Valley around present-day Allentown by William Allen and several other Friends. Although he was new to the colony, the young Penn knew enough to realize that only the Six Nations had the clout necessary to back up these sales and shake loose other lands whose sale monies and quitrents were needed to bail out the financially strapped Penn clan.

Penn and the aging family factotum Logan met with representatives of four of the Six Nations at Philadelphia between late August and early September 1732 to look into ways they might help each other. Penn proposed that they enter into a new relationship in which the Six Nations would serve as the province's strong arm in all matters involving Indians in Pennsylvania. The new policy would depend upon skilled intermediaries. The Six Nations had men like Shikellamy already in place along the Susquehanna. His provincial counterpart would be a uniquely savvy polyglot son of Palatine German immigrants named Conrad Weiser. Weiser had lived among the Mohawks for sixteen years as a young man and was intimately familiar with their language and customs. Fluent in English as well as German, he also understood Delaware and several other Indian languages. What is more, he had begun his career on the frontier in the service of the Six Nations as an intermediary with Pennsylvania.

Having secured Iroquois support, Penn bent his efforts toward ousting the Jersey Indians who had moved to the Lehigh Valley following Weequehela's execution. His first efforts to get Nutimus, who had become leader of the Jersey Indians at the Forks, to give up land there in 1734 failed. One year later, he tried again at another meeting with Nutimus at the Penn family country seat at Pennsbury. Logan started by producing a couple of Indian deeds to lands north of Philadelphia to establish a baseline for Penn's purchase request. One was the well-remembered registered deed to land at the Falls of the Delaware signed on July 15, 1682, by sachems Logan identified at the time as "Idaquahon and several other southern Indians." The second was yet another unrecorded and unendorsed surprise deed, this one with blank spaces in critical places. Bearing a date of August 20, 1686, the document was signed by "Mayhkeerickkishsho, Sayhoppy, and Taughhaughsey, the chiefs or kings of the Northern Indians on Delaware."

The deed purported to convey a substantial tract of land extending "back into the woods as far as a man can go in one day and a half" from a point on Neshaminy Creek. Logan went on to blithely explain that the newly arrived governor had just found the record of the long-forgotten transaction in a box of old family papers. He then introduced several older settlers who came forward to confirm that they had attended the meeting where the deed was signed.

The use of a travel expression to mark deed boundaries was memorably rare. Nutimus admitted that his ancestors had signed a deed to land at Neshaminy bounded in part by travel distance many years earlier. Neither he nor any of the other Forks Indians, however, could remember the document Logan produced or the sachems mentioned therein. Oddly, no one seems to have thought to send a message to Nimham (who was then living far from the Forks) to see if he or a namesake was the "Sayhoppy" in the deed. It was at this time that Logan decided to challenge Nutimus's rights to the land at the Forks by asking how a Jersey man could own land in Pennsylvania. Nutimus responded he had rights to lands on both sides of the river from both his mother's and father's families. Reflecting on Logan's challenge, Nutimus then asked how the secretary, an Irishman from the old country, could have rights to lands an ocean away in Pennsylvania. The meeting broke up with Nutimus promising he would bring knowledgeable elders to sort things out at their next get-together.

Finally realizing that he could not make Nutimus do what he wanted, Penn authorized Logan to begin working behind the scenes to get the Six Nations to make the Indians at the Forks more tractable. Logan started by directing Weiser to get the Iroquois to sign over lands occupied with their permission by Unamis, Shawnees, and other expatriates below the Blue Mountains along the lower Susquehanna River. Although they balked at first, the Six Nations finally deeded over the requested territory on October 11, 1736. Asked to convey Nutimus's land as well, they at first refused to give away the lands of people they characterized in this instance as their cousins. Weiser pressed harder, and Six Nations sachems finally signed over whatever rights they might have to those lands two weeks later. There was only one problem: the Iroquois had no rights to any land at the Forks.

This did not matter to Penn and Logan, who took their next steps toward taking the Forks lands at a special session of the provincial council convened on August 24, 1737, in Philadelphia (a meeting not recorded in that body's regular minutes). Speaking as the principal sachem at Minisink, Manawkyhickon presented Penn with a belt of four rows of wampum to affirm his people's longstanding "mutual love and friendship." He then proceeded to business. He told the governor that his people did not fully understand what lands were involved in the "deed from Mayhkeerichshoe." A hastily drawn-up map showing a northern border marked by what most commentators affirm was represented to the Indians as Tohickon Creek (but inscribed "west branch of the Delaware," actually the Lehigh River, on the only surviving copy of the map) was shown and accepted. Doubtless informed that the Six Nations would not support them against the Pennsylvanians, Manawkyhickon and the other sachems agreed to sign a confirmation deed acknowledging these boundaries so long as their people "may be permitted to remain on their present settlements and plantations, though within that purchase, without being molested." They were promised that would be the case, and the next day, Manawkyhickon, Nutimus, and nearly every other sachem of any consequence with rights to land at the Forks put their marks on the document.

The result was dismally predictable. Penn had a road cut from the starting place at the present-day Bucks County village of Wrightstown due north and away from the Delaware River, straight into Indian territory. He then had Logan hire the three fastest runners he could find to make the one-and-a-half-day walk on September 19, 1737. By noon of the following day, the last remaining runner reached a spot where the borough of Jim Thorpe stands today. The line he had run extended fifty miles from its starting point. Penn then took advantage of the vague wording describing the conveyance's upper border as a line going from "the utmost extent of the said one day and a half's journey . . . to the aforesaid River Delaware." Rather than run the line forming the purchase's upper boundary due east, he ran it at a right angle northeast from the walk's endpoint, extending an incredible sixty-five more miles to a spot where the Lackawaxen River flows into the Delaware River. In one fell swoop, the Walking Purchase took in more than one million acres, five times more land than the Indians had expected to lose and nearly everything the Munsees and their kin had left in Pennsylvania.

Outraged, Nutimus and his people returned home, determined to stop any Pennsylvanian trying to move onto land above Tohickon

Creek. Penn did not move to take the Forks land immediately. Partially honoring the promises he had made to Manawkyhickon in 1737, the Pennsylvania governor set aside a sixty-four-thousand-acre reservation, christened the "Indian Manor," on the upper Lehigh River. He later allowed Moses Tunda Tatamy, a Christian Indian from central New Jersey, to keep a small three-hundred-acre tract at present-day Stockertown, Pennsylvania, land Tatamy had purchased directly from William Allen in 1741.

Most of the buyers moving to the Forks wanted to see all Indians leave the area as quickly as possible. Hard words were soon exchanged and violent threats made. Doubtless reminding the Six Nations that what the Pennsylvanians had done to them could be done to others, Indians at the Forks called on their Iroquois uncles to support them in this time of need. The Six Nations responded by agreeing to come to Philadelphia to discuss the problem. More than four times the expected fifty Iroquois, Munsee, and Unami attendees subsequently gathered in the provincial capital during the last week of June 1742.

The Onondaga speaker Canasatego directly addressed his speech to an expectant Nutimus at the first open session of the meeting on July 12. Nutimus can only have been appalled as Weiser translated the harshest words yet uttered by a sachem from any Indian nation in the presence of colonists in council. Holding up a wampum belt, Canasatego laced into the Forks Indians. He rhetorically shook them by the hair on their heads, called them women with no right to sell land, and upbraided them as selfish children for not sharing goods received for land that had "gone through their guts" (a metaphor likening both goods and land to consumed food that been turned into dung). Imperiously telling them that "we don't give you the liberty to think about it," Canasatego ordered Nutimus and his people to move immediately to lands which the Six Nations had set aside in order to keep an eye on them at Shamokin or Wyoming (a broad stretch of the Upper Susquehanna Valley where Wilkes-Barre stands today). Alone and abandoned, the stunned Forks Indians returned to their towns and pondered their next moves.

11

SOLD OUT, 1743–1766

Cheated by Penn, abandoned by the Six Nations, and suspected of holding a grudge by nearly everyone, most Indians quickly left the Forks after 1742. More than a few decided to join expatriate Shawnees in the Ohio Valley far from colonists and Iroquois. Some moved to Ochquaga on the North Branch of the Susquehanna River. Nutimus and his family stayed closer, moving to one of the Native communities just above the Kittatiny Ridge before relocating to Manawkyhickon's old town at the Great Island between Lock Haven and Williamsport. Manawkyhickon himself remained on the Jersey side of the Delaware, on the shrinking patch of land his people still held at Minisink. Teedyuscung and his people stayed closest of all, remaining in their town of Meniolagomeka, tucked into a small stretch of flat land on Aquashicola Creek at Smith's Gap, just north of the Kittatiny Ridge a few miles west of the Wind Gap.

Other Indians from Munsee country tried to defy Penn's eviction notice and stay in the Lehigh Valley. Some joined the Moravian mission communities at Bethlehem and Nazareth. A few, like Moses Tunda Tatamy, associated themselves with David Brainerd, a missionary who had moved to the Forks to convert Indians there during the early summer of 1744.

Word of another round of fighting between Great Britain and France reached America at around this time. Known in the colonies as King George's War, the new conflict heightened convictions held by settlers at the Forks that angry, alienated Munsees would now turn against them. Colonists there soon joined Penn and the Iroquois in demanding that all Indians leave the Lehigh Valley. Fearing that their nervous neighbors would attack them now that war had been declared, most of Brainerd's followers decided to leave. Most returned to New Jersey by 1746 to settle in small plots that Weequehela's successor, Andrew Wooley, had held on to between Cranbury and Crosswicks.

Colonists in the Hudson Valley also increasingly regarded their remaining Indian neighbors with suspicion. To make matters worse, many settlers feared that the Moravians who had set up missions at mixed Munsee-Mahican communities at Shekomeko and Pine Plains in the Berkshire foothills in 1740 were secret Catholics in league with the French. Giving in to these fears, Dutchess County officials saw to it that the Moravian missionaries left in 1746, along with any loyal converts willing to follow them. Most moved to the small Pennsylvania mission town built for them north of Bethlehem, christened Friedenshuetten, "Huts of Peace." Hostile locals near Bethlehem almost immediately forced the Moravians to relocate the community twenty-five miles farther up the Lehigh River to a place the missionaries named Gnadenhuetten, "Huts of Grace." Situated at Lehighton, Pennsylvania, just above the Lehigh Gap, astride a key communications route to the Susquehanna Valley, the mission lay just across the river from the Munsee town of Pohopoco.

Indians living among worried settlers in New York's Orange and Ulster counties did not wait to be evicted during the anxious winter of 1745–46. They fled to their hunting camps at and around Cochecton after Allamaaseeit, a son of Tatapagh, brought news from the west in mid-December that French and Indians "at Mesasippi" were making large numbers of snowshoes. He reported that they planned to use them in carrying out a midwinter attack "against Albany, Soapus, and Minisink, and likewise the frontiers of Jersey and Pensylvania." The report had chilling credibility in the wake of a combined French and Indian attack on Saratoga some two weeks earlier.

The sudden withdrawal of the Esopus and Minisink Indians from the settlements alarmed the already concerned colonists. New York authorities dispatched a local militia colonel named Thomas De Key to find out what was going on. De Key's small party reached the Indian encampment at Cochecton in late December. In his subsequent report, the colonel stated that he believed the Indians at the camp numbered "about ninety or one hundred together, with their families." Their speaker told him that they had withdrawn into the interior because they had grown afraid of neighbors who were "always under arms." Assuring them that the settlers were not preparing an attack, De Key asked that they keep a sharp lookout for any signs of French raiders. They promised to do so and pledged to help colonists repel any assault launched against the Orange County frontier. Saying that they had recently lost their sachem, they told De Key that they would come to the county seat at Goshen to meet with the governor as soon as they were finished "debating out of which tribe a sachem should be chosen to govern the whole."

The Indians went on to say that they then consisted of the two tribes that De Key identified as Wolves and Turkeys. Neither were mentioned or drawn as signatures on the two deeds signed by Esopus and "Cashicton Indian" leaders shortly thereafter that finally lanced the long-festering boil of Indian resentment over the outrageous amount of land claimed in the Hardenbergh Patent. In early January 1746 the Indians themselves provided some insight into who the Wolves and Turkeys in this instance were when their newly selected sachem arrived with twelve of their chief men at Goshen with a wampum belt to renew their Covenant Chain obligations. De Key wrote that he spent an hour sitting tied to the sachem by this belt in symbolic assurance that their friendship would last "as long as the sun and moon endures." He did not, however, do more than identify the man and his entourage as "Cashighton Indians."

The identity of these Indians from Cochecton was cleared up twelve years later in another treaty meeting. At it, Teedyuscung held up a wampum belt on behalf of "Nimham the eldest principal chief of the Wappingers or Opings . . . living near Aesopus," who was said to be too sick to attend in person. Three years later, the aged Nimham himself held up the same belt at another meeting. This time, the belt was identified as "a large peace belt of sixteen rows with two hearts and the figure 1745 woven into it."

Little was heard of Munsees in corridors of colonial power in the years immediately following the end of King George's War in 1748. Some Indians in northern and central New Jersey got mixed up with rioting farmers still refusing to take out proprietary deeds or pay rents. Andrew Wooley spent years countering suits lodged by Lewis Morris's son, Robert Hunter Morris, aimed at evicting Indian people from their land at Cranbury. Indians repeatedly showed up at Rockaway, Merrick, and other places on Long Island to listen to sermons delivered by revivalist preacher Azariah Horton as he rode his circuit preaching to Native people and enslaved Africans.

Most of the time, however, Munsee people quietly traveled virtually unnoticed through their old homeland, continuing to camp in untenanted back lots or lands specially set aside for them. Many made, sold, and traded baskets, brooms, and herbal remedies to settlers. More than a few supplemented this income by hiring themselves out as seasonal laborers, handymen, and house servants. Able-bodied men often joined other Indians on crews of merchantmen and whalers sailing to Arctic oceans, European ports, and more distant destinations.

No matter how much they traded or how hard they worked, they mostly remained a poor people. Sickness and liquor sapped vitality and spread despair. Colonists in the settlements openly defied laws prohibiting sale of liquor to Indians. Few missed any opportunity to take advantage of alcohol-befuddled Munsees who passed through their neighborhoods. Nakedly manipulative deed deals made at the time were cynically dipped in drink and deceit. Late winters truly became starving times as impoverished families ran through their stocks of corn and flour. Malaria and other fevers racked bodies enfeebled by smallpox, malnutrition, and hard liquor. Many Munsees became apathetic and depressed as they trod through the lands of their ancestors. Selling or pawning furs, guns, and even their clothing for rum and beer may have seemed like little things to people who had bartered away a homeland.

Things were little better on the frontiers. Waves of traders, sometimes hauling few goods other than barrels of rum, descended on Indian towns along the Susquehanna River while Six Nations sachems simultaneously schemed to sell the ground out from under them. Reports reaching New York and Philadelphia were filled with accounts of brawls, assaults, thefts, rapes, and killings. Increasing numbers of reports noted Indian withdrawals farther west into the Ohio Valley. Others warned that Indians everywhere along the frontier were listening more closely to French agents urging them to abandon their Covenant Chain allies.

Although many suffered greatly, few completely gave way to despair. Some Munsees trying to understand why things were going so very wrong decided to hear what missionaries had to say on the subject. More than a few subsequently moved to the missions established by these preachers. These became both homes to converts and way stations for their more itinerant friends and relatives. Diaries chronicling daily life at places like Gnadenhuetten document a constant stream of Indian visitors.

Missions became safe zones where harassed people could take refuge, binge drinkers could dry out, and the hungry could get fed. Although missionaries would only permit converts to settle permanently, few turned away visitors willing to work, hunt, carry messages, or provide other services. Mission Indians often achieved a significant level of economic stability. They built bark-covered longhouses, more substantial log cabins, and frame churches and meetinghouses. Many of their buildings had glass windows and hinged doors. They also erected barns, mills, and millpond dams and races. Many enclosed house lots; fields; apple, peach, and cherry orchards; hog pens; and cattle troughs with stone walls and rail fences.

Only a small percentage of Indians in these mission towns permanently converted to Christianity, however. Some followed the spiritual path trod by Teedyuscung. Immediately after the Six Nations sold his land at Meniolagomeka out from under him, Teedyuscung joined the Moravians and accepted the name Gideon. Gideon's at least superficial conversion may have been inspired by the example set by Tatamy, whose own acceptance of Christianity played a major role in helping him keep his small plot of land at Stockertown on the Forks of Delaware after other Indians were evicted.

Unable or unwilling to buy his people's land at Meniolagomeka, as Tatamy had done at Stockertown, Gideon did the next best thing. He invited Moravians to establish a mission at the place in 1750. The mission lasted until 1754, when Pennsylvania authorities finally ordered the Indians to leave. Some of the townsfolk moved to Gnadenhuetten. Others followed Teedyuscung, who, after disavowing the new religion that had failed to protect his home and his people, finally moved to land under Six Nations control at Wyoming in the Susquehanna Valley.

Other Indians forced to leave the Munsee homeland turned elsewhere for spiritual renewal. Many would soon become followers of Neolin, a man colonists knew as the Delaware Prophet. Neolin called on his people to turn away from Europeans and their religion, guns, drink, and wares. He told followers that Kiisheelumukweenk would drive away the colonists and restore life to the way it was before Europeans arrived if they returned to the old ways.

A few followed the young Munsee mystic Papunhank. A grandson of Mamanuchqua, Papunhank was among the earlier Moravian converts at Shekomeko. He was inspired by dreams to seek a middle way incorporating what he thought were the most workable aspects of traditional and European beliefs. Leaving the Moravian brethren, he established a spiritual community of his own at Wyalusing, on the North Branch of the Susquehanna River, in 1752.

Only the most fervent believers moved permanently to religious communities built by prophets or missionaries. Most Munsees caught up in the religious enthusiasms sweeping through their towns chose to remain at home. Moses Tunda Tatamy and his brethren in New Jersey, and most of the Indians scattered across western Long Island, for example, stayed in their own settlements where they could receive or travel to hear circuit-riding clerics and itinerant preachers.

By 1754, neither prophets nor missionaries nor officials charged with enforcing laws meant to kept the peace could stand in the way of the four hundred thousand or so strangers now living on ancestral Munsee lands. Straining to break beyond the Appalachian mountain wall that had hemmed in settlers for more than a century and a half, they stood ready to sweep down onto the western lands uneasily occupied by displaced Munsees and other Indians under Iroquois suzerainty. Many of these colonists were newcomers alienated in one way or another from the societies they left behind. Most were young. Longing for homes of their own, few wanted to pay rent to Hudson Valley manor lords or buy the high-priced properties then on offer from proprietors in New Jersey and Pennsylvania. Whether they were looking for new lands for themselves or for territory to sell to others, all seemed determined to take what they could from Indians.

Munsees were not the only people threatened by new immigrants. Imperial officials and longtime residents looked for ways to channel the volatile mix of religion and rapacity that seemed to pulse through this land-hungry multitude. Soon Mohawks found themselves in the path of the demographic tidal wave. Unlike their other Six Nations confederates, who had thus far been called on to give up only tiny, albeit strategically placed, pieces of land for some forts and missions, the Mohawks faced the specter of utter dispossession. Colonists claimed nearly all of their lands, brandishing deeds, most of them as usual taking in far more than the Indians had agreed to give, and many of them patently fraudulent.

Fed up Mohawks came to New York in the early summer of 1753 with a long list documenting the worst excesses. They presented their grievances to George Clinton, who was then at the shank end of his ten-year tenure as governor of New York. An indifferent Clinton supported the colonists' claims. On the last day of the meeting an outraged Mohawk sachem, Theyanoguin, known among the colonists as Hendrick, announced that he would be sending a wampum belt to Onondaga demanding that the Covenant Chain be "broken between you and us."

This speech got the attention of the Board of Trade, whose members ordered that every province in British America send representatives to meet with the Six Nations to patch things up. They got their chance the following summer when commissioners from seven colonies got together at what became known as the Albany Congress to coordinate plans to counter French imperial ambitions in North America. Most met with the small embassies of Six Nations and River Indian sachems that trooped in at various times to address the delegates. Although the commissioners did not then know it, these meetings saved the Covenant Chain at a time when they would most need it. Some five hundred miles southwest of Albany, the young Virginian militia officer George Washington had just surrendered his force of four hundred men to six hundred French troops and one hundred Indian warriors at a hastily constructed stockade he dubbed Fort Necessity. The Virginians were there because the French had just started building a post of their own that they called Fort Duquesne at the Forks of the Ohio, on land claimed by their province. Like another killing 160 years later at Sarajevo, this incident would spark the outbreak of a world war.

On May 28, 1754, Washington and his men bushwhacked a French patrol camped unobtrusively in an out-of-the way spot. In the ensuing skirmish, one soldier escaped and made his way back to Fort Duquesne to alert the commander to the patrol's capture. Meanwhile the captured French soldiers denied being in the area to find out what the Virginians were up to, asserting they were on a diplomatic mission. Expecting trouble, Washington scrambled to build the little stockade he called Fort Necessity at a place called the Great Meadow, some miles below the French bastion. Outnumbered and suffering the greater share of casualties when the force from Fort Duquesne showed up for battle, Washington surrendered the place after a one-day siege. The French allowed the chastened young commander to march back to Virginia with his men after signing a piece of paper written in French (a language Washington did not understand) admitting that he had assassinated diplomats sent to parley with him.

Two deeds signed by Six Nations sachems under shady circumstances in Albany during the conference helped Munsees decide which side they would support when the fighting started. Negotiations for the first of these deals dragged on for five days, starting at a local tavern on July 5. The Pennsylvania contingent, led by Thomas Penn's brother John and including Benjamin Franklin, pressed Six Nations sachems to sell all Indian lands in the western region where Washington had just surrendered to the French. Everyone in the room knew that Indians whom they had already betrayed now lived on those lands under their supposed protection. They also knew for a certainty that these Indians would turn against them and join the French once they found out these last lands were sold out from under them.

None of this stopped either the Pennsylvanians or the Iroquois. By the time Conrad Weiser interpreted the last speech, the Iroquois had confirmed the 1736 deed to all lands in the province south of the Kittatinys and had signed a new deed accepting £400 for all land they claimed by conquest west of the Susquehanna River, south of a line running from the mouth of Penn's Creek west to the farthest limits of the province's charter bounds. Just two days later, an Albany trader named John Henry Lydius, representing a cartel of nearly eight hundred Connecticut settlers calling themselves the Susquehannah Company, persuaded eighteen Six Nations sachems to sign over all lands west of the Susquehanna River north of Penn's Creek for £2,000.

As soon as news of Lydius's purchase reached Philadelphia, the Pennsylvanians protested that the Susquehannah Company had no right to buy lands in their province. That did not deter the Connecticut men, who remained confident that their sea-to-sea charter still gave them the right to buy unpurchased Indian lands at their province's designated latitude as far west as the Pacific Ocean. Things soon grew more complicated. In 1755, representatives from another Connecticut cartel calling itself the Delaware Company got Nutimus and several other sachems well lubricated with alcohol to consent to two deed agreements. In these deeds the sachems identified themselves as Ninneepauues (a likely instance of the use of the word *nenapa*, "man"), "otherwise and in English known by the name of the Delaware

Indians." They accepted a total of 718 Spanish milled dollars and un-specified quantities of trade goods for lands taken from them by the Walking Purchase and subsequent disputed deals. They then returned to the Susquehanna Valley to await developments.

They were not the only people in the region waiting on develop-ments. News from the frontier was bad. During the summer of 1754, Abenakis from Canada burned some houses around Schaghticoke and persuaded the sixty or so Indian men, women, and children liv-ing there at the time to leave with them. Thus ended the settlement that Edmund Andros had started nearly eighty years before to protect New York. By winter, Abenakis were traveling through small River Indian encampments below Albany, urging their occupants to join them in Canada.

Relieved colonists welcomed thousands of British troops under the overall command of General Edward Braddock that landed at Boston, New York, and Potomac River shores during the winter of 1754–55. Those Indians still living in the settlements looked on with less en-thusiasm as militiamen began drilling with regulars on local parade grounds. They, like the British, were still formally at peace with the French. Provincial officials and army officers urged those who would listen to sign up for expeditions that were sure to seize Canada and Acadia when the campaigning season reopened in the spring. Politely declining to touch pens to muster rolls, most Munsees chose instead to watch and wait.

They did not have to wait long. Braddock soon announced his plans to take Fort Duquesne and march north to join another Brit-ish army, then gathering at Albany to advance on Fort Niagara. One month later, Braddock began marching his two-thousand-man force and its straggling supply train up the wagon road from Alexandria, Virginia, toward Fort Duquesne. Braddock's axmen and regulars col-lided with 250 French Canadians and 640 Western and Canadian In-dians near the banks of the Monongahela River on July 9, 1755. It is not known if any Munsees were involved in the fight, which turned into one of the most complete defeats the British suffered at the hands of Indians. Only a quarter of more than 1,200 British troops engaged came out of the battle unscathed. The Indians and the French together suffered fewer than fifty casualties.

It was the beginning of a bad summer for the British. News of several other misadventures flashed through the Indian diaspora. Teedyuscung and other sachems metaphorically called women by the Six Nations in councils shed their symbolic petticoats and, to paraphrase Francis Jennings, painted themselves black, summoned their young men to the war dance, grabbed their hatchets, and turned east. By the time winter closed in, hundreds of farmsteads along the Delaware and Susquehanna valley frontier lay abandoned, their occupants killed, captured, or driven away by vengeful Munsee and other Indian raiding parties.

The terrible fighting in the forests was already well under way by the time Great Britain formally declared war on France the following spring. The French, the British, and, soon enough, the breakaway provinces that would become the United States took care to observe the diplomatic niceties still governing war etiquette in Europe. Indians and colonists on the frontier, fighting to save their homes and families, engaged each other by altogether different sets of rules that disregarded notions of just or civilized war. Indians and intruders fought an implacable war that paid only slight regard to formal declarations or solemnly signed treaties. Characterized by wrenching spasms of violence separated by months and sometimes years of anxious waiting, their war would end only after 1815, when Great Britain finally cut Indians off from their last sources of support against the Americans. Scattered and exhausted by sixty years of struggle against overwhelming odds, even the most fervent true believers among the Indians finally gave up their last attempts to regain their lost homelands and instead bent their efforts towards the business of getting through the long years of exile that followed.

The fuel that had kept Indians and colonists fighting one another was a singularly toxic mix of fear and hope. Fear spurred on people who increasingly regarded each other as race enemies. Charismatic prophets and rapscallion provocateurs stoked hopes that eradication of race enemies would end the fear. Outrageous atrocities and ranting threats silenced voices of moderation and confirmed the worst stereotypes. Leaders who held up the hope of celestial victory made promises that sustained followers unable to prevail decisively on battlefields, in boardrooms, or in council rings. The result was the creation of a pervasive atmosphere of terror as dark as some of the deepest forest morasses colonists christened Shades of Death.

The shape this war would take became evident by the fall of 1755. Munsee, Shawnee, and other warriors from Wyoming, Shamokin, and Paxtang (now Harrisburg, Pennsylvania) prepared to head off to war and sent as many of their families as would go much farther north and west to more remote towns like Kittanning on the Allegheny River. Others went east to join Pompton, Cranbury, Crosswicks, and southern New Jersey Indians, who wasted little time assuring New Jersey authorities of their continued friendship. They confirmed their peaceful intentions at a treaty held at Crosswicks in early January 1756. The closer-in towns at the Great Island on the West Branch of the Susquehanna; at Tioga, Atsinksink, and Secaughcung in the Chemung Valley; and at Otseningo and Ochquaga farther up the Susquehanna's North Branch became staging areas for warriors. There they formed themselves into small raiding parties that first struck outlying settlements at Penn's Creek and the Juniata River. Teedyuscung and other sachems assumed the roles of war captains and led their men on raids attacking Minisink and other lands taken from their people. In late November one of these war parties raided Gnadenhuetten, killing eleven of sixteen missionaries and carrying off or scattering most of the town's Indian neighbors.

Settlers and Indians fleeing the war parties spread fear and terror through the settlements. The inclination toward vigilantism seen in the murders at Cacoosing nearly thirty years earlier now metastasized into a mindless viciousness that would soon grow into something much more murderously malignant. In early March a gang of local settlers murdered a family of Indians taking shelter among colonists at Walden, New York. Six weeks later, another mob wantonly slaughtered members of an Indian family in their wigwam at Peapack, New Jersey. Unable to guarantee the safety of River Indians near the settlements, the newly appointed British Superintendent of Indian Affairs Sir William Johnson urged Indians gathered at Wiccopee on Fishkill Creek in Dutchess County to move among other River Indians already settled on Mohawk lands along the Schoharie Valley west of the Catskills. Those not moving west relocated east to Stockbridge. Few at either place would ever return to their Hudson Valley homes for more than the briefest of visits.

The tempo of violence increased as provincial authorities declared war on the Delawares and Shawnees living out west, authorized bounties for scalps of hostile Indians, and looked the other way when settlers casually murdered Native noncombatants in the woods. By the summer of 1756, settlers were fortifying their houses, provincial authorities were building lines of forts on their frontiers, and colonial raiding parties were attacking Kittanning and the Indian towns on the West Branch of the Susquehanna. Although the assault on Kittanning managed to do some damage, militia forces undertaking long-range raids tended to suffer higher casualties than they inflicted on their intended targets.

Having exacted a measure of vengeance on the colonists, hard-headed sachems like Teedyuscung and Nimham began thinking about how they might extract their people from the war. The first two years of fighting had gone badly for the British. Yet Munsees and other Delawares who lived in the British settlements or had been abroad on British merchantmen and men-of-war knew that British sea power and their overwhelming numerical superiority on the ground in North America favored their chances for ultimate victory. They also did not believe French promises that they would not take Indian lands.

Teedyuscung and his colleagues started searching for ways to play the Europeans against one another in the time-honored way of their ancestors. They knew that the British regarded the French as the more dangerous of their enemies in America. Letting on that they might consider leaving the French to fend for themselves, Teedyuscung and his colleagues must have been pleased to find British authorities willing to make separate peaces with them. This was the time when

Teedyuscung, Tatamy, Weiser, Indian Affairs Superintendent John-son's deputy George Croghan, and Moravian lay missionary Christian Frederick Post made their reputations as major frontier diplomats. Crisscrossing the frontier in a colonial form of shuttle diplomacy, they gradually brought Indians and officials together at a series of meetings.

After several preliminaries at Johnson's Mohawk Valley head-quarters, Delawares and Shawnees taking refuge above Tioga made peace with the British at Onondaga during the summer of 1756. The small number of representatives accompanying Nutimus and Wyo-ming Shawnee leader Paxinosa to the meeting suggests that most In-dians refugees were at the very least wary of making any deal with the colonists at that point. Johnson would not be denied, however, and had his supporters among the Six Nations pressure them to change their minds. He soon ceremoniously removed the metaphorical petti-coats from Nutimus's Tioga Delawares and Paxinosa's Susquehanna Valley Shawnees after both leaders joined Six Nations sachems pledg-ing to join in the war against the French.

Although the British wanted to believe otherwise, most Munsee and many Unami, Shawnee, Conoy, and other Susquehanna Valley expatriates remained hostile and unreconciled. Teedyuscung took the lead in diplomatic efforts on their behalf at this time. His influ-ence over all but his immediate followers, however, was shaky at best. Teedyuscung managed to get a large number of Indians from the Susquehanna country to attend a major peace treaty meeting held at Easton from late July to early August 1757. By raising the spec-ter of the Walking Purchase, he almost derailed the proceedings. It would be a while before Teedyuscung would be able to use figurative dirt to metaphorically bury axes still being wielded with deadly ef-fect by Munsee warriors nursing grievances over lands lost and rela-tives killed. Settlers recognized Munsees and Unamis among warriors who continued raiding frontier farmsteads throughout the spring and summer of 1758. These attacks were diminished but not entirely halted as shuttling diplomats persuaded leaders of nearly every Indian community from New York to Ohio to send representatives to Easton for a grand meeting planned for the first weeks of autumn, 1758.

Temporary truces were finally worked out as Munsees and Unamis tied up loose ends with provincial authorities in New Jersey during the run-up to the meeting. Teedyuscung and other descendants of Weequehela gave their powers of attorney to Tatamy and three other countrymen to settle remaining land claims south of the Raritan River. Belts were then circulated through the Jersey communities and Chemung Valley towns, inviting those with outstanding grievances to settle them at a late-summer conference at the old West Jersey capital of Burlington.

Delegates representing Minisinks, Delawares, and Senecas from Chemung country met with recently appointed New Jersey royal governor Francis Bernard at Burlington on August 7, 1758. The Minisink speaker greeted the new governor and his council before deferring to messengers from his uncles, the Senecas. After addressing the Minisinks as "Munseys" and "women . . . who cannot hold treaties by themselves," the Seneca speaker told Bernard that the Six Nations would allow the Munsees to settle remaining land claims in the province with him at the upcoming meeting at Easton. He then displayed a belt and affirmed that the Six Nations, not Teedyuscung, would represent Indians at Easton.

On September 12, Tatamy and his three countrymen representing Munsee interests in New Jersey lands met separately with provincial officials at Crosswicks. They conveyed all but a tract of land owned by Tatamy at the mouth of the Neshanic River and a couple of other small plots south of the Raritan to the New Jersey government. In return, the province promised to purchase lands for a reservation for their people in Burlington county. Using $1,600 allocated for the purpose by the provincial assembly, the officials purchased three thousand acres for the reservation at Edgepillock, soon called Brotherton, in the heart of the pinelands a year later.

On October 7 more than five hundred Indians representing the Munsees and nearly every other Indian nation barring the way to the Forks of the Ohio gathered on the Easton village green. Both sides took care to be as clear in their identifications as in their purposes; all had much at stake. Munsee and other Delaware towns stood directly

astride the intended British invasion route. They were also still formally at war with Pennsylvania. They wanted to secure their lands
and lives. Just as they put their trust in Tatamy and his colleagues to
press their claims in New Jersey, the Munsees must have hoped that
Teedyuscung would help them get the best possible terms for a peace
they very much wanted.

Six Nations sachems also wanted peace, but in keeping with their
unswerving policy on the issue, it had to be a peace made on their own
terms. Still officially neutral even after Seneca and other Iroquois warriors openly joined the French, they wanted a settlement that would
assure their paramount position in the east and support their claims
farther west. The needs of Munsees and other Indians took a back-
seat to these goals. Iroquois diplomats pushed Teedyuscung aside and
took over the meeting. After a month of private meetings and public
declarations, they stood as guarantors for a general peace arranged
on behalf of the Munsees and other Indians who had caused such
mayhem on the Pennsylvania frontier. The blood these warriors had
shed persuaded Pennsylvanians to give up claims to lands west of
the Appalachians purchased illegally from the Six Nations in 1754
but not yet paid for. They knew that bad feelings over this deal were
among the grievances that caused many Munsees to go to war them.
Pennsylvania's surrender of this territory to the Six Nations allowed
the formally neutral confederacy to bloodlessly claim land actually
reconquered by Munsee and other warriors.

Six Nations sachems also sat silently while colonists demanded repatriation of all captives, whether or not they wanted to return. They
also refused Munsee and other expatriate Indian requests that they be
granted secure titles to lands they still occupied in the Susquehanna
Valley. Seeing the way things were going, Teedyuscung withdrew his
allegations accusing the Penn family of land fraud, blaming the war
instead on bad feelings left over from what his people felt was the
judicial murder of Weequehela.

The best Munsees were able to do at Easton was to get Six Nations
help in negotiating a final deed adjudicating their remaining claims
to land in northern New Jersey. On October 23, 1758, Minisink and

Oping sachems accepted one thousand Spanish pieces of eight for all land north of a line running from the Raritan River up to the Lamington Falls and west to the Delaware Water Gap (reserving only their hunting and fishing rights). Manawkyhickon and his compatriots confirmed this and a September 12, 1758, deed to all land south of the line two days later. This done, the assembled colonial authorities made a point of assuring the sachems that outstanding disputes like the Walking Purchase problem would be submitted to the Crown for resolution.

The 1758 treaty at Easton marked the last time Munsees would make decisions that had major consequences for their old lands. Their decision to sell all but their hunting and fishing rights in the northern half of New Jersey and their assent to the creation of a reservation in the southern part of the province ended a relationship that had begun more than a century and a half earlier. And, although they would continue joining other nations in resisting westward expansion for the next fifty years, their decision to sign on to the general peace at Easton ended their last serious military effort to recover territory in New Jersey or any other part of their ancestral homeland.

Settlements made at the Easton treaty had the immediate effect of freeing British armies advancing to the west from the threat of Indian attacks. In Pennsylvania, British troops pushed forward upon receipt of the news. Indian allies of the French just as quickly left their camps around the Forks of the Ohio. Suddenly abandoned by their Indian allies and now overwhelmingly outnumbered by the British, the French blew up Fort Duquesne and withdrew north to Fort Niagara as British troops neared the post in late November. Another army, this one led by Sir William Johnson, took Fort Niagara the following summer. A few months after that, raiders led by Robert Rogers burned the Abenaki stronghold of St. Francis Odanak, where many Mahicans and a few of their Munsee relatives lived. Other victories that year at Ticonderoga, Crown Point, and most tellingly, at Quebec all but ensured final British victory in North America.

Meanwhile, Pennsylvania authorities followed up on their promise to refer the Walking Purchase problem back to the mother country despite Teedyuscung's belated insistence that land had not been the reason they had gone to war in 1755 (he would change his position on this matter several times). Others' interests also were at stake. Imperial authorities were intent on finally imposing the kind of strong centralized control over the provinces they had been struggling to establish since they first conquered New Netherland a century earlier. Proprietors, manor lords, and small freeholders were determined to secure vested rights and interests. Landless tenants and townsfolk were looking for ways to get the rights that property ownership traditionally conferred on landowners. All had supported Indian claims when they thought it was in their interest to do so. Confidence in their now overwhelming power convinced them that the time had come to nullify or ignore Indian rights, especially those claimed by much diminished nations like the Munsees.

The growing impact of these attitudes was seen in the ways authorities handled the endgame in the Walking Purchase dispute. Benjamin Franklin, who represented the Pennsylvania assembly in London at the time, laid the case in front of the Privy Council in 1759. The council, as was its way in such matters, passed the issue on to the Board of Trade. The board punted to Sir William Johnson, directing him to make the final decision on the case. Johnson let three years pass before he got to it. Other problems—like Indian anger over British refusal to honor their promises to leave captured French posts once fighting ended, and colonial impatience over Indian slowness in returning promised captives—made more insistent claims on his time. In June 1762 he finally got "Delawares, Mohiccons, and Opings" represented by Teedyuscung together with Pennsylvania authorities at another meeting in Easton to settle the matter.

Johnson had no direct interest in the issue. His decision, however, was a foregone conclusion. He revealed the considerations foremost on his mind when deciding Indian land disputes in a letter penned a few years later. Johnson was then serving as the Crown-appointed arbitrator in another Indian lawsuit, this one brought by Daniel Nimham. A young man who had just succeeded Nimham as the Oping, or Wappinger, sachem, Daniel was suing the Philipse family and other manor lords for land taken from them in Dutchess County.

As in the Walking Purchase case, where Indians worked with Quakers against the Penn family, the young Nimham made common cause with rent-rioting tenants intent on breaking up vast manor landholdings in the Hudson Valley. Daniel traveled to Great Britain to place the matter before the Board of Trade after being put off by local authorities. Finding merit in the case, the board acted as they had in the Walking Purchase dispute, ordering Johnson to give the Indians justice in the matter.

More introspective in his writings than most of his contemporaries, Johnson was given to unburdening himself in correspondence with trusted confidants and colleagues. In a particularly revealing passage from one of these letters, he wrote that he felt that it was his duty to support just claims made by powerful nations or by people connected with them capable of resenting what he termed "a neglect." Less than clear-cut claims pressed by, as he put it, "long domesticated" nations, he went on, "had better remain unsupported than that several old titles of his majesty's subjects should therefore be disturbed." Acting on these sentiments, Johnson found for the Pennsylvania proprietors in 1762 and the Hudson Valley manor lords three years later.

Johnson might have made different decisions if militant Munsees resenting neglect had carried on the war despite what he called their long domestication. The fact that Johnson was able to make his decisions stick reveals the fundamental shift in attitudes that accompanied imperial victory in the Seven Years' War. Johnson was nearly alone among British commanders, most of whom no longer found it necessary to observe diplomatic niceties when dealing with any Indians. The British refusal to honor their promises to leave the western posts following the formal end of hostilities in 1763 did not go unnoticed by Indians. In a series of counterstrokes made between 1763 and 1764, Indian warriors captured and destroyed all but two of the occupied posts west of the Appalachians. Niagara and Detroit, the two forts that drove off initial attacks, were subjected to sieges that were only lifted by counteroffensives. Chemung Valley Munsees, inspired by their prophet Wangomend, joined in the fighting against the British. Johnson responded by sending a column of 120 Oneida, Tuscarora, and Delaware warriors to destroy the Chemung towns during the summer of 1764. As their ancestors had done so many times before, the Munsees and their compatriots abandoned their towns and withdrew in front of the advancing column. And, as other invaders had done in the past, the advancing force plundered and burned the Indians' houses, destroyed standing crops, and cut down orchards before withdrawing to their base.

This was also the time when vengeful frontier settlers, no longer fearing either Indian retaliation or provincial retribution, began casually slaughtering any Indians they encountered in the Delaware and Susquehanna valleys. The most prominent victim was Teedyuscung, who burned to death in his cabin as a fire swept through his people's town at Wyoming on April 19, 1763. Although Pennsylvanians suspected that Connecticut arsonists set the fire, no one was ever brought to trial. Elsewhere, individual murderers like Tom Quick and a gang of killers known as the Paxton Boys callously killed inoffensive Indians in the most atrocious ways possible to spread the pall of terror that had hung over the frontier since 1755.

By 1765, most Munsees had moved much farther west to the Allegheny Valley of western Pennsylvania. Not all, however, lived in these towns all the time. Despite the danger of sudden attack, Munsees continued to live near or travel through their old homeland during the final years of British colonial rule. Daniel Nimham and other Wappingers forced to abandon their last homes in Dutchess County moved to Indian Town in nearby Stockbridge, Massachusetts. A few Munsees also stayed on with other Delawares on the Brotherton Reservation at Edgepillock. Although Munsees and their fellow expatriates abandoned the Wyoming and Chemung valleys following the destruction of their towns there, others continued to live farther up the North Branch of the Susquehanna River at Otseningo and Ochquaga. Just downriver, Papunhank allowed the Moravians to establish a mission they christened Friedenshuetten next to his town of Wyalusing after his people returned to the locale as the immediate impact of Paxton Boys terror receded.

In 1765, persistent small groups of families and friends continued to hunt, fish, camp, and plant in remote places within their ancestral homeland. One of these groups seen near Ringwood, New Jersey, was described by an ironworking German immigrant named Peter Hasenclever late that summer. He seemed most impressed by their sense of generosity in the face of their extreme poverty. Briefly alluding to their harvests that often seemed to fail, he described them as a people who "dwell in the woods, roaming constantly, and subsisting almost entirely on the chase."

Hasenclever made a telling observation. For the first time in their recorded history, Munsees were cut off from all but the most remote and least productive parts of their former homeland. Mostly living far from ancestral graves and sheltering spirits, they had nothing left but each other. It was enough to see them through the next decades of wanderings and subsequent life on reservations, reserves, and other faraway places. It would not be enough to stop strangers from driving them ever westward. They were adrift on alien terrain far from the ancient hills that had anchored them to the lands of their forebears. Although they would show time and again that they could defy soldiers' bayonets, they had lost the power to prevent those who sent the Long Knives from ultimately intruding into even the most personal parts of their private lives.

12

MANY TRAILS, 1767–TODAY

Very nearly all Munsees had to share their lives with strangers by 1767. The few Munsee families still living on the fringes of their old homeland resided among Unamis at Brotherton in Edgepillock, with Unchechaugs and other eastern Long Island Indians at and around Poosepatuck, with Mahicans and Northern Indians at Stockbridge, and with Western Abenakis at rebuilt Odanak. Some who had moved thirty years earlier to the small River Indian community in the Schoharie Valley were now wedged between Mohawk Indian towns and Palatine German farmsteads just west of the Catskills. Others still trying to make a go of it in the nearby upper Susquehanna Valley lived at places like the Moravian mission town of Friedenshuetten and Papunhank's nearby revivalist Indian community at Wyalusing. More lived in mixed Indian communities like Tioga, Otseningo, and Ochquaga with Mohawk and Oneida Iroquois émigrés and Tuscarora, Unami, Mahican, Shawnee, Conoy, and Nanticoke expatriates.

The majority of Munsees, probably around one thousand people all told, were now living with different strangers much farther west. Some lived in or near Gekelemukpechink in Ohio. More made their homes in Seneca, Mingo, Wyandot, and Mesquakie settlements at Goschgosching and other upper Allegheny River towns near present-day Tionesta, Pennsylvania. Others lived a bit farther south at and around the large town of Kuskuskies on the Beaver River in present-day Lawrence

County, Pennsylvania, with Unami, Mahican, and Mingo neighbors. Many of the people living at Kuskuskies listened attentively to the nativist Delaware Prophet and the relocated Chemung Valley revivalist Wangomend. Increasingly, most people living at these other locales began joining kinsmen and -women already living farther west at and around places like Gekelemukpechink.

Wherever they lived, Munsees began marrying Indians from foreign nations and other strangers, as marriageable partners speaking their own language became harder to find. This necessity created new realities. The problems of fitting into the family of a spouse practicing different cultural traditions multiplied in direct proportion to the rising number of mixed marriages. Clan and family affiliations of one spouse often did not fit easily with those of the other. Other difficulties arose when matrilineal Munsees married people belonging to nations organized along patrilineal principles, like the Shawnees. Patrilineally inclined families often demanded that wives move into their new husbands' households just as determinedly as matrilineal Munsee and Unami households expected the opposite arrangement. Couples unwilling to break off their relationship when they could not agree on a residence increasingly struck out on their own elsewhere.

Traditionally, even in their homeland, many Munsee children had grown up in households where multiple dialects, and sometimes entirely different languages, were regularly spoken. Munsees now found that their traditional encouragement of fluency in several languages served them well. Spouses in mixed marriages often had to learn to speak each other's languages while raising their children in one or the other family's household. Fluency in multiple languages went far in smoothing over rough patches when it came time for people to make difficult choices. In the past, Munsee men had often had to decide whether their primary loyalty lay with their mother's family or with the family they married into. This choice could be particularly difficult when the man in question was the sachem of his wife's community. Although primary data documenting choices made by Munsee sachems in their homeland are lacking, colonial records amply chronicle the overpowering sense of belonging felt by many captives adopted into Indian families. This suggests that most sachems took their obligations to the people of the communities they guided very seriously.

The need to choose one's nationality after marriage made matters even more difficult for Munsees living in multicultural communities after 1767. Increasingly, Munsee women as well as men now had to make this decision. Although documentation chronicling such decisions is spotty, their effects can be seen. Many Munsee family names later turned into surnames primarily found in other Indian communities, as Munsee spouses took on new nationalities. The Munsee Nimham family name, for example, gradually became a prominent Oneida surname as the children of Munsee Nimham men married to Oneida women adopted the nationality of their Oneida mothers but kept their father's surname.

Munsee lineages finally lost cohesion and purpose during the nineteenth century as members married into neighboring communities like the Oneidas and into other more distant nations. The larger multiclan Wolf, Turkey, and Turtle phratry groups lasted longer. These, too, eventually fell by the wayside as Munsees and other Delawares found it necessary to look farther afield to find marriage partners. As their traditional matrilineal extended family, lineage, and phratry organizations lost numbers and ceased to function effectively, most Munsees increasingly chose to adopt the American and Canadian form of bilateral social organization centering on nuclear families.

Traditional phratry affiliations served as a way to divide up ritual responsibilities among those continuing to observe the annual Big House ceremonies in increasingly scattered and shrinking Munsee, Delaware, and Mahican exile communities. Even the phratries gradually disappeared as Christian conversion and increasing interest in the Native American Church drew adherents away from Big House congregations. The Eastern Oklahoma Delaware community, the last to observe the ceremony, gathered for its final full-scale Big House observance in 1924. After that the associations of particular people and families with particular phratries finally faded from the memories of all but a dwindling number of traditionalists who continued to speak their ancestral language.

Many paths led to changes great and small in Munsee life after 1766 (see map 9). None, however, traced a direct route. Like the roads and rivers Munsees traveled into exile, their personal lives traversed tortuously twisty terrain. Munsees embarking on these journeys had to develop new habits of mind in order to meet new challenges in strange lands. A bewildering and seemingly ever-changing assortment of parties, coalitions, and interest groups united and divided them along the way. Feelings of love and hate for and against Moravian and Presbyterian missionaries, nativists like the Delaware Prophet, revivalists like Papunhank and Wangomend, and traditional metewak joined and split Munsee families and factions along the Upper Susquehanna during the first decades in exile.

Divergent loyalist, neutral, and pro-American sympathies roused during the American Revolution divided Munsees for decades after the war ended. Later on, Munsees living on American reservations and Canadian reserves had to choose between Indian parties advocating continued tribal communal governance versus Citizen parties calling on members to take personal ownership of allotted lands and assume rights and obligations of private citizenship. Munsees in a society dominated by racially obsessed whites discriminating against people of color and generally looking down on Indians had to choose a racial identity or have one thrust on them. Many Munsees have only recently begun again regarding their Indian identity as a good thing.

All this does not mean that Munsee history after 1767 was a confused jumble of random, unrelated events. No nation, not even one with a track record for flexible adaptability as strong as that held by Munsees, can withstand overwhelming chaos for very long. Difficult as things sometimes were, catastrophically chaotic conditions seldom lasted very long. Munsees confronting change were helped, as ethnologist Edward Spicer would have said, by their enduring sense of themselves as members of families and communities and, perhaps most important of all, as custodians of cultural traditions worth

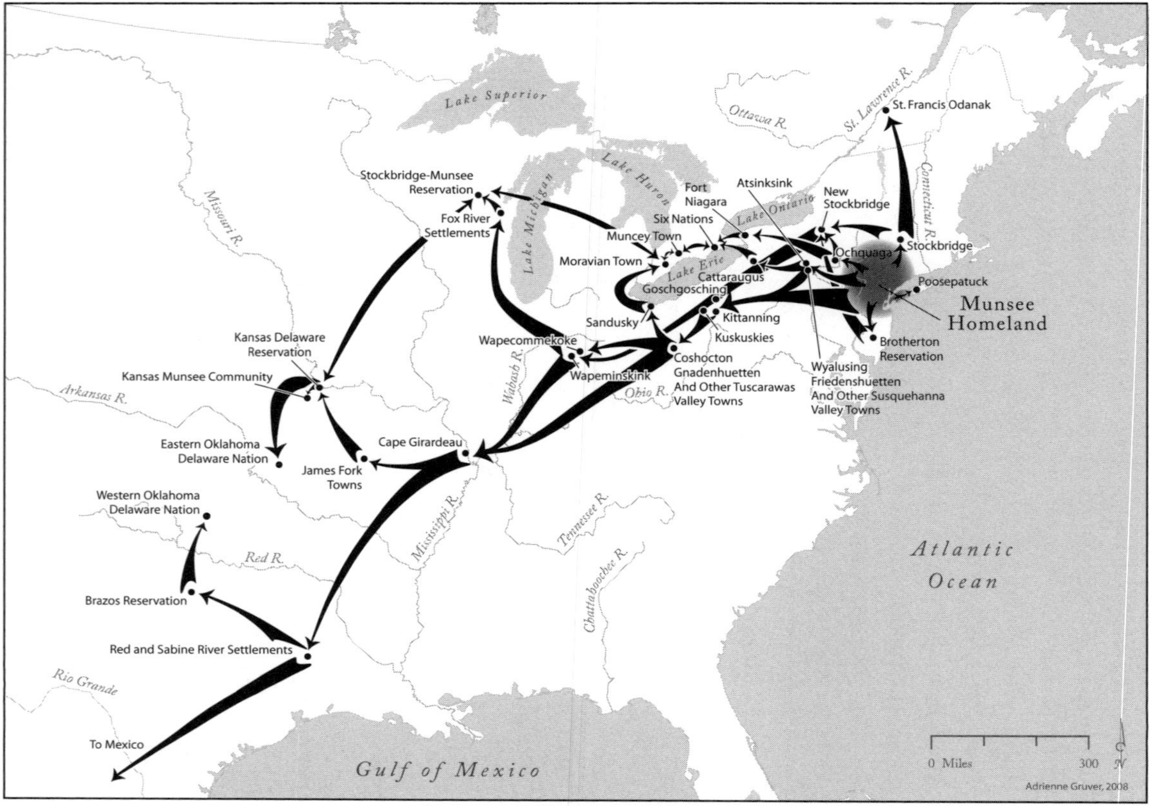

Map 9. Munsee relocations in exile, 1770s–1860s.

Munsee Homeland

Atlantic Ocean

Gulf of Mexico

St. Francis Odanak
St. Lawrence R.
Ottawa R.
Lake Superior
Lake Huron
Lake Michigan
Lake Erie
Lake Ontario
Connecticut R.
Stockbridge
Poosepatuck
Brotherton Reservation
New Stockbridge
Wyalusing
Friedenshuetten
And Other Susquehanna Valley Towns
Atsinksink
Fort Niagara
Six Nations
Cattaraugus
Goschgoschink
Kittanning
Kuskuskies
Coshocton
Gnadenhuetten
And Other Tuscarawas Valley Towns
Muncey Town
Moravian Town
Sandusky
Wapencommikonk
Wapeminskink
Ohio R.
Wabash R.
Tennessee R.
Chattahoochee R.
Stockbridge-Munsee Reservation
Fox River Settlements
Cape Girardeau
Mississippi R.
Kansas Delaware Reservation
Kansas Munsee Community
Eastern Oklahoma Delaware Nation
James Fork Towns
Missouri R.
Arkansas R.
Red R.
Western Oklahoma Delaware Nation
Brazos Reservation
Red and Sabine River Settlements
Rio Grande
To Mexico

0 Miles   300
Adrienne Gruver, 2008

230

preserving. Not all Munsees always felt the same way, and many chose paths that took them far from their roots. A sufficient number, however, always thought that their identities as Munsee people were important enough to preserve.

The few who continued living in the east in mixed communities at Poosepatuck, Stockbridge, Brotherton, and the Upper Susquehanna towns found themselves at the center of the drift toward colonial rebellion in the years immediately following 1767. Many but not all of Tackapousha's and Suscaneman's descendants moved, along with Southern New England Indian adherents of the Brothertown Movement, from Long Island to Stockbridge, Scaticook, and other Housatonic River mission towns during the last quarter of the eighteenth century. Many people living on the Brotherton Reservation in New Jersey later joined their near-namesake co-religionists during the first decade of the nineteenth century.

The Unchechaug language was probably last spoken by Indian people at Poosepatuck sometime after constitutional framer and future president James Madison collected a small vocabulary of their words while visiting the locale in 1801. Several hundred Unchechaug descendants, including some whose ancestors may have spoke Munsee, continue to live on the Poosepatuck Reservation in Mastic.

Other people tracing their descent to Indian forebears also continued to live in Brooklyn, Staten Island, and parts of New Jersey and adjacent sections of New York. Although the small reservations in present-day Nassau County completely fell from documentary notice sometime during the 1700s, several families claiming descent from Tackapousha's brother Chopeycannows and other Matinecock ancestors continue to make their homes on western Long Island. Other families claiming Munsee ancestry live in small enclaves throughout the Hudson River valley.

At Stockbridge, increasing numbers of Massachusetts settlers flooding into the Berkshires bought or leased much of the town's lands after 1767. Soon outnumbering the Native population, non-Indians held a controlling interest at Stockbridge by the time the Revolutionary War broke out in 1775. Daniel Nimham and his son

Abraham joined other Stockbridge Indians helping rebel forces drive British troops from Boston, capture Fort Ticonderoga, and defeat Burgoyne's army at Saratoga. Abraham was given command of an all-Indian Stockbridge rifle company formed while Washington's army was encamped at Morristown, New Jersey, during the winter of 1777–78. Ordered to join troops covering British positions north of New York City, the company fought in several skirmishes. Both Abraham and his father, along with most of the company, subsequently were killed in a fight with British dragoons at Cortlandt Ridge in the north Bronx on August 31, 1778.

Most of the few Munsees living with other River Indians in Mohawk territory at Schoharie sided with the British when the war broke out. Surrounded by rebel sympathizers, nearly all had to leave in early 1777 after it became clear that Mohawks still mourning the recent death of their patron Sir William Johnson in 1774 would remain loyal to the Crown. A few joined the Delaware main body in Ohio. Some moved in with other Mohawks at Ochquaga and nearby Upper Susquehanna towns. Most moved to the Iroquois refugee encampment at Fort Niagara, set up and supplied by the British Indian Office run by the late Sir William's son and successor, Guy Johnson. Esopus warriors taking refuge at Niagara, like Harman Hekan's descendant Jacob Hagan, joined Loyalist rangers raiding outlying settlements along the New York, New Jersey, and Pennsylvania frontiers. These men were led by Mohawk captain Joseph Brant and Loyalist officer Walter Butler. Raiders going to and from Niagara often stopped at Ochquaga for rest and resupply.

As much divided in their sympathies as the residents of the Delaware capital at Coshocton, Ohio, the inhabitants of Ochquaga suffered the same fate as the Delawares. Like Coshocton, Ochquaga was hastily evacuated during the early fall of 1778, when news reached the town of the imminent arrival of a rebel column led by New York militia colonel William Butler (no relation to Walter). And, like the soldiers who laid waste to Coshocton and the other Delaware towns in Ohio, Butler's militia column systematically destroyed houses, fields, and orchards at Ochquaga and every other Indian community along the Upper Susquehanna. The only house they left standing among the forty log cabins (some, Butler noted, with leaded glass windows and hinged doors) at Ochquaga belonged to an Oneida family. It was spared because the Oneidas and Tuscaroras were the only Iroquois nations openly supporting the American war effort.

Loyalist Indian families burned out of their homes at Ochquaga mostly moved to Niagara for the duration of the war. Pro-American townsfolk subsequently mostly sought shelter in Oneida country. The latter families were probably burned out of their homes a second time when a Loyalist column led by Brant burned the chief Oneida town of Kanonwalohale and the nearby fort built by the Americans in 1780. Many of these people joined other Oneidas swelling Indian refugee ranks at Fort Niagara.

After the war, victorious Americans refused to allow Munsees and other Indian people forced from their homes on the upper Susquehanna to return, no matter which side they had taken during the conflict. Pro-American Tuscaroras, for example, had to leave their Susquehanna homes and move farther north among the Oneidas. Many pro-British Munsee refugees either stayed around Fort Niagara with exiled Mohawks or settled nearby with Senecas at Cattaraugus.

Surviving Stockbridge Indian soldiers returned to a community that was no longer their own. What was worse, they were no longer welcome in their own homes. Some three hundred Indian Stockbridgers, mostly Mahicans but including members of the Nimham family and a few other people from Wappinger and Esopus countries, took up a longstanding Oneida invitation to settle among them in Madison County, New York, in 1785. Some Stockbridgers also moved north to the Abenaki town at St. Francis Odanak. A few trekked west to join the Delaware Indian main body in Ohio. Family traditions affirm that a small number of families refused to leave, settling in remote hollows in the mountainous country above Stockbridge.

British authorities set aside land in Ontario for Indians sheltering at Niagara who were unable to return to their old homes after the war ended. The overwhelming majority of Munsees at Niagara joined Mohawks and other Loyalist Indians moving to these reserves.

Some may have been in the group led by Mohawk leader John Dese-rontyon that relocated to the ninety-four-thousand-acre Tyendinaga Reserve established at the Bay of Quinte on the northeast shore of Lake Ontario. Most, however, moved with nearly 450 Mohawks and 1,400 other Iroquois and their allies following Joseph Brant to land reserved for them on the Grand River in Ontario during the winter of 1784–85. Situated some fifty miles west of Niagara, the Six Nations Reserve originally covered a six-mile strip on either side of the lower fifty miles of the Grand River, from the present-day city of Brantford to the river's mouth at Lake Erie.

Some 162 Ochquagas and 231 Delawares were living among 1,843 Indians on the nearly one-million-acre Six Nations Reserve by 1785. Although this census does not break these numbers down further, later records noting Esopus and other River Indian residents on the reserve indicate that a goodly number of the enumerated Ochquagas and Del-awares were Munsees, Mahicans, and people closely linked to both na-tions. Some of these people later moved on to other places. More than a few moved to the sites of the upper and lower Muncey towns built on Chippewa land northwest of the Six Nations Reserve near the headwa-ters of the Thames River. Most staying on at Six Nations moved along-side Cayugas, who established themselves along the lowermost reaches of the Grand River around Dunnville and Port Maitland. Today, many descendants of these Munsee people continue to live in and around the much-reduced reserve farther north near Brantford.

Slightly more than half of the one hundred Munsees who had held on at Sandusky, Ohio, from the time of the Revolution to the end of the War of 1812 joined the main body of their people when they moved to Missouri, as did the few Munsees left at the Ohio Moravian town of Goshen. The other half of the Sandusky Munsee community moved north to the Muncey towns in Ontario or to the New Fairfield community. New Fairfield was a town rebuilt by Moravian Indians across the Thames from the Fairfield mission destroyed by the Ameri-can army after the Battle of the Thames in 1813.

While these relocations were going on out west, Munsees and their relatives in New Jersey and New York were finding it impossible to stay in their remaining enclaves. Most of the few Munsees living with Unamis at Brotherton in Edgepillock moved with them among the Brothertowners at New Stockbridge in Oneida country after they sold their reservation to the state of New Jersey in 1802. Their stay in New Stockbridge was brief. Oneidas who had returned home after the Revolution were facing strong pressure to sell their lands. They were forced to part with all but a few hundred of the original six million acres in their homeland in twenty-three treaties with New York authorities concluded between 1795 and 1846.

In 1818, the beleaguered New Stockbridgers living among the Oneidas finally accepted a Miami invitation first made ten years earlier to join the Delaware main body then on the White River in Indiana. A party of seventy-five men, women, and children arrived just after Delawares sold their Indiana lands in the St. Mary's Treaty and moved west to Missouri (and later on to Kansas). The hapless New Stockbridgers found nothing set aside for them. Unwilling to join the main body on its trek west into the prairies of the Great Plains, they lingered briefly in Indiana until their leaders back east convinced the federal government that they were ideal intermediaries to bring Protestant religion and civilization to the Catholic and traditionalist Indians in the deep forests of Wisconsin. In 1822, federal authorities brokered a deal in which the Menominee Indians allowed people they called New York Indians (mostly Oneidas, Mahicans, and Munsees) to settle along the Fox River between Green Bay and Lake Winnebago. By 1830, nearly all of the 225 to 350 Indians from New Stockbridge, and a sizable number of Oneidas, were living on Menominee land in Wisconsin.

Stockbridge and Brotherton immigrants were not happy with the swampy ground initially allotted to them. In 1831, they managed to get the federal government to sell them two townships (containing a total of seventy-two square miles) of land in public domain fifty miles farther west. These tracts, sold earlier to the United States by Menominees, were allocated to the mostly Mahican Stockbridge immigrants. An additional adjoining township (thirty-six square miles) was sold to the primarily Delaware Brotherton descendants. One year later, an elder named Bartholomew S. Calvin (his Indian name was

Shawuskukhung, "Wilted Grass"), who had been born in New Jersey, petitioned for and received $2,000 from the New Jersey legislature for the hunting and fishing rights in northern New Jersey his ancestors had reserved at Easton in 1758. These funds helped impoverished Brothertons who traced their ancestry to Weequehela and his kin maintain themselves on lands that became the nucleus of the present-day Stockbridge-Munsee Reservation.

Word of the move to Wisconsin and the relocation of the Delaware main body from Missouri to Kansas in 1832 reached Munsees living at New Fairfield and the Muncey Town settlements in Ontario. Increasingly surrounded by Canadian settlers flooding into Upper Canada, Indians along the Thames finally agreed to see how things stood out west. Some 230 mostly Munsee and Mahican people left the Thames Valley in 1837. Passing through Green Bay, they made their way to the Kansas Delaware Reservation. A party of Stockbridge and Brotherton people from Wisconsin also came to Kansas a year later. Those who liked what they saw elected to stay, purchasing land of their own from the Delawares. The first of these purchases was made in 1851 in what is today Wyandotte County. Three years later, most of these people moved to modern-day Leavenworth County when the Delawares were compelled to sell off a substantial portion of their original reservation. Discouraged by the frequent moves and not particularly fond of life on the prairie, many of these Munsees gradually moved back to Wisconsin and the Thames River Indian towns.

Back in Ontario, Methodists and Baptists were converting most Moravian and traditional Munsees. The last Moravian missionary preached his final sermon in Unami and left New Fairfield on November 6, 1864. Most of the remaining Moravian Indians moved from the already nearly abandoned town shortly thereafter. The majority settled nearby on lands within the present-day reserve of the Moravian of the Thames First Nation. Around the same time, Protestant missionaries finally persuaded new converts at Muncey Town to give up their Big House ceremony. Today, a few people in both reserves still speak Munsee, and interest in traditional culture is strong. Some 450 enrolled Moravian Indians live at Moraviantown while another

580 or so live off-reserve, mostly in nearby towns and cities. Farther upriver, 163 of the 524 enrolled members of the Munsee-Delaware First Nation enumerated in the 2000 census live on their band reserve at Muncey Town.

In 1859, a number of Delawares and Munsees, many belonging to the Killbuck family directly descended from the Ohio Munsee sachem Gelelemend, decided not to join the main band in its projected move to the new Indian territory in Oklahoma. They joined with Black River and Swan Creek Chippewas to establish a twelve-square-mile reservation of their own at Marais des Cygnes, "Marsh of the Swans," in what is now Franklin County, Kansas. They maintained their reservation there until 1900, when the Chippewas and the seventy Munsees still on the tribal roll (twenty-one of whom were Killbuck family members) accepted a final lump-sum payment of all outstanding federal monies owed to them, dissolved the tribe, and became American citizens. Unlike the Stockbridge Munsees, who made a similar decision in 1910 then managed to reverse it in 1934, the Kansas Munsees chose to keep their U.S. citizenship. The last elders speaking Munsee among them probably passed away shortly after the tribe disbanded, and most descendants married out into other families. At present, Kansas Munsee descendants are developing a growing interest in their Indian ancestry.

Memories of the traditional religion lingered on in several families who continued to speak the Delaware language among themselves. Today, a number of eastern Oklahoma Delaware people maintain their traditional language and culture on and near reservation lands only recently acknowledged as sovereign Delaware territory by both the Cherokee Nation and the U.S. government.

Today, Americans take pride in remembering nations like the Iroquois Confederacy, celebrated for its determined, if doomed, resistance. Mahicans and Delawares are remembered as tragic figures and wronged friends. Many like to see Indians as valiant opponents whose courageous defense of their homeland and traditions does honor both to their memory and to the descendants of those who defeated them. More than a few prefer to think of Indians as nature's nobility, exemplars of lost innocence, custodians of ecological wisdom, spirit guides, and role models for right living. Until recently, however, few besides descendants of the Munsees themselves evidently gave much thought to their ancestors' culture or history.

Since much of modern collective memory is preserved on paper, some of this forgetfulness has to be chalked up to bad press. From the beginning, bad experiences of intercultural contact led Europeans and Indians in the Hudson and Delaware valleys to regard one another as thievish, murderous, and treacherous. Although we can only imagine what went on before Hudson sailed into New York Harbor, at least some of that history must have been unpleasant. When Hudson's sailors first met Indians living around the harbor a Dutch sailor promptly killed an Indian trying to carry off a pillow, leading the two sides to slash, shoot at, and club each other. Colonists who followed could not see that they themselves were foreigners, preferring instead to treat Indians as aliens. Perceiving themselves as good, civil Christians, they called Indians savages and barbarians, and believed what they said.

In contrast to their later reassessments of other Indians tarred with the same ethnocentric brush, the invading colonists and their immediate descendants did not seem to think that Munsees did much to redeem themselves. Most people like their heroes, both winners and losers, to stride majestically across the pages of history. An American fondness for nobly lost causes goes far in explaining why the numbers of books about wars with Indians are exceeded only by those devoted to the Civil War. Munsee warriors who gave themselves totally to battle died early and often, as did Mayane, who reportedly in 1644 single-handedly attacked three colonists, killing two before being shot by the third. It is difficult to make out what colonists thought of those of his nation whom they surprised in their villages, indiscriminately shot down, and roasted alive in burning houses and forts. The terse tone of their reports suggests that these brutalizing slaughters gave their perpetrators neither a sense of moral uplift nor the euphoria of martial glory.

After colonists broke their power, Munsees did not do the noble thing and resist to the death, quietly disappear, or join their feeble strength with the Iroquois and other militant nations. Instead, they put up with affronts and abuses and held on to what they could. They endured colonial contumely and Iroquois insult, let pompous governors address them as children, and sat quietly as the Iroquois called them women. When it came to their land, they refused to court certain disaster by defying the colonists. Instead, they put off would-be purchasers and did what they could to hold on to their remaining lands. Many sold tracts with overlapping boundaries. Sometimes they sold the same ground two or three times in ways pejoratively called "Indian giving" to the present day.

Colonists buying the land assured themselves that the Indians were submitting to their power and rule. Most would not see that Munsees accommodated the settlers on their own terms and, as often as possible, at times of their own choosing. These responses could only baffle and infuriate thwarted colonists, who did not appreciate and could not admit that they were being outmaneuvered by people they often called savages and heathens to their faces.

Colonists had greater success plying Munsees with liquor in order to pry furs, land, and more from them. Settlers comparing their Munsee neighbors to the more distant Iroquois fell victim to the contempt born of familiarity; those Indians living farther away seemed nobler, purer, and somehow better. They increasingly regarded the Munsees they regularly encountered in their towns and villages as debauched and dissipated drifters. By the nineteenth century, such attitudes had hardened into the venomous species of biological racism that equates intimate interracial contact with degeneration. Racial purity was extolled. Intermarriage was condemned. Today, we wince at accounts deploring the mixed ancestry of Munsees, accounts written at a time when it was thought that one drop of blood of any color other than that imagined to be white somehow diminished a person's character and identity. Many modern Americans are also ashamed when they compare such intolerance with the way Munsees accepted strangers and cried when forced to part with adopted captives of other nationalities.

Yet Americans have not forgotten other Indian nations who intermarried with foreigners and whose people suffered slaughter and insult. Even the murderous hatred for Indians that terrorized the frontier could not erase the memories of many of its victims. Why, then, are the Munsees forgotten? Part of the answer lies in the role they played in the early history of the American nation. They frequently appear in accounts as treacherous and dangerous enemies suspected of harboring escaped slaves and criminals and supporting rebels and renegades. In many ways, they seem to resemble the maroon societies of escaped slaves and outcasts in Latin America and the American South, who banded together to form outlaw nations of their own in the backcountry.

Just as accounts of burnings provide the only known descriptions of many Indian towns, chronicles of attacks furnish much of what is known about maroon societies. Like other nations fearing resistance, raids, and possible resurgence of conquered peoples, the U.S. government relentlessly sent armies to hunt down and destroy maroon communities. During and after the War of 1812, they defeated and re-enslaved free blacks who had escaped southern bondage. The most extensively documented of these attacks occurred at Fort Mose near St. Augustine in east Florida and at the Negro Fort on the Apalachicola River. The presence of Cherokees (who were widely known to willingly harbor escaped slaves) among Indians resisting expansion into the Midwest may have helped fuel fears that similar maroon societies might also emerge on the Ohio. Munsees—who had a long history of accepting strangers—may have been regarded as a particular dangerous threat. Such fears may partially explain why white Americans, particularly slave owners like Virginians and Kentuckians, were so persistently determined to conquer and control the Ohio country.

Fears of this sort are not inconsiderable, especially when felt by people who get their history from books. Anyone looking at the past swiftly realizes that big things mostly grow from small beginnings. A short millennium ago, English was spoken only by a tiny tribe on a remote island. Armed mainly with swords, spears, and bows and arrows, the few people speaking the Old English tongue managed to forge the island's tribes into a formidable nation. Only a few more centuries passed before musket-toting, seafaring, English-speaking soldiers, sailors, and settlers carried their language to every part of the world.

What if the situation in Munsee country had been slightly different before the English or their Dutch cousins showed up? Instead of an Alfred the Great or a Queen Victoria, imagine, say, a particularly enterprising Munsee woman blessed with strong spirit power and an even stronger constitution—someone like Mamanuchqua. She is seized by a dream of imperial proportions. The dream may come fully formed, stirred perhaps by legends and stories. Or she herself may have seen massive cities like Cahokia or Tenochtitlan on her travels. Whatever the source of her visions, she would have known how to turn them into prophetic power that mobilized her people's energies. With the tactical skill and strategic guile shown by Powhatan, Pontiac, Tecumseh, and other great Indian leaders, she could have forged a vast empire by the time European sailors started venturing to Munsee shores. Further suppose that people belonging to this Munsee-speaking empire perhaps were immune to the diseases striking down remnants of European populations already ravaged by the Black Death and other plagues. It is not hard to imagine that ultimately they could have used their own guns and sailing ships to colonize and dominate "new-found Golgothas" in the Old World.

History, of course, did not turn out that way. But the fact that it didn't probably was more of a near miss than might be imagined. And because near misses are the very stuff of history, it makes good sense to recover forgotten histories of enduring people like the Munsees, whose past record of survival against great odds preserves survival skills that can come in handy at any time.

Personally, the story told in these pages is more than just a handy survival guide or a usable history filled with object lessons. As I look back on a career largely devoted to reconstructing the facts and understanding the broader significance of Munsee and other North American Indian cultures and histories, I am still struck by the passionate love of country exemplified by forgotten forebears who once called the Hudson and Delaware valleys home. Their homeland, and the nation that has risen up on its soil, I also love above all others.

Like others who love reading but always have trouble writing, I've long taken comfort in the old saw asserting that reading makes a learned mind but writing makes a precise one. Writing has given me a sharper focus on the kinds of choices made by one group of people during a critical time in their history, helping me get a clearer grasp on questions that still perplex me. Whereas the Munsees and countless other exiles throughout history always had somewhere else to go, we have now filled up most of the world's habitable places. How can different people, each confident in the validity of their own beliefs and ways of doing things, survive in a world where they have to live together? It seems to me that greater awareness and fuller understanding of the kinds of creative misunderstandings and working disagreements that helped Munsees and colonists live together during trying times can go far in helping people today adjust stubbornly idealistic hopes to the equally unyielding realities of life on our crowded planet.

NOTE ON SOURCES

The thousands of artifacts and documents preserved in public and private collections throughout Greater New York show that the forgotten history of the first Manhattans has been hidden in plain sight for a long time. Vast as it is, the record is widely scattered and fragmentary. Those trying to make sense out of it must troll through endless bits of documentary data like archaeologists looking for patterns among scraps and shards piled on lab tables. Cultural differences and the ravages of time and accident further obscure the view. Ceramic and stone materials are discarded or misidentified. Ink fades and paper yellows and becomes brittle. Microfilms intended to make fragile records available to researchers frequently are blurry, incomplete, and often nausea inducing. Fires, trash cans, and recyclers also take their toll. Dutch West India Company records in the Netherlands were pulped for their paper following the corporation's dissolution. In Albany, old records in the New York Archives that survived the flames that destroyed the State Library building there in 1911 still bear scorch marks from the conflagration.

Materials that have survived frequently are hard to find. Many are scattered in separate manuscript groups in different departments of the same institution. Others in deep storage are all but inaccessible. Many are too fragile for direct viewing and some are simply lost. Only tiny portions of the important archaeological collections curated in the National Museum of the American Indian,

the American Museum of Natural History, the State Museum of
New York in Albany, and the Trenton State Museum, for example,
are on public display at any time. Documentation recording more
than the find locations of many of these materials, moreover, has
disappeared.

Although a portion of the material evidence documenting Munsee
life is available in print, these publications are also scattered, mostly
produced in small numbers, and largely out-of-print. Some published
compilations, like the *Documents Relative to the Colonial History of
the State of New York,* successively edited by Edmund O'Callaghan
and Berthold Fernow from 1853 to 1887, have been digitized and are
available on compact discs. Although increasing amounts of published and manuscript material are appearing in print and online,
quantities and quality currently are still limited.

The State of New York still conserves papers originally published
by O'Callaghan and Fernow and others not destroyed in the Albany
fire. These include the New York Colonial Manuscripts series, notably the Minutes of the New York Executive Council from 1668 to
1783 (surviving portions of which continue to be published by New
Netherland Project scholars) and the Indorsed Land Papers of the
Province of New York (a guide to which was first published in 1902),
both curated in the New York Archives. New York State Library collections stored in the same building contain most published primary
sources and a very wide range of secondary studies. The New Netherland Project, housed in the same building, curates many Dutch-
language materials unavailable elsewhere.

Elsewhere in New York, the Municipal Archives of the City of New
York preserves the Westchester town records and town records from
Kings County saved from destruction by Saint Francis College archi-
vist Roger Kelley during the 1960s. The Ulster County Archives in
Kingston contain an extraordinarily large body of land records and
minutes of meetings with Esopus Indians held there between 1665
and 1783. Copies of other Indian deeds contracted when New York
was a colonial province (and, like other colonial-era transactions, recognized by the state government that replaced it) are also preserved in

the record offices of Dutchess, Orange, Ulster, and Westchester counties. Particularly extensive bodies of documents recording Indian land issues at local levels are found in the records of the town of Bedford in Westchester County (published from 1962 to 1978) and the western Long Island towns of Oyster Bay (published between 1916 and 1940) and Hempstead (published between 1896 and 1904).

New Jersey governments also preserve considerable amounts of material. The New Jersey Archives in Trenton curates a number of significant manuscript groups documenting Indian relations. Foremost among these is the large body of deeds and other land papers contained in two sets of records, those of the East Jersey Board of Proprietors and of the West Jersey Council of Proprietors. Other holdings include survey books, meeting minutes, and a wide range of court and other legal proceedings. The records offices of Bergen, Hunterdon, Middlesex, Monmouth, and Somerset counties also preserve copies of Indian deeds to lands within their colonial boundaries.

In Pennsylvania, the State Archives in Harrisburg preserves most Indian-related land, administrative, and diplomatic records generated during colonial times. Many but by no means all of these materials have been published in an ongoing series of publications begun during the nineteenth century.

Private societies, museums, and their libraries in the three states containing traditional Munsee homelands preserve a substantial percentage of the surviving materials. Papers of several prominent individuals and families stored in the library of the New-York Historical Society contain many relevant documents. The library also possesses an unparalleled selection of colonial maps and published sources. The Brooklyn Historical Society (formerly known as the Long Island Historical Society) likewise houses many treasures, the most prominent of which is the original manuscript of Jasper Danckaerts's *Journal of a Voyage to New York in 1679–1680*. Other important holdings include the Livingston Family Papers and anthropologist William C. MacLeod's unpublished manuscript, "The Indians of Brooklyn in the Days of the Dutch," produced in 1941 under a Works Progress Administration contract.

The New Jersey Historical Society in Newark houses a number of important collections. In Pennsylvania, several privately owned repositories contain important bodies of material. Two of the more notable of these are in Philadelphia: the Historical Society of Pennsylvania (which holds several significant manuscript groups as well as the Penn Wampum Belt and a number of important paintings), and the American Philosophical Society, whose collections contain a wide range of manuscript materials and the most comprehensive extant collection of Delaware word lists, recordings, and texts.

Also in Pennsylvania, the Records of the Moravian Mission among the Indians of North America, on file in the Moravian Archives in Bethlehem, represent one of the most important bodies of manuscript material bearing upon the final half century of Indian life in and around the ancestral Munsee homeland. Elsewhere, other materials may be found in the Special Collections of the Alexander Library of Rutgers University, the Scheide Collection in Princeton University's Firestone Library, the Allinson Collection in the Quaker Archives housed at Haverford College, the Library of the Friends Historical Society in Swarthmore College, and the Ayer Collection of manuscripts in the Newberry Library in Chicago.

The Internet has made a number of maps and other illustrated material showing Munsee community locations, portraits, tools, and other subjects readily available for the first time. Many maps, for example, may now be seen online at sites like nnp.org and antiquemaps. co.uk. Several of the small number of images depicting Munsee people are also available. These include the painting from the British Library entitled "Indiens des Manathans." This watercolor was painted by an unknown artist sometime in the late 1700s. Long forgotten and only first published in the 1960s, it is particularly notable for its accurate depictions of clothing, tools, weapons, and the male figure's coif, shaved and painted in red on one side and left long on the other in the manner of shamans documented other early colonial illustrations. Other images preserved in Great Britain by the British Library and kindred institutions include an etching of a Munsee or Mahican man made by Flemish engraver Wenceslaus Hollar in 1645 and a portrait of the Upper River Indian leader Etow Oh Koam painted by John Verelst in London in 1710. In the United States, the Pennsylvania Historical Society houses the widely reproduced painting of the Munsee sachem Lappawinza from the Forks of Delaware made in 1735 by Pennsylvania artist Gustavus Hesselius.

Numerous journals, diaries, and other eyewitness accounts mentioning Munsee Indians have been published. J. Franklin Jameson gathered together many of the most useful of the early Dutch writings in *Narratives of New Netherland* (first published in 1909). Other notable sources include William Penn's 1683 *Account of the Lenni Lenape or Delaware Indians,* Danckaerts's aforementioned journal (first published in 1867), and Adriaen Van der Donck's *A Description of the New Netherlands* (the first edition appeared in 1655; the latest in 2008).

Gaps in existing records impose limitations that subsequent writers have dealt with in a variety of ways. Novelists deal with the absence of dialogue in original sources by putting words in the mouths of long-silent or wholly invented characters. Most also use literary devices like narrative flow, plot complication, and character development to help readers experience feelings of identification, emotional immediacy, and dramatic involvement rarely communicated in colonial documents. James Fenimore Cooper was one of the first Americans to master this art. Inspired by the romances of Sir Walter Scott, Cooper almost single-handedly invented the western novel in a series of books published during the second quarter of the nineteenth century. Cooper set his frontier epics in his native Northeast, casting events in the deep forests that still covered wilder parts of the region. Conversations and adventures of the fictional characters Chingachgook, Uncas, and Hawkeye from his best-remembered work, *Last of the Mohicans* (first published in 1826), still reveal surprisingly nuanced insights into attitudes toward race, class, and ethnicity along the New York frontier during the Seven Years' War. Strong-minded and conflicted, Cooper's protagonists ultimately became prototypical pop culture icons endlessly recycled in literature, film, and every other form of mass media.

Cooper was only the first of a long line of novelists whose strong interests in Indians in general, and colonial- and revolutionary-era history in particular, placed Munsees and other Northeastern Indians at the center of historical narratives. Three other representatives of this genre will have to serve as examples for the rest. The first two are bookends set, respectively, at the beginning and end of the colonial era. Mark Raymond Harrington's often reprinted and much-loved 1940 volume, *The Indians of New Jersey: Dickon among the Lenapes,* takes place in 1612 during the first years of contact. Drawing upon a lifetime of library research and fieldwork with Munsees and other Delawares in Ontario and Oklahoma, Harrington describes Delaware life as it was at that time through the eyes of his protagonist, a young English boy named Dickon.

As Harrington tells it, Dickon is rescued by a Delaware family after being washed overboard during a storm off the Jersey shore. Initially compelled to cook, clean, and perform other women's work, he is eventually adopted and grows to manhood among the Indians before boarding a ship sent from Jamestown to reunite him with his father. Harrington lets the details of Delaware life unfold gradually as Dickon is taught their language, woodcraft skills, and religious beliefs. Illustrations by Clarence Ellsworth help readers share Dickon's growing appreciation of his adopted people. Executed in the gracefully detailed naturalistic style popular in woodcraft books produced during the early 1900s, Ellsworth's pen-and-ink sketches depict characters, events, artifacts, and step-by-step production methods mentioned in the text.

Light in the Forest, first published by Conrad Richter in 1953, tells the story of another English boy, this one forcibly taken captive by the Delawares toward the end of the colonial era in 1754. The title is a tip of the hat to Harrington's protagonist, whose Delaware family named him Day'kay-ning, "In the Forest," for the way his name, Dickon, sounded to them. Richter names his protagonist True Son. His story turns on an actual event, the forced repatriation of all captives living among the Delawares that colonial officials demanded at meetings in Pittsburgh ending Pontiac's War in 1765. Captured at the age of four, True Son is eleven when his adoptive parents reluctantly turn the unwilling boy over. What follows is a story of divided loyalties as True Son, caught between two worlds, tries to make his peace with both. True Son's agonies of ambivalence and alienation have resonated among young readers since the book first appeared.

Katherine Kirkpatrick's *Trouble's Daughter* (1999) is one of the more recent contributions to the genre. Like Dickon and True Son, Kirkpatrick's Susanna Hutchinson is a captive. Unlike her literary precursors, Susanna was an actual person, the only member of her family who survived the attack that killed her siblings and her mother, New England religious exile Anne Hutchinson. Kirkpatrick's Susanna is also a more complex character than her literary predecessors, confronting feelings of terror, grief, disgust, and hatred as she gradually learns to accept and empathize with her captors. She is a very modern heroine, a strong visionary open to insight and self-discovery. Her personal growth among her captors helps her become, in the soft tones of Indian songs she sings for her children years after her repatriation, a bridge between Indian and English worlds.

A spate of novelesque auto-histories has appeared in recent years. Among the more notable of these books are Theodore L. Kazimiroff's *The Last Algonquin* (1982) and Evan T. Pritchard's *Native New Yorkers* (2002). Kazimiroff presents a narrative based on stories told by his father, the late Bronx historian Ted Kazimiroff, Sr. of an old Indian living in a remote wooded island in Pelham Bay Park he met when he was young. Pritchard adopts a seemingly more scholarly approach, complete with bibliography and footnotes. These support an idiosyncratic presentation that can perhaps best be described as a mix of identity politics and spirituality informed by a postmodern sensibility privileging what he regards as authentic indigenous texts and testimony.

Novelists and their kin produce fictions best known to the public. The overwhelming bulk of writers devoted to understanding the culture and history of Indians in Munsee country, however, use more traditional scholarly methods to discover or reinterpret documentary, archaeological and linguistic sources. Most numerous are antiquarian historians and amateur archaeologists who literally love the past for its own sake. Many tend to be passionate partisans touting the virtues of particular places and local heritage. Free to focus their attention on the objects of their affection, amateurs frequently know far more about local history and circumstances than their professional counterparts do. Today, many amateurs are academically trained. Some are retired. Others have independent means or make their living in other professions. Few, however, are formally trained in the fields of history, anthropology, or linguistics.

This situation has two consequences. On the positive side, the works of rigorous amateurs, like Edward M. Ruttenber's *History of the Indians of Hudson's River* (1872) and William Wallace Tooker's *Indian Place-Names of Long Island* (1911), are still-useful, pioneering studies. On the more problematic side, others fill voids left by silent documents and empty map spaces with names, places, and events their authors think would belong there if since-vanished sources were still available. To remedy deficiencies in the Munsee historical record, nineteenth-century ethnologist Henry Rowe Schoolcraft and local historian Reginald Pelham Bolton both used this approach in several still widely consulted studies.

More recently, ethnohistorians combining the disciplines of anthropology and history have crafted innovative approaches to address problems posed by cultural distance and the passage of time. Some of the pioneering works on the ethnography of the region, such as *Teedyuscung: King of the Delawares* (1949), Anthony F. C. Wallace's methodologically sophisticated application of psychosocial theory, continue to be models for present-day ethnohistorians.

Building on this work, scholars belonging to the following generation began trying to prove whether particular practices predated or postdated colonial intrusion. The late anthropologist Lynn Ceci, for example, challenged assumptions that aboriginal Long Islanders used fish for fertilizer, produced wampum, and grew corn before contact. Other scholars marshaled evidence showing that splint baskets, maple sugar, and log cabins were products of colonial contact.

Growing numbers of ethnohistorians began using written records to produce historical accounts of Delawares at this time. Allen W.

Trelease's *Indian Affairs in Colonial New York* (1960), Clinton A. Weslager's *The Delaware Indians: A History* (1972), and Herbert C. Kraft's *The Lenape-Delaware Indian Heritage* (published posthumously in 2001) all draw deeply on sources documenting Munsee people and history.

Two studies published in 2006 focus on Munsees' relations with colonists in New Netherland. While both emphasize what they call Munsee cultural otherness, each does so to make a particular point. Paul Otto's *The Dutch-Munsee Encounter in America* uses the extensive body of existing primary and secondary sources to argue that different cultural worldviews governed the responses of Indians and colonists along the Hudson Valley frontier. Donna Merwick's *The Shame and the Sorrow* is largely devoted to showing how Dutch failure to live up to peaceful mercantile ideals, caused in part by their inability to penetrate Indian cultural opacity, led to violence that still shames and saddens their descendants.

Those interested in seeing more detailed discussions of the sources mentioned in this essay, and of numerous others that could not be included in this abridgement, should consult the essay on sources in my 2005 report, *From Manhattan to Minisink,* on file in the National Park Service Northeast Region Ethnography Program office in Boston, Massachusetts.

INDEX

Canada/Canadians, 5, 23, 34, 91, 117–
18, 126, 139, 148, 152, 155, 158,
169, 179, 190, 197, 214, 228–29,
236
Canarsie, Kings County (N.Y.), 11
Canasatego (dates unknown), 204
Capellen toe Ryssel, Hendrijck Van
der (d. 1659), 80–82, 84
Caribbean, 25, 51
Carolinas, 5, 23, 113, 127, 181–82;
Indians from, 127
Carteret, Elizabeth (1615–96), 132
Carteret, George (1610–80), 89, 132
Carteret, Philip (1639–82), 89, 94,
99–101, 103–104, 108, 110, 118–19
Cartwright, George (dates unknown),
90
Castine, Hancock County (Maine), 105
Catholics. *See* Christians and
Christianity
Catskill Creek, 121
Catskill Indian community/country,
55, 121, 128, 164–65
Catskill Mountains, 3, 164–65, 176,
187, 217, 226
Cattaraugus Indian community and
reservation, 233
Caughnawaga Mohawk Indian
town, N.Y., 93; Catholic mission,
Montreal, 155
Ceci, Lynn (1931–89), 250
Chanongong Indian town, 189
Charles II. *See under* Stuart
Charleston, S.C., 183
Chechong Indian plantation, 189
Cheesecocks Patent, 174
Chemung River and Valley, 216, 219,
223–24, 227
Cherokee Indians, 181, 237, 240
Cherries. *See* Plants/planting
Chesapeake Bay, 20, 110, 118, 123,
130, 169
Chickataubut (d. 1669), 93. *See also*
Kinaquariones, Battle of; Massa-
chusetts Indians; Northern Indians

Children: Indian, 6, 8–9, 11, 17, 20,
32, 35, 40, 42, 49–51, 102, 131, 139,
157, 166, 186, 227–28, 235, 249;
colonial; 37, 42; Munsees metaphorically addressed as, 125, 153,
204, 239
Chingachgook, 247
Chippewa Indians (Anishinabeg),
234, 237
Chopeycannows (fl. 1658–96),
younger brother of Tackapousha,
12; descendants, 231; Matinecock
sachem, 231; Suscaneman's sister's
husband, 12; war leader, 54
Christians/Christianity, 35, 80, 138,
186, 204, 209–10, 238; Baptists,
236; Calvinists, 171; Catholics, 32,
133, 155, 167, 190, 206, 235; Jesuits,
137; Lutherans, 171; Methodists,
236; missions and missionaries,
17, 23, 138, 155, 167, 186–87, 190,
198, 205–206, 209–11, 216, 218,
224, 226, 229, 231, 234, 236, 246;
Moravian Brethren, 205–206, 210,
218, 224, 226, 229, 234, 236, 246;
Presbyterians, 229; Protestants,
32, 235–36; Quakers, 44, 69, 119,
132, 144–45, 152, 171, 223. *See
also* Spirits/spirituality; *individual
missions and missionaries*
Claes de Wilt. *Also* Claes the Indian,
Towackhachi (fl. 1666–1714), 103,
110, 130–31, 133, 135, 157, 159, 174
Clans. *See* lineages *under* Kinship and
marriage
Clinton, George (1686–1761), 211
Clothing and apparel, 7, 14, 21, 25, 35,
91, 208, 246
Coalitions. *See* Social and political
organization
Coats. *See* Clothing and apparel
Cochecton Indian town, 188–89,
206–207
Colve, Antonij (dates unknown),
105–106